CONSTITUTIONAL LAW AND

CONSTITUTIONAL LAW
AND
CONSTITUTIONAL RIGHTS
IN IRELAND

BRIAN DOOLAN

GILL AND MACMILLAN

Published in Ireland by
Gill and Macmillan Ltd
Goldenbridge
Dublin 8
with associated companies throughout the world
© Brian Doolan 1984
7171 1330 0
Print origination in Ireland by
Galaxy Reproductions Ltd
Printed in Hong Kong

PREFACE

Most books are written because the author is in love with his subject, which he wishes to share with others. The level of enthusiasm for a subject will often depend on the availability of understandable material. That there is general interest in constitutional law and rights is indisputable. It is therefore surprising to find, that although the Constitution of Ireland was enacted 46 years ago, there is a noticeable absence of easily understood material on this, our fundamental law. This book aims to fill that gap.

There are at least two ways of studying the Constitution. The first would begin with the Preamble and work in sequence through to Art. 50, giving each Article attention in turn. Such a method is, because the same subject may be found in many Articles, repetitive and diffuse. The second method, which is adopted here, is to arrange related Articles under subject headings and then to consider each in turn together with the relevant case law. This method brings order and hopefully leads to understanding.

Our Constitutional law lends itself to a natural division of the subject into political rights and personal rights. This division underlies the scheme of this book. Part One considers such political matters, from a legal viewpoint, as the Nation, the State and the institutions of Government. Part Two concentrates on the various constitutional rights available to the individual. Like most legal subjects a study of constitutional law would be incomplete without a study of the appropriate case law. The inaccessibility of law reports has forced an innovative feature. Over 100 leading constitutional law cases are contained in Part Three. Explained in easy terms the reader is referred in the text to the appropriate case by a distinctive number. A quick reference to the case acquaints the reader with the facts and decision.

While this book was in preparation the Criminal Justice Bill, 1983 was introduced into Dáil Éireann. From the reactions to it, it is probable that it will be enacted substantially in its published form. I have set out in an Appendix the proposals which will impinge on constitutional law.

My thanks are due to those who assisted with the preparation of this book. The tables of cases and statutes were prepared by Paul Cleary. For patient and skilful editorial assistance Bridget Lunn must receive credit.

Brian Doolan
Dublin
December 1983

To my sisters
Maura, Sheila and Eileen

CONTENTS

TABLE OF CONSTITUTIONAL ARTICLES

TABLE OF STATUTES

xiii

TABLE OF CASES

Chapter 1

THE NATURE OF THE IRISH CONSTITUTION

Meaning of Constitution and on Constitutions in General

In political and legal affairs the word *constitution* is used in at least two differing senses: the wide and abstract sense and the narrow and concrete sense. The constitution of a state in the wider sense is the system of laws, customs and conventions which create and validate the organs of government and which regulate the interaction between those organs with one another and with the individual. Most of these rules are legal in the sense that courts of law will recognise and apply them where appropriate. Other rules, non-legal in nature, consisting of customs and conventions, will be adhered to, though not having the force of law; all combine to give a wide and abstract meaning to the word constitution. In a sense the most appropriate expression to encompass this meaning is *constitutional law*. A constitution in its narrow and concrete sense means the document or documents in which the basic legal rules of the constitution are authoritatively declared. It is *the* source of law for a community. The law of the constitution is readily and easily ascertained by reference to one or a few documents which have, by some legitimating means, been given the stamp of approval which marks them down as being the law above all else and by which all other legal norms and rules are to be judged.

In every modern state there exists a readily identifiable document or collection of documents which embodies a selection of the most fundamental rules about the government of that state. A comparative study indicates a series of features common to all or most of these constitutions.[1] The first common feature is that some special process will have been used to enact the constitution, and this process has two effects. In the first place it gives to the constitution a legitimacy not given to other forms of law, while secondly the constitution is given a primary character as law: it is the fundamental law of the state over and above all the other forms of law. The second common feature is that many constitutions contain a power given to courts to pronounce ordinary laws inconsistent with the constitution and therefore null and void. The courts measure the compatibility of ordinary laws and administrative action against the provisions of the constitution and those found wanting are condemned. The word *constitutional* means 'in conformity with the constitution' and the word *unconstitutional* means 'in violation of the constitution'. Since the constitution is the fundamental law of the state it follows that to retain this character it must be immune from easy and unconsidered amendment.

1

The protection from mutilation is the third feature common to many constitutions. A special procedure is required before the constitution can be amended. If an amendment was permitted by ordinary law the constitution would be denied this badge of speciality which it claims because of its special enactment and its fundamental character.

Having looked at the character of constitutions let us now examine the contents of constitutions. Constitutions are primarily about political authority or power. The constitution will usually locate, confer, distribute and limit authority and power among the organs of government of a state. More often than not it is concerned about procedure as much as substantive rules of law. The organs of government will interact with each other to prevent abuse, and all the organs will interface to form a system which will have, as its aim, good and just government. In a political society the individual must yield to government. How far he must submit will depend on the type of society in which he lives. Government and individual freedoms of an absolute nature are incompatible. Good government will permit the greatest freedoms. For freedoms to flourish, government must be controlled. The purpose of a constitution, apart from establishing the State and its institutions, is to limit the power of government. There can be no unlimited power under a constitution: the word *constitution* denotes limitation. A perusal of constitutions will show how the various organs of government are limited and controlled. These restrictions are imposed so that tyranny can be prevented and the individual, subjected to the least amount of control, can develop his personality and assert his individuality to the fullest.

Because they signal a new political beginning, many constitutions contain explicit guarantees of rights and freedoms to be enjoyed by the individual. Remembrance will be made of the injustices that went before because of a colonial or dictatorial regime. A new political beginning demands a new attitude towards the individual. He is elevated into constitutional significance. His role is not alone that of the governed but of the governing and as far as it is practicable the individual is allowed to exist and develop and be possessed of rights that cannot easily be negatived. Sometimes a constitution will incorporate ideological pronouncements, that is principles by which the community ought to be guided or to which it might aspire. These principles must be given effect when interpreting the constitution and when ordinary laws and actions are to be judged. Such ideas will depend on the political and moral beliefs of the community.[2] While a perusal of constitutions will exhibit an array of differing philosophies, a central feature of constitutions will be some idealistic foundation.

The Irish Constitution and Constitutional Law

Having looked at constitutions in general we can approach our Constitution with some preconceived expectations. The Constitution when enacted in 1937 marked a new political beginning in that it was a document drafted without reference to any other government[3] though it incorporated institutions which had been tried elsewhere. It was enacted by the People[4] ; it established the State and the organs of government; it contained a statement of individual rights; it declared its objective to be the attainment of stated social aspirations and it provided a special method of amendment. It thus contained many of the characteristics of other modern constitutions while it in turn exhibited these characteristics as the typical foundations of a modern constitution.

When we speak of the Irish Constitution we mean the document enacted by the People. This is the narrower meaning which can be given to constitutions. But a reading of the Constitution, worth while in itself, does not introduce the reader to all the rules of our constitutional law. That the Constitution is a basic document denotes the idea that upon this foundation will be built a structure that must include other documents and customs. The Constitution is the legal skeleton upon which must be hung legal rules and interpretations which give it life. This book attempts to examine the Constitution together with its implementing statutes and in the light of judicial interpretation to prove that constitutional law is a real and vital force in our law and society. One of the unique features of such a study will be the conclusion that our constitutional law, more than any other branch of our law, has developed in a way peculiar to our own ideals, aspirations and needs.

The Legitimacy and Supremacy of the Constitution

For a measure to have the force of law it must have the appropriate legitimacy. Legislation is law because it was enacted by a competent authority. In what circumstances can a constitution claim to have this legal authority? By what criteria do those whose task it is to administer the the law recognise that a certain document, described as a constitution, is part of the law? The general rule, as already explained, is to seek a body competent to make law. But the dilemma is obvious: since the constitution itself creates the law-making body, can there exist another body competent to enact a consitution before the constitution itself is in being? To resolve this puzzle it becomes necessary to conceive of a body which can give the force of law to a constitution before the constitution itself authorises the establishment of a law-making body. Who then are these original primeval law-givers? To this question there are three possible answers. In the first type of case the original law-giver will be an assembly specially constituted for that purpose. The assembly will be directly elected by the people though the latter do not take part directly in the acceptance or rejection of the constitution. In India a special constituent assembly was elected to adopt the Constitution. The Constitution of Saorstát Éireann was enacted by this method. The second method is to acknowledge the original law-giver to be another parliament. The Constitution of Australia is a statute of the British Parliament.

In the third type of case the original law-giver will be the people. The

3

constitution will be voted on by popular franchise and the decision of the majority will prevail. The people are the fountainhead of authority. This method was adopted when the Constitution of Ireland was framed and proposed. It was put to the People in a plebiscite and enacted by them.[5] That the People are the first and primary authority has been accepted by judicial pronouncements. This authority has been re-emphasised regularly by the necessity of ascertaining the will of the People before the Constitution can be amended: permission to alter has been both given and refused.

The supremacy of the Constitution over other forms of law was achieved by giving it a quality of uniqueness against which all other laws are to be judged. If the latter infringe upon the Constitution they are declared to be null and void no matter how necessary and useful they may in themselves appear to be. The Constitution is our legal yardstick.

The Ethos of the Constitution

It can be expected, since the Constitution was enacted by the People, that the ethical values on which it is based will reflect the morals of this society. That this society is Christian in character is undeniable: that the Constitution will give voice to Christian values and virtues is therefore hardly surprising. The Preamble acknowledges the Christian God and seeks to promote the common good with due observance of prudence, justice and charity.[6] To see such sentiments as sectarian is to be possessed of a high level of intolerance. No constitution could give expression to the beliefs of every individual or group. Because this cannot be attained is no argument for the complete absence of sentiments which have the support of the majority.[7] The majority are entitled to this consideration provided the sentiments expressed are not used to persecute and alienate those who do not subscribe to such ideals. The tyranny of a minority can be as destructive as any majority persecution.

It is generally accepted that the Constitution is based on natural law teachings.[8] The natural law is based on value judgments which emanate from some absolute source such as, for example, God's revealed word. These absolute value judgments reflect the essential character of the universe and are immutable and eternally valid. They can be grasped and understood by the proper employment of human reason. When perceived, they must overrule all positive, or man-made, law. Indeed the positive law is only truly law if it conforms to the natural law. There are thus two kinds of law, the natural law and the positive law. Both are necessary in society but the positive law must yield to the natural law. Some oppose the notion that natural law exists or that it should be used to measure positive law. If the notion that natural law does not exist is accepted it is difficult, if not impossible, to argue for the existence of natural rights. If only positive law exists then rights can be awarded and abrogated by positive law. The Constitution and the courts refuse to countenance that rights are given by positive law.

4

Apart from the Christian nature of the Constitution there is another broad concept which pervades it. The People enacted the Constitution by popular vote and they can and do amend it by the same method. That the People decide issues is evidence of the democratic nature of this society. Not alone do the People vote on what are directly constitutional issues; they vote from time to time in elections to decide who should carry out various constitutional functions. The People are an integral part of government: it is government by the People for the People

The Interpretation of the Constitution

A reading of the Constitution, like the reading of other material, leads to some conclusion as to its meaning. Because it is a legal document some legal terminology must be used though essentially the Constitution is a document that can be read by the lay person.[9] The politician, the lawyer, the moralist and the sociologist can, with differing emphases on different nuances, argue in favour of particular conclusions. This may appear to cause confusion. On the contrary, if the Constitution is to remain vibrant and relevant it is imperative that it lends itself to differing interpretations. It is when the Constitution loses this quality that its importance will fade.

Of course there must be some institution or person who can give the Constitution an authoritative interpretation. The Constitution grants this power to the courts and consequently the Constitution means what the superior courts declare it to mean. The High Court has jurisdiction, having regard to the provisions of the Constitution, to question the validity of any law, and the Supreme Court has appellat jurisdiction* from such decisions. 'In this country,' said Walsh J. in *McGee v. Attorney General* (Case No. 50), 'it falls finally upon the judges to interpret the Constitution ... the judges must, therefore, as best they can from their training and experience interpret these rights in accordance with their ideas of prudence, justice and charity.' This is an acknowledgement that any interpretation of the Constitution is subjective: it cannot be otherwise. While the judges interpret the Constitution it does not follow that the People must accept such interpretations. A decision of the courts could be negatived by a referendum, or the People could amend the Constitution by removing this power of interpretation from the courts. An interpretation once given may be altered. 'It is natural that from time to time the prevailing ideas of these virtues may be conditioned by the passage of time,' said Walsh J. in the same case. 'No interpretation of the Constitution is intended to be final for all time.'[10] The Constitution declares that in case of conflict between the Irish and English texts the text in the Irish language prevails.[11]

Amendment of the Constitution

Constitutions are often classified as flexible or rigid.[12] The former is

*The definition of this word appears in the Glossary, and this is true of all the words that are followed by an asterisk throughout the text.

one which can be changed with the same ease and in the same manner as ordinary law. An example of a flexible constitution is that of Britain. A rigid constitution is one which requires some special procedure before it can be altered. Amendment of the United States Constitution requires either initiation by two-thirds of both Houses of Congress and ratification by the legislatures of three-fourths of the states or initiation by two-thirds of the states and ratification by conventions in three-fourths of the states. Few constitutions require a referendum of the electorate but since our Constitution was enacted by the People it is hardly surprising that the amendment must be enacted by the same method. But the possibility of amendment is controlled in that any proposal must be initiated in Dáil Éireann and be passed or deemed to have been passed by both Houses of the Oireachtas.[13] No initiation by the electorate is possible.[14]

Every proposal submitted to the People in a referendum is approved if a majority of the votes cast are cast in favour. Referenda, apart from deciding particular questions, give the People an opportunity of confirming their faith in the Constitution (Art. 47).

Part One

THE NATION, THE STATE AND THE INSTITUTIONS OF GOVERNMENT

Chapter 2

THE NATION

The People are the Nation

In the first chapter we laid out the scheme on which our constitutional law rests. As the primary law-makers the People enacted the Constitution which established the State and the organs of government. The Preamble speaks of the 'people of Éire' and this impersonal and imprecise subject is identified in Art. 1. 'The People', the primary law-makers and the ultimate source of authority, under God, is the Irish nation: so the People and the Irish nation are synonymous. A power reserved in the Constitution to the People can only validly be exercised by the Irish people.

The Constitution declares that the Irish nation has the inalienable, indefeasible and sovereign right to choose its own form of government (Art. 1). The form chosen is republican and democratic. The nation determines its relations with other nations. Being a sovereign nation it is free to develop its life, political, economic and cultural, in accordance with its own genius and traditions.

There are two possible definitions of a nation. First, it can be an aggregation of a people or peoples of one or more cultures or races organised into a single state. Applying this test, it must be positively admitted that there is a state and within its borders are a people who share a common heritage and aspirations. Secondly, a nation can be a community of persons not constituting a state but bound by common descent, language, religion and history. Applying this definition it can be seen that the Irish nation spreads beyond the borders of the State to encompass persons who identify closely with the people of the State. The Constitution intends the second definition to be the operative one as will be seen when we examine the extent of the national territory a little later.

One of the attributes of nationhood is a distinct language which need not be widely spoken by the people. It might, rather, be of historical importance and while the possibility of restoring it to common usage might not be real, the sympathy shown towards it is sufficient to identify it as the national language. The Constitution declares Irish to be the national and first official language (Art. 8). The English language is recognised as a second official language. The Constitution was drafted, proposed and enacted in both languages. Both have played and continue to play an important role in the life of the nation. The Constitution does not either expressly or by implication attempt or aspire to substitute one language for the other.

The National Territory

The Constitution declares that the national territory consists of the whole island of Ireland, its islands and the territorial seas (Art. 2). Here is an unambiguous declaration that the Irish nation is the inheritor and the rightful possessor of the whole island of Ireland. The reality of the political division of the island does not detract from that factual statement which is also in the nature of an aspiration that the Irish nation will one day possess the whole island incorporated into some political structure independent of outside control. This declaration is not a claim by the State established under the Constitution to exercise jurisdiction over the whole of the island. On the contrary it is an acknowledgment that the Irish nation and not any particular state existing on the island are the possessors of the national territory.

Art. 3 of the Constitution accepts the political division of the national territory by stating that the jurisdiction of the State has the same kind of application as the laws of Saorstát Éireann. This is an acceptance that the State called Ireland is composed of the same geographical area as was the Irish Free State, and no more. This is a *de facto* recognition that the national territory consists of more than one political entity. This acknowledgment of reality cannot be paraded as a claim of jurisdiction over that part of the national territory not under the political control of the State established under the Constitution.

Art. 3 contains the words: 'without prejudice to the right of the Parliament and Government established by this Constitution to exercise jurisdiction over the whole of that territory' which, it has been suggested, contain a *de jure* claim by this State to exercise jurisdiction over the whole island. A reading of the complete Article cannot support such an argument. The Article speaks of the reintegration of the national territory and acknowledges that the State established under the Constitution has the same jurisdictional extent as Saorstát Éireann. The realities of these admissions dilute any *de jure* claim if such a claim can be found. It is indisputable that the Irish nation has a right to the whole island of Ireland. But the State established under the Constitution has not and does not make such a claim. By accepting these realities the State does not abandon its aspiration to national unification.

Art. 3 does not define the geographical State established under the Constitution though it declares that the laws, and therefore the jurisdiction, are to have the same application and extent as the laws of Saorstát Éireann. This latter entity was not defined in the Constitution or in the

8

Constitution of the Irish Free State or in the Treaty between Great Britain and Ireland. To resolve the matter recourse must be made to the *Government of Ireland Act, 1920.* This statute of the British Parliament divided the island into two political entities: Southern Ireland and Northern Ireland. Only Northern Ireland was defined as the parliamentary counties of Antrim, Armagh, Down, Fermanagh, Londonderry and Tyrone. Southern Ireland was to consist of the remainder of the island. This entity became Saorstát Éireann and is now the extent of the State established under the 1937 Constitution.

Various statutes set the extent of the territorial waters of the State. There is a ribbon of water around the State over which exclusive jurisdiction is exercised. There are other areas of water over which the State exercises limited jurisdiction and the concept of extra-territorial jurisdiction is considered in the next chapter.

Chapter 3

THE STATE

Nature of a State and the Irish State

In international law the legal criteria of statehood, set out in Art. 1 of the Montevideo Convention on Rights and Duties of States,[15] are a permanent population, a defined territory, a government and the capacity to enter into relations with other States. The concept of independence is represented by the capacity to enter into external relations with other States. Guggenheim distinguishes the State from other legal orders by two tests.[16] First, the State has a degree of centralisation of its organs not found in the world community and secondly, in a particular geographical area, the State is the sole executive, legislative and judicial authority. If an entity has its own organs of government and, according to Brownlie, a nationality law of its own,[17] there is *prima facie* evidence of statehood.

Applying these criteria to the circumstances existing in 1937, and currently pertaining, Ireland in international law has the status of a State. It has a permanent population, it occupies a defined territory, it has organs of government and it enters into relations with other States.

It was open to the People in 1937 to decide whatever kind of State they wished to establish. A monarchy, a dictatorship or an oligarchy could have been established. It could have been structured as a unitary state or a federation. In international affairs the State could have aligned itself with any other State or group of States it chose. Instead Art. 5 of the Constitution declares Ireland to be a sovereign, independent, democratic State.

9

A Sovereign State

Despite the remark by Stark[18] that sovereignty is a term of art rather than a legal term capable of precise definition, Schwarzenberger[19] defines sovereignty in the context of the constitutional theory of the unitary state as meaning omnipotence. Sovereignty may be external or internal. In international law a state's external sovereignty reflects its autonomy or independence. It is positive in that power is exercised in pursuance of objectives such as the maintenance of status and power. It is negative in that it involves the absence of subordination to any foreign or exterior power. This view of external sovereignty accords with judicial thinking. 'The declaration of sovereignty' according to Walsh J. in *Byrne v. Ireland* (Case No. 19), 'means that the State is not subject to any power of government save those designated by the People in the Constitution itself, and that the State is not amenable to any external authority.'

In international law a sovereign state is possessed of rights and duties. It has the exclusive right to control its own domestic affairs, to admit or expel aliens and the sole jurisdiction over crimes committed within its territory. A state has the duty

— not to perform acts of sovereignty over the territory of another state,
— to abstain and prevent agents and subjects from committing acts constituting a violation of another state's independence or territorial supremacy,
— and not to interfere in the affairs of another state.

At the present time there is hardly a state which has not accepted restrictions on its liberty of action in the interests of international comity. Most states belong to the United Nations. Such membership limits the unfettered discretion of a state in matters of international policy. Sovereignty is lost, according to Brownlie, where foreign control overbears decision-making on a wide range of matters of high policy on a systematic and permanent basis.

Does our membership of the European Economic Community dent our sovereignty in a serious way? In economic matters the answer is yes though this, important as it is, hardly excludes this State from being sovereign, on the Brownlie test. Ireland formally became a member of the EEC in January 1972. In order to permit laws of the community made externally and not by organs of government established under the Constitution it was necessary to amend the Constitution, which was done by the People on 10 May of that year.[20] The amendment reads: 'No provision of this Constitution invalidates laws enacted, acts done or measures adopted by the State necessitated by the obligations of membership of the Communities or prevents laws enacted, acts done or measures adopted by the Communities, or institutions thereof, from having the force of law in the State.' This gives a constitutional basis to the limitation of our sovereignty.

The laws of the EEC have found their way into domestic law in a number of ways. The *European Communities Act, 1972* made the Treaties part

10

of the domestic law and Ministers of State are empowered to incorporate further laws into domestic law by statutory instruments.* Some statutes have been passed to give effect to Community law though Community law, in the nature of Regulations, has automatically become the law of the State. The Community issues Directives which set out objects to be achieved while leaving it to each member state to choose its own method of achievement.

What is the status of the State in domestic law? While it is sovereign in international affairs how far does this concept extend in the domestic forum. It was not until *Byrne v. Ireland* (Case No. 19) that the status of the State with regard to internal sovereignty, and the extent of its rights and liabilities, were convincingly established. In that case the State was sued for the wrongful acts of its servant. The defence was raised that by reason of its sovereignty the State was not liable in its own courts and that there was vested in the State an immunity from action, a prerogative formerly vested in the Crown. The Supreme Court rejected these contentions. The State was the creation of the People and consequently could only exercise powers given to it by the People. In several parts of the Constitution duties were imposed on the State to bestow rights on the citizen. The Constitution sets restrictions on the exercise of the powers of the State and every such restriction tended to prove that the State was not sovereign. If the Constitution had intended the State to have immunity it would have said so. The concept of immunity from action was a medieval one based on feudal theories contained in the maxim that 'the King can do no wrong'. These concepts were irreconcilable with modern ideas. Ireland was a State established in modern times and its Constitution was of recent enactment. The Crown was completely absent from the Constitution and gone with it was any idea of the Crown as the personification of the State.

The Jurisdiction of the State

The sovereignty of the State in international law is essentially a negative concept; the *jurisdiction* of the State is its positive counterpart. Jurisdiction is concerned with legislative, executive and judicial competence and can be divided into personal and territorial jurisdictions.

Personal jurisdiction is the authority asserted over individuals on the basis of fidelity and loyalty. In the evolution of contemporary international law, personal jurisdiction preceded territorial jurisdiction. By this concept the subject of a sovereign was considered to remain under his authority wherever the subject went. This concept finds a place in our constitutional law. The Constitution draws a distinction between the status of the citizen and that of the non-citizen. Because fidelity and loyalty is demanded of the citizen, the State acknowledges that certain fundamental rights are available to him and not to others. The concept of personal jurisdiction was enforced by the common law. This was done on the basis of domicile. Irish courts may apply our law to citizens dying abroad provided they retained an Irish domicile and conversely an Irish court might apply foreign law where a person dies in Ireland but is domiciled elsewhere. Irish courts recognise a divorce obtained by persons whose domicile at the time of the divorce permitted divorce though there is no law of divorce available to persons domiciled within this State.[21]

The trend in international law was away from personal jurisdiction and towards a territorial jurisdiction. Sovereigns insisted on exclusive jurisdiction over every person and every thing within their borders. The most noticeable exception was diplomatic personnel. In most areas of our law this jurisdiction operates: everyone regardless of nationality is subject to the criminal and civil laws. This jurisdiction is extended to ships and aircraft while on the high seas or in international air-space. In *The People (A. G.) v. Thomas* a person was convicted of a crime committed aboard an Irish registered ship while on the high seas between Ireland and Britain.

So far we have looked at the exercise of personal and territorial jurisdictions. It remains for us to examine the extraordinary jurisdictions of a state. The principle that the courts of a place where the crime is committed have jurisdiction over the offender is one of universal application. This principle has a number of advantages including the convenience of the forum and the presumed involvement of the interests of the state where the crime was committed. The question had been mooted whether extra-territorial jurisdiction was permissible under our law. There were some judicial views that it did. In *R (Alexander) v. Circuit Judge for Cork* two judges of the former Supreme Court, without citing authority, felt that it did. Kennedy C.J. said: '.. I refer of course to territorial jurisdiction. If specific legislation of such a kind were passed (without reciprocal enactment by the Parliament within whose territorial sovereignty were the persons attempted to be bound) it would *prima facie* offend against the conventions of international law by impinging upon the exclusive sovereignty and jurisdiction of another ...' FitzGibbon J. said: 'But by constitutional usage, and by the comity of nations and so-called international law, the Courts of one country do not, as a rule exercise jurisdiction over the subjects or citizens of another ... I would be prepared to hold that in any case, outside that class of enactment of the Oireachtas, conferring upon the Courts of the Saorstát jurisdiction over foreigners was valid, provided I was satisfied that it was essential for the peace, order and good government of the Saorstát.'

The actual question of extra-territorial jurisdiction came up for discussion in *Art. 26 and the Criminal Law (Jurisdiction) Bill, 1975* (Case No. 3) which provided for the trial within this State of certain offences committed elsewhere. The Supreme Court upheld the constitutionality of the Bill on two grounds both of which are open to criticism. The Supreme Court held that Art. 3 of the Constitution did not prohibit the Oireachtas legislating with extra-territorial effect provided the parliament of Saorstát Éireann had had the same power. O'Higgins C.J., said: 'The Court has no doubt that in 1937 Saorstát Éireann had power to legislate with extra-territorial effect ... The Court is satisfied that Saorstát Éireann had full power to legislate with extra-territorial effect from 1922. This was the view of FitzGibbon J. in *R. (Alexander) v. Circuit Judge for Cork* . . .' This bald statement is not convincing. It ignored the 1929 report of the Conference on the Operation of Dominion Legislation which noted that the question was 'full of obscurity' in favour of s.3 of the *Statute of Westminster, 1931,* a statute incidentally not binding on Irish courts, which declared that the parliament of a Dominion had full powers to pass laws having extra-territorial effect. But that raised the unanswered question whether the Oireachtas of Saorstát Éireann was a Dominion parliament.[22] Reliance on the views of FitzGibbon J. is unsound because the actual point was not argued in that case, no authority was cited for his *obiter dictum,* because his views were contrary to existing judicial opinion,[23] and because, from the question above, it was obvious that FitzGibbon J. envisaged a situation where the person was outside the jurisdiction of the Irish courts, unlike the situations envisaged in the Bill where the person was apprehended within this jurisdiction.

The Supreme Court relied on the decision of the Permanent Court of International Justice in the *Lotus* case[24] for the authority in international law that every sovereign state has power to legislate with extra-territorial effect. The facts of the *Lotus* case may show how the Supreme Court misunderstood the question at issue there. A collision took place on the high seas between a French steamer and a Turkish collier. The latter sank and when the French steamer put in to a Turkish port its officers were tried and convicted of the manslaughter of those aboard the Turkish ship. France contended that the flag state alone of the vessel had the jurisdiction over acts performed on the high seas. By the casting vote of the President of the Court the decision was that Turkey had not acted in conflict with the principles of international law by exercising criminal jurisdiction. This decision has been criticised by a number of authorities[25] and its emphasis on state discretion has been contradicted in two later cases.[26] The Permanent Court was dealing with a case where one state purported to exercise jurisdiction over the high seas whereas the *Criminal Law (Jurisdiction) Bill* was purporting to exercise jurisdiction over actions committed in another state.

An Independent and Democratic State

The word 'independent' as used in Art. 5 of the Constitution may be a synonym for sovereign or it may imply something different. 'Sovereign' means freedom from external authority. 'Independent' could mean not affiliated or reliant on other states. Does this mean that this State must not take a partisan attitude to world affairs. Does the word independent imply neutrality?

Democracy can be defined as government by the people or their elected representatives. The common people are the political force within a state.

13

Democracy must be more than the citizens having a periodic say in the election of their leaders: it must mean the correlative right to offer oneself for election. It must mean that the affairs of state be conducted fairly. There must be equity in the taxation system: one section of the community must not be over-burdened with taxes nor must another section reap all the benefits without contributing. Public funds must be evenly distributed. In a democratic state public service posts must be open to all in fair competition: the fostering of an elite must not occur.

Different regimes lay claim to the title of being democratic. Most countries in the western world claim to be democratic. In these pluralist regimes the most notable feature is peaceful political struggle which takes place openly and freely under the glare of publicity. There are several political parties: the struggle for power is open to public attention. Liberal concepts of freedom are accepted: there are freedoms to express opinions, to establish and join political organisations and to hold meetings and disseminate political beliefs and opinions. But in unitarian regimes, such as the USSR and East Germany, political conflict does not officially exist except in the form of individual struggle to win the favour of the party in power. The official doctrine is above the fray of political battle: there is no freedom to organise opposition groups to challenge the monopoly of the established order. There are elections but all the candidates belong to the one recognised party.

Which meaning would the courts adopt if called on to consider the meaning of the word 'democratic' in Art. 5? Would the meaning given to it prevent the establishment of a one-party State? The answer is probably in the affirmative though support for this proposition cannot be found in the political rights in the Constitution but rather in the personal rights. It seems that once there is a plurality of candidates allowed in an election, the citizen's political rights are vindicated. The prevention of a one-party State is found in Art. 40 which guarantees freedom of expression and association. What more fundamental way of exercising these rights could be found than offering oneself for election? But the spirit of the Constitution demands positive incentives towards political activity. While there is no constitutional or legal restriction on the establishment of a political party, the State through its existing political establishment may create a hegemony: while not forbidding new activity it may create a climate in favour of the existing order, thus preventing the dissemination of new ideologies and ideas. There is some evidence which suggests that such is the position in this country. A registered political party can place its name on the ballot papers of its candidates: in order to be registered a party must fulfil requirements set down by those already elected. The state-owned radio and television station, while not bound by law to cover political activities, does so by giving the largest party represented in the Dáil the greatest amount of coverage while the others are covered according to size in descending order of representation. A new party gets little or nothing.

For Dáil elections a deposit is payable: this discriminates in favour of those in power who have the means by drawing earnings from the State, and against those seeking it. Existing political parties represented in the Dáil are favoured by the payment to their leaders of sums of money from public finances. Elected representatives are favoured by the provision of travelling subsidies and free postage over those seeking office. Do these restrictions prevent the State from being a true democracy, and what approach would the courts take should any of these restrictions be challenged?

A Republican State

The one concept noticeably absent from Art. 5 is the declaration that the State is a republic. A republic can be defined as a form of government in which the head of state is elected by the people, or by some body itself directly elected by the people. This republican form of government is evidenced by the presidential system, the most impressive example being the American one. In the United States the people elect their head of state whereas in India it is the Congress, itself an elected body, which has this function. Under the Constitution the head of state, the President of Ireland, is elected by the People. Surprisingly, until 1948 the executive function in relation to external relations was performed by the British Crown on the advice of the Government. This power was repatriated with the passing of the *Republic of Ireland Act, 1948*. This Act declares that the description of the State shall be the *Republic of Ireland* whereas Art. 4 of the Constitution declares the name of the State is *Éire* or in the English language *Ireland*.

A Unitary State

Art. 5 establishes Ireland as a unitary State. In such a state the legislature of the entire country is the supreme law-making body. It may permit other legislatures to function but it retains the power in law to overrule them: they are subordinate to it. On the other hand in a federal constitution the powers of government are divided between a government for the entire country and governments for parts of the country in such a way that each government is legally independent within its own sphere. The government for the entire country has its own areas of powers and it exercises these without any control from the governments of the constituent parts and these latter in turn exercise their powers without being controlled by the central government. Among examples of federal constitutions may be mentioned those of the United States, Switzerland and Australia. In each the Constitution sets out the matters on which the legislature of the entire country can make laws and it reserves to the states or cantons a sphere in which their legislatures may operate in legal independence of the central government and of each other.

The Government of Ireland Act, 1920 established a federal Ireland with institutions for each part of the island and all-Ireland institutions. One of

15

the possible constitutional solutions to the partition of Ireland may be the establishment of a federal State similar to that provided in that Act.

The Ownership of the State

The 1916 Proclamation declared the right of the People of Ireland to the ownership of Ireland, a sentiment restarted by the First Dáil in 1919. The Constitution of Saorstát Éireann declared that 'all the lands and waters, mines and minerals, within the territory of the Irish Free State hitherto vested in the State, or any department thereof ... and all the natural resources of the same territory (including the air and all forms of potential energy) ... belong to the Irish Free State, subject to any trusts, grants, leases or concessions then existing ...' Art. 10 of the Constitution declares that 'all natural resources, including the air and all forms of potential energy ... belong to the State subject to all estates and interests ... lawfully vested in any person or body'. Does this mean all the land of Ireland belongs to the State in the same manner as all the land of the United Kingdom is held from the Crown? If this is the meaning, then the State has done nothing to vest the land in itself as ultimate owner. Large tracts of Irish lands are owned by old feudal landlords who reside abroad, and have little interest in the affairs of this State. It is even possible that rents leaving this country find their way from landlord to landlord to the British Crown. The placing of the State in the position of ultimate owner could be done without any interference with the right of private ownership. On the other hand Art. 10 can be construed as placing the State in the category of private owner together with other private individuals. The State cannot abrogate interests which existed in others at the time the Constitution was enacted: these continue to exist and can be alienated without hindrance. On this construction the State owns some of the land and the remainder belongs to others.

The Constitution of Saorstát Éireann prohibited the permanent alienation of State property and this limitation was not continued. The temporary or permanent alienation of State property is permitted: this power adds weight to the construction that the State should be classified as a private owner of property.

A Citizen of the State

Nationality is important on two levels. It is significant in international law in matters such as diplomatic protection abroad, immigration, deportation and the negotiation of treaties. In constitutional law the distinction between nationals and aliens is relevant because the latter are subject to disabilities. Nationality is founded on the doctrine of allegiance which is considered to bind the citizen to the State. The Constitution demands fidelity to the nation and loyalty to the State as political duties of the citizen and in return the State protects and vindicates the citizen.

The Constitution in Art. 9 confers citizenship on any person who was a

16

citizen of Saorstát Éireann just before the coming into effect of the Constitution. The further acquisition and loss of citizenship is to be determined by law, currently the *Irish Nationality and Citizenship Act, 1956.* It permits the acquisition of citizenship in a number of ways. Every person born in Ireland is a citizen from birth. Every person is a citizen if his father or mother was a citizen at the time of his birth: the birth can take place anywhere and it is immaterial whether the child's parents are married. The child of a foreign accredited diplomat here is not a citizen.

Pending the re-integration of the national territory, a person born in Northern Ireland on or after 6 December, 1922[27] is not a citizen unless that person declares himself to be a citizen. If that person is not of full age his parent or guardian may declare for him. In either case he takes citizenship from birth. A person born of parents who themselves were born outside Ireland is not a citizen unless the birth is registered in a diplomatic or consular office or in the Department of Foreign Affairs.

A woman not a citizen at the date of her marriage to a citizen, other than a citizen by naturalisation, does not become a citizen merely on marriage. She must lodge a declaration with the Minister for Justice or with any diplomatic or consular office either before or at any time after her marriage accepting citizenship as her post-nuptial citizenship. If the declaration is lodged before marriage citizenship dates from the marriage: in other cases it dates from the lodgment. There is no similar provision applying to non-citizen males who marry citizens though they may apply for citizenship by naturalisation. This inequality was challenged in *Somjee v. The Minister for Justice* (Case No. 85) where the High Court in upholding the statute said that it was not the act of marrying which conferred citizenship but the law. The two different methods of acquiring citizenship did not create an invidious discrimination but were merely a diversity of arrangement. Even if the Court ruled the statute unconstitutional it availed the alien nothing because the Court could not instruct the Oireachtas to legislate in a manner which would confer on the alien the benefit sought.

A child born posthumously whose father at the date of his death was a citizen acquires citizenship as if his father was alive at his birth. Every deserted infant first found in the State is, unless the contrary is proven, a citizen. On the making of an adoption order under the *Adoption Act 1952* the adopted child, if not already a citizen, becomes one if the adopter, or where the adopters are a married couple either spouse, is a citizen.

The President may grant citizenship as a token of honour to a person (or to his child or grandchild) who in the opinion of the Government has done signal honour or rendered distinguished service to the nation.[28]

Citizenship may be conferred on an alien by means of a certificate of naturalisation granted by the Minister for Justice in his absolute discretion. Certain formalities must be complied with and before it is granted the person must in open court before a District Justice make a declaration of fidelity to the nation and loyalty to the State. A citizen by naturalisation has all the political and personal rights of a citizen by birth or descent except that his citizenship may be revoked.

A person not a citizen is an alien, and the *Aliens Act, 1935* gives wide power of control over non-citizens. Whether or not an alien can avail of the personal rights acknowledged in the Constitution is considered in Chapter 10. One undoubted right they do not possess is the right of entry to the State and it seems that aliens can be deported whereas citizens cannot. In *The State (K.M.) v. The Minister for Foreign Affairs* (Case No. 92) the High Court in declaring a constitutional right to leave the State must by implication have acknowledged the corresponding right to enter the State. If the citizen has a right to leave he must have the right to return which may be curtailed when the common good requires though not in any arbitrary or unjustifiable manner.

The Separation of Powers

The ability or the capacity to perform, act or to exercise a choice may be limited or unlimited. In legal affairs the very meaning of the word 'law' denotes limitation. When something is done according to law we mean that only that which is permitted to be done is done and nothing more. In constitutional law when speaking of an act or power being *unconstitutional* we mean it was performed without there being justification for it in the Constitution. It is clear from our constitutional framework that the State is the creation of the People. It has only limited powers and duties: the State is not all-powerful. The People is the only possessor of unlimited power in our constitutional law. How does the Constitution insist on the limitation of power? It relies on the doctrine of the separation of powers. There is a maxim, the truth of which can be seen throughout history, that all power corrupts and that absolute power corrupts absolutely. The doctrine of the separation of powers accepts that maxim unquestioningly and attempts to frustrate its effect. Tyranny is inevitable if too much power is placed in too few hands. 'Personal liberty is to be found', according to Montesquieu, 'only where there is no abuse of power. But constant experience shows us that every man invested with power is liable to abuse it, and to carry his authority as far as it will go ... To prevent this abuse, it is necessary from the nature of things that one power should be a check on another ... There would be an end of everything if the same person or body, whether of the nobles of the people, were to exercise all ... powers.'[29]

Montesquieu[30] divided the powers of government into three and this forms the basis of the present classification for most modern states. The legislative function is the making of new laws and the alteration or repeal of existing ones: in this country the legislative organ of the State is the Oireachtas. The executive function is the general administration of the State including the framing of policy: this function is performed by the Government. The judicial function consists of the interpretation of laws and their

18

application to the facts of particular cases: this function within the State is exercised by independent courts. Of course a complete separation of powers in the sense of a distribution of the three differing functions among three independent organs of government with no co-operation would bring government to a halt. There must be interaction if good and fair government is to flourish. The doctrine does not forbid co-operation provided that each organ operates as a check on the others.

The United States Constitution goes far in this doctrine. The executive power is vested in the President who is elected directly by the people for a fixed term, the federal legislative power is vested in the Congress and the federal judicial power is vested in the Supreme Court. The President and his advisers cannot be members of Congress, nor are they responsible to Congress, nor can they initiate legislation though they can recommend it in a message to Congress. In Britain the separation of power is not so clear. Parliament legislates and operates a check on the executive who are all members of Parliament. The judges are independent though some judges are members of the House of Lords, one of the Houses of Parliament. The Lord Chancellor is a member of Parliament, the Cabinet and the judiciary. These examples prove and misprove the doctrine. They contradict it on the ground that there is some contact between the organs of government and they support the doctrine in that in both systems there are checks and balances which do not allow the concentration of all power in the hands of one organ of government.

The Constitution declares that all powers of government, legislative, executive and judicial, derive from the People (Art. 6). This is an emphatic direction that the organs of government are divided threefold and limited. A reading of the Constitution reinforces this direction which has been supported many times in judicial comment. The Oireachtas can control the Government by refusing to enact its policies into law and Dáil Éireann can, by withdrawing its support, force the Government's resignation. The Oireachtas checks the Courts by deciding the content of the law, legal procedures, the structure of the court system and by being empowered to remove judges from office. The Government balances the power of the Oireachtas by having the exclusive right to recommend the appropriation of public monies. The Courts check the Government by demanding that it acts *intra vires* the Constitution and checks the Oireachtas by denying it the ability to enact unconstitutional legislation. Apart from these general checks by one organ of government on the other two, there exist internal checks and balances within each organ of government which are considered in the appropriate places later.

While the rigid separation of powers is not contained in the Constitution, the Courts have not hesitated to condemn actions or strike down measures on the ground that one organ of government has trespassed into the domain of another. There are three possible clashes. The first can be between the legislature and the executive, the second between the legislature and the

19

judiciary and the third can be between the executive and the judiciary. From the decided cases it will be seen that the courts are the organ of government most jealous of its preserve and most willing to repel encroachments on its functions.

We will examine in the first instance cases where the legislative and judicial functions have clashed. In *Buckley v. Attorney General* (Case No. 17) the Oireachtas passed a statute concerning a case which was then being litigated. The High Court refused to stay the proceedings because to do so would, according to Gavan Duffy P., be to 'abdicate its proper jurisdiction to administer justice in a cause whereof it is duly seized'. The Supreme Court upheld that decision on appeal. O'Byrne J. explained that 'in bringing these proceedings the plaintiffs were exercising a constitutional right and they were, and are, entitled to have the matter in dispute determined by the judicial organ of the State. The substantial effect of the Act is that the dispute is determined by the Oireachtas . . .' In *In re Haughey* (Case No. 41) the Courts, in rejecting the argument that the Committee of Public Accounts of Dáil Éireann had tried and convicted the applicant, warned, per Ó Dálaigh C.J. that 'the trial of a criminal offence is an exercise of judicial power and is a function of the Courts, not of a committee of the Legislature . . . The Committee of Public Accounts is not a court and its members are not judges . . . Trial, conviction and sentence are indivisible parts of the exercise of this power.' In *Maher v. Attorney General* (Case No. 53) the Supreme Court in rejecting a statutory provision which gave a badge of conclusiveness to a certificate in a criminal trial said, per FitzGerald C.J., that 'the administration of justice, which in criminal matters is confined exclusively by the Constitution to the courts and judges set up under the Constitution, necessarily reserves to those courts and judges the determination of all the essential ingredients of any offence charged against an accused person'.

The prevention by statute of a person remanded in custody from being returned to the court on the remand day was in *The State (C.) v. The Minister for Justice* (Case No. 88) found to be an unwarrantable interference with the administration of justice. 'In the year 1875', explained Ó Dálaigh C.J., 'it was for an omnipotent parliament to determine what should be done . . . no question could arise as to whether the provision made by parliament was or was not an intrusion into the judicial domain. It is otherwise now because the Constitution effects a separation of legislative, executive and judicial powers . . . the provisions of the Act of 1875 . . . is about as large an intrusion upon a court's proceeding as one could imagine.' Whether the power of the Attorney General to return a person for trial after the District Court had refused to do so was an administration of justice was decided in *The State (Shanahan) v. Attorney General* (Case No. 99). The High Court held it was. Davitt P. explained that 'if the Attorney General can be, within the terms of Constitution, empowered to reverse such a judicial decision of the District Court then he, and anyone else, can be empowered constitutionally to reverse any judicial decision of any Court.' This decision was reversed on appeal by the Supreme Court because a person could be put on trial without any preliminary examination. If the power given was to change or modify the order of the District Court there might be some objection. 'The direction of the Attorney General', according to Walsh J., 'is not an intervention in the particular controversy before the District Court which has, in the event, already been brought to an end ... Rather is the direction of the Attorney General the initiation of a different justiciable controversy, namely, the trial upon indictment.'

What the courts have objected to in these cases is the direct interference with actual litigation rather than the proper ordering of the judicial system. The Oireachtas can and does interfere with the administration of justice without complaint from the courts. Statutes have declared and limited the civil jurisdictions of the courts; created new procedures, criminal offences and torts; given new remedies; abolished civil wrongs; created courts and rule-making committees. All of these are vitally necessary if the legal system is to cater for the needs of society.

We will now examine the occasions on which the courts and the executive have clashed. In 1939 the High Court had to consider the nature of the power given to a Minister of State to order the internment without trial of a person in *The State (Burke) v. Lennon* (Case No. 86). In striking down the function Gavan Duffy J. remarked that 'the authority conferred on a Minister ... is an authority, not merely to act judicially, but to administer justice and condemn an alleged offender without charge or hearing and without the aid of a jury ...' The Oireachtas retaliated by changing the offending word 'satisfied' to 'opinion' and the President referred the Bill to the Supreme Court: *Art. 26 and the Offences Against the State (Amendment) Bill, 1940* (Case No. 7). The Supreme Court rejected the argument, and by implication the decision in Burke's case, that the Minister when ordering an internment was hearing a criminal charge and imposing punishment. Comparing the judgments the High Court decision is to be preferred but the judiciary, particularly the Supreme Court, must have been aware, when giving their decisions, that the Constitution could be amended by ordinary legislation and they may have feared some curtailment of judicial functions if they appeared to challenge and frustrate the legislature and executive. They were yet to stand over even further abuses of executive power. These short-term failures ensured long-term advantages.

In *Deaton v. Attorney General* (Case No. 31) the Supreme Court struck down legislation which permitted the executive to choose which of two penalties a court should impose. 'In my opinion', said Ó Dálaigh C.J., 'the selection of punishment is an integral part of the administration of justice and, as such, cannot be committed to the hands of the Executive.' But it must be noted that in *Conroy v. Attorney General* (Case No. 25) the Supreme Court held that the mandatory disqualification from driving was not a punishment but the withdrawal of a privilege. The courts had to decide in *Murphy v. Dublin Corporation* (Case No. 59) whether the executive could claim privilege over documents which were considered essential in pending litigation. The Supreme Court was not enamoured with the common law rule that once the claim of executive privilege* was made, the courts were bound to accept it. 'The division of powers', according to Walsh J., 'does not give paramountcy in all circumstances to any one of the organs exercising the powers of government over the other. ... it is, however, impossible for the judicial power in the proper exercise of its functions to permit any other body or power to decide for it whether or not a document will be disclosed or produced. In the last resort the decision lies with the courts so long as they have seisin* of the case.' The Court acknowledged that different rules might apply where the vital interests of the State were involved.

But the courts will not interfere with the policy of the executive which falls short of constitutional transgression. This was decided by the Supreme Court in *Boland v. An Taoiseach* (Case No. 14) though only because in the case under consideration intervention was inappropriate. 'In the event of the Government', said Griffin J., 'acting in a manner which is in contravention of some provision of the Constitution it would in my view be the duty and the right of the Courts, as guardians of the Constitution, to intervene when called upon to do so if a complaint of a breach of any of the provisions of the Constitution is substantiated in proceedings brought before the Courts.' The courts will not permit the executive to introduce legislation and, when it is challenged as to its constitutionality, suspend its operation. This was decided in *Condon v. The Minister for Labour* (Case No. 24) where O'Higgins C.J. explained: 'Serious consequences could ensue if this Court pronounced that temporary legislation ... should be immune from judicial review merely because it had expired before the question of its validity could be examined. All legislation passed by the Oireachtas is presumed to be valid. If the Oireachtas were free to enact temporary legislation ... and if that legislation, on its expiry, escaped examination in the Courts, a form of legislative intimidation could be exercised.'

From a review of these cases it can be seen that the doctrine of the separation of powers is not an empty political theory but a constitutional reality implemented to ensure that power is exercised in the manner prescribed by the People.

Chapter 4

THE OIREACHTAS

Nature of the Oireachtas

One of the three arms of government is the Oireachtas,* created by Art. 15.1 and consisting of the President and two Houses, a House of Representatives called Dáil Éireann and a Senate called Seanad Éireann. The legislative function under the separation of powers falls to the Oireachtas though the powers of the Oireachtas extend far beyond the single role of legislating. The expression 'parliamentary government' means government by an executive in and through the Oireachtas. The Oireachtas supervises the Government's conduct by giving or withholding its approval and being responsible for the Government's continuation in office. It controls the judicial arm of government by limiting the scope of the courts, by organising the system of courts and by having the power to remove judges from office.

While exercising checks on the other branches of government the Oireachtas operates an internal system of balances on its component parts. Thus the President can request the Supreme Court's advice on the constitutionality of legislation passed by the Houses of the Oireachtas; and Dáil Éireann, with its greater powers, can be checked by the Seanad. A study of the Oireachtas encompasses both these aspects: its role as an organ of government and the roles of its components. This chapter deals with the Oireachtas proper while the President, the Dáil and the Seanad are given separate chapters.

Supremacy of the Oireachtas?

The legislative supremacy of the British Parliament was, before its entry into the Common Market, the most important characteristic of its constitutional law. In its positive sense it meant that Parliament could pass *any* law and negatively it meant that there was no person or body whose legislative power overrode it. How far do we accept this principle of parliamentary supremacy in our constitutional law? The simple answer is that we do not because we reject the notion of unlimited power. One of the purposes of a constitution is to divide, and thus limit, power among different bodies. It must follow that the Oireachtas, like the other organs of government, is confined to the functions laid down for it in the Constitution and that these functions may be limited or curtailed. In this chapter we examine the areas of government which the Constitution has assigned to the Oireachtas and the limitations imposed.

The Oireachtas must not enact any law which is repugnant to the Constitution (Art. 15.4.1°). Unfortunately a declaration of constitutional invalidity will usually come after the law is enacted and operating. Apart from the limited scope of Art. 26 there is no constitutional machinery for ascertaining whether legislation is constitutional or not before its enactment.

23

In France legislation considered unconstitutional is referred before its enactment to a constitutional court. If the court holds it constitutional it may be enacted into law; if unconstitutional it cannot be enacted. Once laws are passed in France they cannot be challenged. In this country there are two ways of testing the constitutionality of legislation. After a Bill has been passed by the Houses of the Oireachtas, the President may seek the advice of the Supreme Court. The second way is by a person affected by the legislation taking an action in the courts to have it declared constitutionally invalid.

Apart from this general direction the Constitution prohibits the Oireachtas from legislating on certain matters. The Oireachtas must not declare acts to be infringements of the law which were not so at the date of their commission (Art. 15.5). The creation of criminal offences and civil wrongs cannot act retrospectively: they can only operate prospectively because a person should know at the time he performs an action whether it is lawful or not. This constitutional provision does not mean that no law can act retrospectively. For example the *Marriage Act, 1972* regularised certain marriages celebrated abroad. But for a statute to have retrospective effect its provisions must, according to the Supreme Court in *Dunne v. Hamilton,* clearly displace the presumption of prospectivity. In that case the *Family Home Protection Act, 1976*, which renders void a conveyance of the family home by one spouse without the consent in writing of the other spouse, was held not to apply retrospectively to a transaction begun before the passing of the statute and not completed until after its enactment, because to do so would frustrate contractual rights and thus constitute an unjust attack on the property rights of the purchaser contrary to Art. $40.3.2°$ of the Constitution.

No law can disqualify on the ground of sex any citizen from either membership of Dáil Éireann or voting in Dáil elections (Art. $16.1.1°$). No law can be enacted which provides that the number of members to be returned for a Dáil constituency can be less than three (Art. $16.2.6°$).

No law can be passed which removes the appellate jurisdiction of the Supreme Court in cases which involve the question as to whether a law is invalid having regard to the Constitution (Art. $34.4.4°$). No law can be enacted which permits divorce (Art. $41.3.2°$). The State guarantees to pass no law attempting to abolish the right of private ownership (Art. $43.1.2°$), and legislation providing State aid for schools must not discriminate between different religious denominations (Art. $44.2.4°$).

Apart from these constitutional limitations the Oireachtas is free to legislate as it pleases. It can pass unreasonable laws. An Oireachtas could not fetter the freedom of its successors by enacting laws which it claims are unamendable or irrepealable.

Duties and Powers of the Oireachtas

A distinction must be drawn between the duties and the powers of the

24

Oireachtas. There are instances when the Oireachtas *must* act: it is placed under a mandatory duty, and there are instances where the Oireachtas *may* act: it is given a discretionary power. The functions of the Oireachtas will be considered under these headings of duties and powers. But it must be noted here that each House of the Oireachtas does not possess the same powers and duties. This difference stems from the fact that Dáil Éireann, directly elected by the people, is the possessor of greater powers than the Seanad which is elected by a limited electorate.

Duties of the Oireachtas

Some appointments to constitutional offices are made by the Oireachtas. The Taoiseach* is nominated by, and the other Government members are approved by, Dáil Éireann. All are then appointed by the President (Art. 13.1.). The Houses of the Oireachtas must hold at least one session every year though the Constitution does not provide for the length of such sessions. Sittings are in public but in special emergencies a private session may be held with the assent of two-thirds of the members present.

The right to raise and maintain military forces is vested in the Oireachtas (Art. 15.6.1°). The constitutional practice in Britain of authorising the keeping of a permanent army for one year only was a device by Parliament to force the Crown to hold at least one annual session of Parliament. This practice was continued here after 1922 until the *Defence Act 1954* provided for the raising and maintaining of permanent Defence Forces.

Each House must make its own rules and standing orders with power to attach penalties for their infringment (Art. 15.10). The question whether this duty was fulfilled was raised in *In re Haughey* (Case No. 41). It was argued that the standing orders in operation were those of the former Dáil Éireann, the chamber of deputies, established under the Constitution of Saorstát Éireann and not those of the Dáil established under the 1937 Constitution. There was truth in this contention. Before the coming into force of the Constitution, the Committee of Procedure and Privileges met and recommended certain amendments which were adopted by the new Dáil on 12 January 1938. 'This was', said Ó Dálaigh C.J., 'a tacit adoption by the new Dáil Éireann of the standing orders of the former House, as amended, as the standing orders of the new House.' The comment by the Chief Justice that 'taciturnity is uncharacteristic of parliaments' is still true because as yet Dáil Éireann has not adopted a new set of standing orders. The power of punishment for breach of standing orders is considered later.

Each House must elect from its members a Chairman and a Deputy Chairman. The Chairman of the Dáil is known as the Ceann Comhairle and the Deputy as the Leas-Cheann Comhairle. The Chairman of the Seanad is known as the Cathaoirleach and the Deputy as the Leas-Chathaoirleach. Apart from taking the Chair in each respective House these officers have other constitutional functions; both are members of the Presidential Commission and the Council of State. The law may confer extra functions. Both are members of the Appeal Board which hears appeals arising from the refusal to register a political party and both are members of the Appeal Board which hears appeals arising from the refusal to register a body as a Seanad nominating body.

Because the Ceann Comhairle of the Dáil restricts his political activities by not, for example, asking parliamentary questions or contributing to debates he is given a privilege under Art. 16.6. The Ceann Comhairle, should he wish to stand for election, is automatically re-elected. The *Electoral Act 1963* provides that he is re-elected for the constituency for which he was a member or if a revision of the constituencies has taken place the constituency declared to correspond to that constituency. It can be argued that the citizens who voted for a member of Dáil Éireann who subsequently is elected Ceann Comhairle are denied representation by that member, though in the multi-seat constituencies this does not amount to total non-representation. A case can be made for appointing a Ceann Comhairle from outside the membership of the Dáil. This privilege of automatic re-election does not extend to the Cathaoirleach of the Seanad.

The Government must prepare Estimates of the receipts and Estimates of State expenditure in each financial year (Art. 28.4.3°), and these must be presented to and be considered by Dáil Éireann. Presumably this constitutional requirement of consideration gives to each member a right to raise questions and debate their contents. The Seanad has no power to consider the Estimates. More attention is given to the finances of the State in Chapter 8.

Every member of the Government has the right of audience in each House of the Oireachtas. Each Minister can explain policy and answer questions and reply to debates. This provision, Art. 28.8, clarifies the standing of a Minister in relation to the House of which he is not a member. In general there is no right of audience given to Oireachtas members to speak in either House nor is there a constitutional provision for the meeting of both Houses.

Every international agreement to which the State becomes a party must be laid before Dáil Éireann (Art. 29.5). This seems to be for information purposes only because the expression 'laid before' is used. There seems no right to debate and vote upon such agreement. The State and international agreements are fully discussed in Chapter 8.

Powers of the Oireachtas

The Power to Legislate

Legislation is the laying down of legal rules by a competent authority. Generally these rules are purely for the future though occasionally actual situations are legislated for. Law-making is the central function of the

26

legislator and includes every expression of the will of the legislature irrespective of its purpose and effect. Legislation may be superior or subordinate. The former proceeds from the superior legislator in the State and is incapable of being repealed, annulled or controlled by another legislative authority though in this country a judicial act may do so. Subordinate legislation proceeds from any authority other than the superior authority but is dependent for its continued existence and validity on the superior authority.

The Oireachtas is the superior law-making authority: superior must not be confused with supreme. The Oireachtas is the sole and exclusive lawmaker (Art. 15.2.1°). The law may create and recognise subordinate legislatures. With this two-tier system constitutional law confines itself to the superior legislature and leaves subordinate legislation to administrative law. Suffice to explain that the superior legislator grants to subordinate legislators the power to make rules which have the force of law. Some control is maintained by the superior legislator.

Applying procedural criteria, legislation can be divided into three categories. Ordinary legislation is that which does not fall within the two other categories. Financial legislation is the second, and abridged-time legislation is the third.

Ordinary legislation can cover a multitude of subjects: a profession can be regulated, conditions of employment controlled, a new coinage created, succession rights altered, semi-state bodies established, criminal offences created, legal procedures provided and civil actions abolished. A Bill to amend the Constitution is subject to the same procedure as ordinary legislation. Every ordinary Bill initiated and passed by the Dáil is sent to the Seanad. A Bill may lie on the order paper of the Dáil indefinitely but once passed to the Seanad a time limit applies. The Seanad has a maximum of ninety days to consider an ordinary Bill. There are two possible consequences if the Seanad either (a) rejects a Bill completely, or (b) amends it in ways not agreeable to the Dáil, or (c) neither passes or rejects the Bill within the ninety days. The Dáil may allow the Bill to lapse or may insist that it becomes law. If the latter is desired the Bill is deemed to have passed both Houses of the Oireachtas if the Dáil so resolves within a 180-day period after the expiration of the ninety days. The Seanad cannot thwart the will of the Dáil, the popularly elected House, by holding a Bill indefinitely, or by rejecting it ensure its permanent defeat. A Bill must always be passed by each House separately as there is no constitutional provision for a joint meeting of both Houses to consider and pass legislation. An ordinary Bill may be initiated in the Seanad and when passed go to the Dáil. If the Dáil amends it the Bill is then considered to have been initiated in the Dáil and must proceed again to the Seanad if passed by the Dáil.

Financial legislation has its own procedure and this is the second category of legislation. A Bill containing a financial proposal, or a Money Bill, to use its constitutional term, is one which contains only any of the following:

27

(1) the imposition, repeal, remission, alteration or regulation of taxation; (2) the imposition for the payment of debt or other financial purposes of charges on public money or the variation or repeal of any such charges; (3) supply; (4) the appropriation, receipt, custody, issue or audit of accounts of public money; (5) the raising or guarantee of any loan or its repayment; and (6) matters incidental to any of these matters.[31] (Art. 22). If the Ceann Comhairle is of opinion that a Bill is a Money Bill he so certifies. A Money Bill can only be initiated in the Dáil and if passed is sent to the Seanad for its recommendations. The Seanad has only twenty-one days to make such recommendations before the Bill is returned to the Dáil which may accept or reject them. If the Seanad fails to return a Money Bill, or if it makes recommendations unacceptable to the Dáil, the Bill is deemed to have passed both Houses at the expiration of the twenty-one days. Here is another example of the Dáil having a greater prerogative than the Seanad. But Seanad Éireann is not left without some remedy. (Art. 21).

A challenge can be made to the certificate of the Ceann Comhairle. The Seanad may by a resolution, passed at a sitting at which not less than thirty members are present, request the President to refer the question whether the Bill is or is not a Money Bill to a Committee of Privileges. If the President, after consultation with the Council of State, accedes to this request he appoints the Committee which consists of an equal number from each House with a judge of the Supreme Court as Chairman who has a casting vote only in the event of an equality of votes. Though the President must consult with the Council of State before acceding to the request he has a discretion as to the number of members and their choice. The Committee must report within twenty-one days after the day on which the Bill was sent to the Seanad. Their decision is final and conclusive. If the President does not accede to the Seanad's request, or if the Committee fails to report within the time allowed, the certificate of the Ceann Comhairle stands confirmed.[32] (Art. 22).

The third category of Bills, known as Abridged Time Bills, have a different procedure from the other two categories. Art. 24 declares that if a Bill is passed by the Dáil and the Taoiseach certifies in writing to the President and to the Chairmen of both Houses of the Oireachtas that in the Government's opinion the Bill is urgently needed for the preservation of the public peace and security, or by reason of a domestic or international emergency, then the time for the consideration of such a Bill by the Seanad will, if the Dáil so resolves, and the President concurs, be abridged to such period as the Dáil specifies. The concurrence of the Seanad is not necessary though the President's role in this procedure offers some protection against abuse. Time for consideration can only be abridged and not abolished.

If such a Bill is (a) rejected by the Seanad, or (b) passed with amendments to which the Dáil objects, or (c) neither passed nor rejected within the abridged-time period, it is deemed to have passed both Houses at the expiration of that period. Such abridged-time legislation only remains in force for ninety days though this period can be extended by resolutions of both Houses. This procedure has never been resorted to but is necessary because of the obvious need to act quickly in times of emergency.

Promulgation of Laws

The Taoiseach must present a Bill to the President for his signature and promulgation as law as soon as it has passed both Houses (Art. 25). A Bill is promulgated as law by the publication at the President's direction of notice in the *Iris Oifigiúil** that the Bill has become law. The President must sign a Bill between the fifth and seventh day after presentation though he may at the Government's request, and with the Seanad's concurrence, sign a Bill earlier than the fifth day. Every Abridged Time Bill must be signed on the day it is presented. Every Bill becomes law on the day it is signed though it may not come into operation until later, on the making of a statutory instrument by the appropriate authority.

Reference of Bills to the Supreme Court

The President is under a duty to sign Bills into law. But this is a duty coupled with a power. The President has a discretion not to sign a Bill, but for one reason only: in order to obtain the views of others, either the People or the Supreme Court. This power to obtain the advice of the Supreme Court before the signing of a Bill into law is unknown in other jurisdictions. It was included in the Constitution because it was not foreseen that the courts would entertain individual constitutional actions brought by the citizen. The President may after consultation with the Council of State refer any Bill to the Supreme Court for a decision whether it or any of its specific provisions is repugnant to the Constitution (Art. 26). He may not refer a Money Bill, an Abridged Time Bill or a Bill to amend the Constitution. The reference must be made not later than the seventh day after it was presented for promulgation. Pending the Supreme Court's decision the President refrains from signing the Bill.

The President may refer the whole Bill or only part of it for decision and he may ask the Supreme Court the general question whether what he is referring offends the Constitution or he may confine the question of possible repugnance to specific Articles. A Supreme Court of at least five judges must consider the reference by hearing counsel on behalf of the Attorney General, who argues in favour of a constitutional construction, and counsel assigned by the Court, who generally argue against its constitutionality. The Supreme Court must pronounce its decision in open court within sixty days of a reference. To satisfy this constitutional requirement, a simple yes or no would suffice but in keeping with judicial tradition a reasoned decision is given. The Constitution is silent on the consequences of the Supreme Court failing or refusing to give a decision within the sixty days.[33]

29

The decision of the majority of the judges is the decision of the Court and no opinion either assenting or dissenting is to be pronounced or even disclosed. It is difficult for a number of judges to agree on a unitary decision. Judges may disagree on the conclusion or agree on the conclusion but disagree on how to reach it. It is within the judicial tradition to dissent. This Art. 26.2.2° when originally enacted permitted the disclosure of whether the decision was unanimous or by majority. The former Supreme Court in its first referral, *Art. 26 and the Offences Against the State (Amendment) Bill, 1940* (Case No. 7), gave a majority decision. This loophole was closed by the *Second Amendment of the Constitution Act, 1941* which was passed as ordinary legislation within the three-year period in which such amendments could be made.

No court may question the validity of a law the Bill for which was referred to the Supreme Court by the President (Art. 34.3.3°). The consequences of a referral are important: that law can never be challenged again no matter how long it remains on the statute book and how circumstances change.[34] Of the four referrals which the Supreme Court held to be constitutional two are still in force. The Supreme Court has ingeniously suggested that the referrals up to 1961 may not be immune from further challenge because they were decisions of the old Supreme Court of Justice established under the Constitution of Saorstát Éireann which had not the jurisdiction to hear such questions.[35] The Supreme Court which had such jurisdiction was not established until late 1961.

Six referrals have been made. The first was the *Offences Against the State (Amendment) Bill, 1940* (Case No. 7) which permitted internment without trial. It was upheld by the former Supreme Court and remains in force.[36] The President referred only one section of the *School Attendance Bill, 1942* (Case No. 8) to the Supreme Court which advised him that it was unconstitutional.[37] Twenty years passed before the next referral which was the *Electoral (Amendment) Bill, 1961* (Case No. 4) which was found unobjectionable and has since been repealed.[38] The *Criminal Law (Jurisdiction) Bill, 1975* (Case No. 3) was held to be constitutional and is still in force.[39] Later the same year the President referred the *Emergency Powers Bill, 1976* (Case No. 5) to the court and was advised that it was constitutional. It has since lapsed.[40] The last referral was the *Housing (Private Rented Dwellings) Bill, 1981* (Case No. 6) which was considered repugnant to the Constitution.[41]

The Presidential Commission which acts in certain circumstances has never referred a Bill to the Supreme Court though it has that power.

In the last referral, *Art. 26 and the Housing (Private Rented Dwellings) Bill, 1981*, the Supreme Court commented on Art. 26. The obvious shortcoming was that matters raised could only be dealt with as abstract problems in the absence of evidence and the Court left open the question as to whether it could hear evidence in referral cases. On the general value of Art. 26 O'Higgins C.J. said: 'Whether the constitutionality of a legislative

30

measure of that nature which has been passed by both Houses of the Oireachtas is better determined within a fixed and immutable period of time ... rather than by means of an action in which specific imputations of unconstitutionality would fall to be determined primarily on proven or admitted facts, is a question on which we refrain from expressing an opinion.' The conclusion from this comment is that the Supreme Court is unhappy with the Art. 26 procedure.

The President must decline to sign a Bill which the Supreme Court has advised is unconstitutional. If the Court only finds objection in part of a Bill it cannot be signed because there is no procedure which allows the President to delete the offending sections. The remaining sections become law if the Oireachtas incorporates them in another Bill. If the Oireachtas were to persist in its intention to pass unconstitutional legislation it has a number of options. It could propose an amendment to the Constitution, or it could propose to either abolish the Supreme Court or curtail its powers, or it could enact the legislation under Art. 28 which is discussed later.

Reference of Bills to the People

In a parliamentary democracy the majority govern with the consent of the minority. To prevent the oppression of the minority Art. 27 provides a procedure by which the views of the People may be ascertained before a Bill becomes law. A majority of the Seanad and at least one-third of the Dáil may jointly petition the President to decline to sign a Bill into law because it contains a proposal of national importance on which the will of the People ought to be obtained. The petition must be in writing, signed by the petitioners and contain the reasons on which the request is based. It must be presented to the President within four days after it has passed or deemed to have passed both Houses.

The President must after consultation with the Council of State give his decision within ten days. If the petition relates to a Bill which has been referred to the Supreme Court the President may defer his decision until after the Court's judgment. If the President concurs with the petition he so informs the Taoiseach and the Chairman of each House. This is an example of the President exercising his discretion. He declines to sign the Bill until the proposals contained in the Bill are approved *either* by the People in a Referendum or by a resolution of a new Dáil after a general election: either of which must be performed within eighteeen months of the President's decision. If the People approve, or if the new Dáil resolves, the Bill must be signed by the President.

If the President dissents from the petitioners' request, he informs the Taoiseach and the Chairman of each House and signs the Bill not later than eleven days after it was passed or deemed to have passed both Houses.

This is a forgotten constitutional procedure for ascertaining the wishes of the People on a piece of legislation. It has never been used, which is a

31

pity because some proposed legislation causes public controversy and a simple way of resolving the issue is by consulting the electorate. The often-made claim by elected representatives that they are the sole law-makers is not constitutionally correct.

Authentication of Legislation

There must be some method by which a statute can be recognised as an Act of the Oireachtas. Art. 25.4.5° declares that the text signed by the President must be enrolled in the office of the Registrar of the Supreme Court and is conclusive evidence of that law. Thus the document enrolled is the law and no other document can prevail against it. All copies of the law must correspond exactly with the enrolled copy. If the President signs a text in one official language an official translation must be issued in the other official language. If the President signs texts in each official language, both must be enrolled, and in case of conflict the text in the national language prevails.

Procedural Invalidity

Can the courts look behind enacted legislation to ensure that the proper constitutional procedures have been observed? This question has never been litigated. In Britain the courts refuse to concern themselves with the procedure of Parliament. But in Ireland the courts have the function of policing the Constitution. They presume that things done are done according to the Constitution. But a litigant who could show some procedural indiscretion, the fact that the Bill never passed the Seanad for example, might be able to have it declared null and void. While the Oireachtas can make law it can only make law in the manner prescribed in the Constitution and not in any other way.

Judicial Power of the Oireachtas

The Houses of the Oireachtas exercise a judicial power when they remove certain constitutional officers from office. The President, judges and the Comptroller and Auditor General can be removed. Another possible judicial function is the punishing of outsiders for contempt of the Oireachtas but as will be seen later in this chapter, it is unlikely that the Oireachtas has this power.

Declaration of War

War must not be declared and the State must not participate in any war without the assent of Dáil Éireann (Art. 28.3.1°). In the case of an actual invasion the Government may take whatever steps they consider necessary for the protection of the State and the Dáil if not sitting must be summoned to meet at the earliest practicable date. In the United States it is the Congress and not the President who declares war, whereas in Britain the declaration of war is vested in the Crown as an executive function.

State of Emergency

The Houses of the Oireachtas may by resolutions declare a national emergency (a) in time of war; (b) in time of armed rebellion, and (c) when there is taking place an armed conflict in which the State is not a participant but which affects the vital interests of the State (Art. 28.3.3°). This Article was more limited when originally enacted but was amended by ordinary legislation by the *First Amendment of the Constitution Act, 1939* and the *Second Amendment of the Constitution Act, 1941.*

Since 2 September 1939 a state of emergency has existed. On that date resolutions were passed on account of the conflict in Europe. Despite pacification in Europe after 1945, the emergency was not revoked until 1 September 1976, only to be renewed. The Houses of the Oireachtas passed resolutions that 'arising out of the armed conflict now taking place in Northern Ireland a national emergency exists affecting the vital interests of the State'.

The consequence of a national emergency is that nothing in the Constitution can be invoked to invalidate any law enacted for the purpose of securing the public safety and the preservation of the State. At one fell swoop the Constitution and fundamental freedoms can be set aside. Rather than take part in idle speculation about what could be done, let us look at what was done under the umbrella of the 1939 resolutions. Military courts which alone could impose the death sentence, from which there was no appeal, and which could disregard the rules of evidence, summarily tried a large number of persons, who were executed. In *In re McGrath and Harte* (Case No. 51) the ordinary courts held themselves incapable of reviewing the emergency laws. This was a period, now deliberately ignored, of which the legislature and the courts can be ashamed. Only one statute was passed on foot of the 1976 resolutions. The *Emergency Powers Act, 1976* empowered the detention of persons without charge for seven days. This statute operated for a year and while it could have been renewed it was allowed to lapse.

The effect of Art. 28.3.3° is to remove from judicial review statutes passed under its provisions. The courts in earlier times tended to stand aside. This attitude was devastatingly explained in *The State (Walsh) v. Lennon* by Gavan Duffy J.:

> The function of the judiciary is to co-operate with the Legislature and the Executive in the government of the State for the people, and in the exercise of that function the judiciary may be called upon from time to time to pronounce a statute unconstitutional or to declare the act of an executive Minister illegal. But in time of war or armed rebellion the apprehension of judicial intervention may at some delicate moment hamper the legislative or the executive authority when Government needs all possible strength and freedom to steer the ship of State through the crisis, consequently the Constitution has placed in the hands of the Oireachtas, as law-giver, special authority to suspend judicial control

over the other organs of government during any such emergency.

This timid approach at that time is understandable because the judiciary may have feared that a more robust attitude would have jeopardised the continued existence of judicial review. The new Constitution could be amended by ordinary legislation for a period of 3 years and a confrontation at that time between the judiciary and the legislature and executive could have had only one conceivable result: the curtailment of judicial power.

The courts by 1976, secure in the role of vindicator of constitutional rights against encroachment by the legislature and executive for 20 years and having seen with hindsight the results of giving *carte blanche* to the other organs of government in the 1940s, reacted less generously when the issue came before the Supreme Court in *Art. 26 and the Emergency Powers Bill, 1976* (Case No. 5). The Supreme Court accepted that once the procedural requirements affecting a Bill to which Art. 28.3.3° applied had been complied with, its provisions could not be invalidated. But it left open the important question as to whether it could look behind the resolutions of the Houses of the Oireachtas to ascertain whether the facts on which they were based existed. O'Higgins C.J. explained: 'It was submitted by the Attorney General that there is a presumption that the facts stated in the resolutions are correct. The Court accepts the existence of that presumption and the corollary that the presumption should be acted upon unless and until it is displaced. In this case it has not been displaced ... The Court expressly reserves for future consideration the question whether the Courts have jurisdiction to review such resolutions.' This comment suggests that had there been evidence which contradicted the facts on which the resolutions were based, the Supreme Court might have held against the legislature. It follows that once the armed conflict in Northern Ireland is past, these resolutions are spent. An interesting dilemma for the courts would be legislation passed under a state of emergency which purported to abolish the Supreme Court. Could a court consider legislation which purported to abolish it?

The Privileges of the Oireachtas

The members of each House are, except in the case of treason, felony or breach of the peace, privileged from arrest while going to, within, and coming from the relevant House (Art. 15.13). A member is free from arrest in civil and criminal matters and an abuse of this constitutional right results in an action for damages rather than punishment by the appropriate House. Freedom of debate is an essential feature of every free legislative assembly. A member is not amenable to any court, or other authority, for any utterances made within the House (Art. 15.13). A member cannot be sued for slander should he defame a citizen in debate. What is said is absolutely privileged. Nor is the member answerable to any tribunal of inquiry though he is answerable to the House itself. How widely does this privilege extend? Does it apply only to words spoken within the chamber of each House or within the wider precincts of each House? In 1970 when the Public Accounts Committee was directed by Dáil Éireann to examine certain public expenditure it reported a fundamental difficulty in that it did not know the extent of this protection. Concern about the liability of the Committee members and witnesses was expressed and the Committee was legally advised that it enjoyed absolute privilege but as a safeguard a statute was passed giving legal protection to the Committee, its advisors and witnesses and to its papers. This statute fell foul of the Supreme Court for other reasons in *In re Haughey* (Case No. 41).

All official reports and publications of the Oireachtas are privileged (Art. 15.12). Each House has power to protect its official documents and the private papers of its members (Art. 15.10). Each House has power to protect its members against interference, molestation and corruption in the exercise of their duties (Art. 15.10). To implement these protections a statute defining the offences is necessary.

Each House makes its own rules and standing orders with power to attach penalties for their infringement. Can each House punish its members only or can it punish anyone improperly treading on its domain? In Britain, Parliament is the High Court of Parliament and calls those who offend its dignity to account before it. The Committee on the Constitution in 1967 concluded that Art. 15.10 was confined to internal matters of procedure and discipline. That this was the correct view was echoed in *In re Haughey* (Case No. 41), per Ó Dálaigh C.J., 'But the trial of a criminal offence is an exercise of judicial power and is a function of the Courts, not of a committee of the Legislature. Art. 34 of the Constitution provides that justice shall be administered in courts established by law by judges appointed in the manner prescribed by the Constitution. The Committee of Public Accounts is not a court and its members are not judges.' While each House may not be able to punish outsiders directly, statute could define offences relating to the Oireachtas and these could be tried and punished by the ordinary courts.

Offences relating to the Oireachtas

The *Offences Against the State Act, 1939* prohibits the setting up, maintaining or taking part in a body purporting to be a legislature, which is not authorised by the Constitution. The prevention or obstruction by force of arms or other violent means of the legislature is an offence, and if murder is committed the offence is capital, and under the *Criminal Justice Act, 1964* the punishment is death. It is unlawful to hold a public meeting or procession within a half-mile of the Oireachtas when it is sitting, or about to sit, if forbidden by a member of the Gárda Síochána.*

35

Chapter 5

THE PRESIDENT OF IRELAND

The Office of President

Head of State

The Constitution, in Art. 12, in keeping with its republican nature, establishes the office of President of Ireland.[42] This office is more than a formal Head of State. The President is cast by the Constitution as the defender of the People's rights. By being placed outside the mainstream of political life the President can exercise some restraint on the powers exercised by others under the Constitution. But the powers of the President are so arranged as to prevent him from becoming an overpowering political figure.

In some countries, such as the United States and France, the President combines the roles of head of state and head of the executive. In Ireland the powers of the President are, under the Constitution, non-executive in nature. Other functions may be conferred by law but these, in so far as they are executive in nature, are limited and on the periphery of executive government.

Art. 12, in establishing the President as Head of State provides that he takes precedence over all other persons in the State. The President is not above the law. The notion that *le Roi ne peut mal faire,* which applied to the French kings before the Revolution of 1789 and to the Crown in Britain until 1947, has no application in our constitutional law. As the State created by the People cannot be equated to the feudal concept of the Crown, neither can the presidency be identified with the Crown. The President is answerable for his criminal and civil wrongs in the same way as other citizens.

Selection and Eligibility for Office

In western democracies the head of state can be selected in one of three ways. By the first method the constitution permits a hereditary monarchy as in Britain and Belgium. Secondly, the selection may be made by an elected body, as in the Federal Republic of Germany, where the President is chosen by Parliament. Thirdly, the head of state can be chosen directly by the people. In Ireland, as in the United States and France, the President's link with the People is forged by his election by popular franchise.

Every citizen who has reached his 35th year is eligible for election. In this respect no distinction is made between natural-born citizens and citizens by descent and naturalisation. Only a natural-born citizen of 35 years with a residency of at least fourteen years is eligible for the United States presidency. Apart from these qualifications, the Constitution does not empower the Oireachtas to impose disabilities by statute. If the President on his election is a member of either House of the Oireachtas he is deemed to have vacated his seat. But it is not a prerequisite of candidature that Oireachtas membership be resigned.

Nomination as Candidate

Art. 12.4 provides the only three methods by which a candidate may be nominated. The first method empowers nomination by not less than twenty Oireachtas members. The material date is that of nomination and not the latter election date. The nomination paper must be signed by each nominating Oireachtas member and be delivered to the presidential returning officer.

The second nomination method is by 4 administrative county councils, including borough councils. The intention to propose a nomination resolution must be given in writing to every member of the council at least 3 days in advance. If the resolution is passed, the nomination paper must be sealed with the seal of the council and delivered to the presidential returning officer. Four valid nomination papers nominating the same person by the council of a different county or county borough constitutes a valid nomination. When a presidential election is declared, a county or borough council may stand dissolved under the *Local Government Act, 1941* and its powers be transferred to another body or person. In such a case the *Local Government (Nomination of Presidential Candidates) Act, 1937* provides that such body or person does not have the power to nominate a presidential candidate.

No person or council is entitled to nominate more than one candidate in the same election. Where an Oireachtas member signs two or more valid nomination papers the one first received by the returning officer is regarded as valid. Where the returning officer receives from a council two or more nomination papers he must declare invalid any two or more passed on the same day. He must also deem invalid a nomination paper passed on any subsequent day. If one nomination paper is earlier in date than the others he may accept that one as valid and regard the remainder as invalid.

The third nomination method empowers a former or retiring President to nominate himself. Such a nomination paper must be signed by the candidate and delivered to the returning officer.

The nomination procedures are contained in the *Presidential Elections Act, 1937* as amended by the *Electoral Act, 1963*. At noon on the last day for receiving nominations, the presidential returning officer must attend at the place appointed and rule upon nomination papers received by him. Every question relevant to the nomination of a candidate, such as his citizenship and age, the sufficiency or correctness of his name, address or description, may be raised by the returning officer and any person entitled to take part in the proceedings. The President of the High Court acts as judicial assessor. Any matter referred to the judicial assessor must be immediately decided and his decision is final and cannot be reviewed by a court. Every candidate or his representative must attend and furnish all relevant information which is reasonably required by the returning officer or judicial assessor. Evidence, either oral or written, may be tendered and may if necessary be given on oath. The nomination may be disallowed if the candidate does not attend or attending refuses relevant information.

A candidate for the presidency, unlike the candiates for Dáil Éireann, is not required to lodge a deposit with his nomination paper.

Desirability and Necessity for an Election

In recent times the politicians, in whose grace the nomination for the presidency rests, have for convenience, party political economy and the fear of their candidate losing, decided upon an agreed candidate. The spirit of the Constitution envisages the office being open to any citizen with the corresponding expectation that every citizen has a voice in choosing the President. The dignity of the office and respect for the constitutional functions of the President are not enhanced by the absence of elections for the office. Either politicians operate the Constitution or abolish the office of President. An easing of the nomination requirements would ensure regular elections. One method would be to require a candidate to receive the nominations of, say, 50,000 voters.

Art. 12.4.5° declares that no election is necessary if there is only one candidate. If only one person is nominated the returning officer declares such person to be elected. He notifies the Taoiseach and publishes the fact in the *Iris Oifigiúil*. If there is more than one candidate he adjourns the election for the purpose of taking a poll. If no candidate stands nominated, the procedure must be recommenced. If after the adjournment the returning officer is satisfied before the taking of the poll that one candidate has died, he must countermand the poll and the procedure is recommenced.

The Election

Art. 12.3.3° declares that the election must be held not later than, and not earlier than, the sixtieth day before the expiration of the incumbent President's term of office. If the President resigns, is removed, dies or is declared permanently incapacitated, the election must be within sixty days of such event. The Minister for the Environment sets the date and appoints a fit and proper person to be the presidential returning officer whose duty it is to conduct the election, count the votes cast, ascertain and declare the result. The country is divided into constituencies. Those used in the previous Dáil elections are maintained. Local returning officers are appointed.

Every citizen who has the vote in Dáil elections has the vote at a presidential election. The voting is by secret ballot on the system of proportional representation by means of the single transferable vote. As soon as the presidential returning officer declares a candidate elected he must so inform the President, the Taoiseach, the Chief Justice, the Chairmen of Dáil and Seanad Éireann and the Secretary to the President. He must also inform the successful candidate.

Term of Office

The President-elect enters office on the day following the expiration of his predecessor's term. If his predecessor had resigned, was removed, died or was declared permanently incapacitated, the President elect enters office as soon as may be after the election. On entering office the President must make the declaration, set out in Art. 12.8, publicly in the presence of members of the Oireachtas, the judges of the superior courts and other public personages. He declares he will 'maintain the Constitution of Ireland and uphold its laws'. Whether the making of this declaration is mandatory or merely directory is unclear. A judge's office is terminated, under Art. 34.5.4°, if he fails to make the required declaration. There is no similar provision regarding the President in the Constitution. No President-elect has failed or refused to make this declaration which invokes the name of Almighty God and pleads for direction and sustenance. A problem would arise if a President-elect objected to making this declaration or wished to make it in a modified form. A President-elect might have conscientious grounds for his action. Whether a refusal simply prevents a President taking office or amounts to misbehaviour is debatable. The President of the United States must make a similar declaration though he has the option to swear or affirm.

The President holds office for seven years from the date he enters office, which is presumably the day on which he makes the declaration. This term is curtailed if he resigns or dies, events precipitated by the President. The death of a President sets in train an election, but how does a President resign? The Constitution and statute law is silent in this regard. A constitutional dilemma would arise if a President who had resigned withdrew his resignation during a presidential election campaign or after a successor was elected. A President would probably effect his resignation by publicly announcing that fact, surrendering his seal of office, vacating Arus an Uachtaráin and refusing to act as President; as Ó Dálaigh did.

Art. 12.3.1° declares that the President holds office unless he becomes 'permanently incapacitated' in the opinion of not less than five judges of the Supreme Court. This expression is not defined in the Constitution and while it is open to the Oireachtas to define it, it has not. Until statute law offers a definition it falls to the Supreme Court to instil it with meaning. The expression is wide enough to cover physical and mental incapacity though it must be of a nature which interferes with, and prevents, the President from carrying out his functions. Because the President must sign Bills into law, it is implicit that he must be able to read and write. Would any illness which affected either capacity, or the advance of senility, come within this expression? Mental disorder, more difficult to define and prove, must be included.

39

What meaning is to be given to the expression 'satisfaction' of not less than five judges of the Supreme Court. The law of evidence has two differing standards. In a criminal case the standard is beyond a reasonable doubt, while in civil proceedings the standard is the balance of probabilities. Because the consequences are so grave, the standard of beyond a reasonable doubt seems the more appropriate one. It also seems that the decision of the five judges must be unanimous though if there are more than five judges then a majority of at least five is necessary to remove the President. The Constitution is silent as to who may bring such a motion before the Supreme Court. In the absence of qualification it is fair to assume that any citizen may initiate and prosecute this procedure. Had the Constitution placed this initiative in specific hands, such as in the Government or Oireachtas, it might have been seen as a covert threat to the President. Art. 30 declares that all crimes and offences must be prosecuted by the Attorney General or other person authorised by law. This procedure is not a criminal one, so is not caught by this restriction. The hearing itself probably must be in open court though the Constitution does not expressly say so. In keeping with the rules of fair procedures the President must be informed of the charge, the nature of the evidence to be given, be given an opportunity to call rebutting evidence and to be professionally represented. If it is alleged that the President is mentally ill the preliminary question as to whether he understands the proceedings, and can give instructions in his defence, may have to be decided.

The second way in which the President can be removed from office is by 'impeachment' for stated misbehaviour. Impeachment is an old English device for bringing formal charges against a public official with the intent of removing him from office. It was a judicial proceeding for a state offence beyond the reach of the law and is now considered obsolete in Britain. Impeachment is possible under the United States Constitution.[43] In this country it is the function of the Houses of the Oireachtas to impeach a President and is the only instance in which they administer justice, which function in general is confined under the Constitution to the courts.

A President can only be impeached for stated misbehaviour, an expression not defined in the Constitution though the Oireachtas may do so by statute. This behaviour must, according to Art. 12.10.7°, be 'such as to render him unfit to continue in office'. Obvious examples of misbehaviour are the refusal to appoint a Taoiseach and leaving the State without the consent of the Government. It cannot be misbehaviour to refuse an exercise of his discretionary powers or to exercise any of them in a particular way. A more difficult decision concerns indiscretions of a President in his personal life. The conviction for a serious criminal offence probably amounts to misbehaviour whereas matters of a domestic nature would not. The American Constitution confines impeachment to 'treason, bribery or other high crimes and misdemeanours.'

A proposal for impeachment may be made in either House upon a notice of motion in writing signed by not less than thirty members of that House and cannot be adopted except by a resolution of that House supported by not less than two-thirds of its total membership. It is not sufficient to gain the support of two-thirds of the members present and voting. On adoption by one House it is passed to the other House for investigation though it is not constitutionally necessary for that other House itself to investigate the charge. Art. 13.8.2° permits 'any court, tribunal or body appointed or designated by either House of the Oireachtas' to investigate the charge. The President has the right to appear and be represented. If, after investigation, a resolution is supported by not less than two-thirds of the total membership of that House declaring that the charge has been sustained and that the behaviour was such as to render the President unfit to continue in office, such a resolution operates as a removal from office.

Can the courts exercise jurisdiction over the impeachment process? They can in a limited way. They could not become involved with the merits of the allegations but they could supervise to ensure that all the constitutional requirements were met, such as the requisite thirty members signing the motion and the two-thirds of the membership to support the resolution. The courts could probably insist that the rules of fair procedures were observed. A clash between the courts and the Oireachtas on any question relating to impeachment would be of high constitutional importance as indeed would the impeachment process itself. The Oireachtas might not welcome such intervention and might take action to curtail the powers of the courts. On the other hand the courts could hardly shrink from their constitutional duty by failing to protect the President from *ultra vires* actions by the Oireachtas.

The impeachment or removal of a President sets in motion a presidential election. Surprisingly the Constitution does not prohibit a President removed from office in either of these ways from seeking re-election on his own nomination though he can do this only if he has served one term of office because a former President can be re-elected only once.

Seal of Office

The Constitution by implication provides that the President should have a seal of office though there is inconsistency in when it must be used. When removing a judge or the Comptroller and Auditor General from office the President must do so 'under his hand and seal' whereas when a member of the Government is being dismissed 'his appointment shall be terminated by the President.' While the Constitution expressly provides for its use in a limited number of cases, in practice all proclamations, such as that dissolving Dáil Éireann, and all warrants of appointment, such as those appointing judges, have the seal affixed.

The *Presidential Seal Act, 1937* provides that the President shall have an official seal which shall be in his custody while exercising and performing the powers and functions of his office. It is affixed to instruments

41

made by the President and when affixed is authenticated by his signature. This seal must be officially and judicially noticed and must be admitted in evidence in legal proceedings without further proof.

Presidential Independence

If the President is to carry out his discretionary constitutional functions according to his own dictates it is essential that the Constitution provides him with protection from undue or improper influences. A President must be amenable to requests and approaches as to how he should perform his functions. For example it is not improper for a citizen to request the President to refer a Bill to the Supreme Court. Such a request is not undue pressure. But a request, either openly or obliquely made, coming from the Government might be more difficult to resist. To aid the President preserve an independence from the legislature and executive, the Constitution provides two safeguards. Art. 12.11.3° provides that the emoluments and allowances of the President must not be diminished during his term of office. Financial intimidation cannot be used as a lever of pressure against a President. These amounts may be increased and of course they may be reduced in the interregnum between Presidents.

The second safeguard is security of office. It is difficult to remove a President from office. This procedure has been explained earlier.

Presidential Immunity

Art. 13.8.1° declares that the President is not answerable to either House of the Oireachtas, or to any court,[44] for the exercise and performance of the powers and functions of his office. The exception to this is the impeachment procedure. The failure by the President to perform his non-discretionary duties would be misbehaviour, while the exercise or non-exercise of his discretionary powers are immune from action. Since the President is part of the Oireachtas his official papers are, under Art. 15.12, privileged.

The Duties and Powers of the President

Duty and Power Distinguished

A distinction must be drawn between a duty and a power. A *duty* denotes obligation: it is *mandatory*. There is no discretion in a duty; it must be performed. On the other hand a *power* denotes *discretion:* there is a choice as to whether it is or is not performed. Broadly speaking the functions of the President can be divided into duties *simpliciter* and powers *simpliciter* though there is also the hybrid of a duty coupled with a power. Each of these will be examined individually.

Duties of the President

The President must not hold any other position of emolument so that the impartiality needed in the carrying out of his office will be seen to be untainted (Art. 12.6.3°). The President must not leave the State without the consent of the Government (Art. 12.9). The President has an official residence in or near the City of Dublin (Art. 12.11.1°). The Constitution does not expressly require the President to reside or work in Arus an Uachtarain: it is probably implied. The purpose of having an official residence and of not leaving the country without the knowledge of the Government is that access to the President may be required in the event of an emergency.

The President appoints the Taoiseach on the nomination of Dáil Éireann (Art. 13.1.1°), and appoints the other Government members on the nomination of the Taoiseach with the approval of Dáil Éireann (Art. 13.1.2°). On the advice of the Taoiseach the President accepts the resignation, or terminates the appointment, of the Attorney General on the advice of the Taoiseach (Art. 30). This appointment does not constitutionally require the approval of Dáil Éireann. The President appoints the Comptroller and Auditor General on the nomination of Dáil Éireann, and on the receipt of resolutions of both Houses of the Oireachtas he terminates this appointment (Art. 33). The President appoints all the judges for the courts established under Art. 34 of the Constitution. On the receipt of resolutions of both Houses of the Oireachtas he removes from office a judge of the Supreme or High Courts (Art. 35.1 and 35.4).

The supreme command of the Defence Forces, under Art. 13.4, is vested in the President though its exercise may be regulated by law. The *Defence Act, 1954* vests this exercise in the Minister for Defence.

The right of pardon and the power to commute or remit punishment imposed by a criminal court vests in the President (Art. 13.6). This duty is exercisable only on the advice of the Government. This is a judicial function and its scope can be judged from the language used. 'Commute' means to reduce and 'remit' means to relax. Any punishment can thus be mitigated. The President has altered a death sentence to one of forty years' penal servitude. This duty of commutation may, except in capital cases, be conferred by law on other authorities. Capital cases are crimes for which the death penalty is imposed. The *Criminal Justice Act, 1951* confers this power on the Government. There is no power to remit any punishment of a civil court. Usually this punishment is damages by way of compensation but occasionally a civil court may impose imprisonment for disobedience to an injunction or a contempt of court.

The President on the advice of the Taoiseach fixes the date on which Seanad Éireann first meets after a general election (Art. 18.8).

Powers of the President

The President may at any time, after consultation with the Council of State, convene a meeting of either or both Houses of the Oireachtas (Art. 13.2.3°). He may, after consultation with the Council of State, communicate with the nation or the Houses of the Oireachtas by message or address on any matter of national or public importance (Art. 13.7.1°). Every message or address must have the prior approval of the Government. To give such address or issue such message without Government approval would amount to misbehaviour. President de Valera did, in January 1969, address the Houses of the Oireachtas on the 50th anniversary of the 1st Dáil. The President of the United States is bound annually to address the Houses of Congress but one must remember that he is the chief executive.

The President in his absolute discretion may appoint, and later dismiss, not more than seven persons to be members of the Council of State.

Duties coupled with powers of the President

The President summons and dissolves Dáil Éireann on the advice of the Taoiseach though he may, in his absolute discretion, refuse to dissolve it on the advice of a Taoiseach who has ceased to retain a majority of the Dáil. The Presidents to date have never refused a dissolution to a Taoiseach who has ceased to retain the support of a majority, probably because the will of the people, and not his own view, should prevail.

The President must, under Art. 25, sign Bills into law but, under Art. 26, he has the power before signing a Bill to refer it to the Supreme Court for advice as to its constitutionality. Under Art. 27 the President may on the petition of some members of the Houses of the Oireachtas refer a particular Bill to the People in a Referendum. Under Art. 24 the stated periods of time which Seanad Éireann has to consider legislation may be abridged if the President concurs. Art. 22.2.2° empowers some members of the Seanad to request the President to refer to a committee whether a Money Bill is such a Bill. He may or may not accede to the request. These last four functions are all considered fully in Chapter 4 when discussing the legislative process. Here it is sufficient to note that while the President must act he has discretion as to how he acts.

Duties conferred by Law

Art. 13.10 permits statute law to confer additional powers and functions on the President though all functions so conferred can only be exercisable on the advice of the Government. The *Republic of Ireland Act, 1948* conferred the executive function of the State in connection with its external relations on the President. He accredits Irish diplomatic personnel abroad and accepts the credentials of foreign diplomats to this country. Strangely this function was performed by the British Crown until 1948 even after the enactment of the Constitution. S.12 of the *Irish Nationality and Citizenship Act, 1956* empowers the President to grant Irish citizenship as a token of honour.

Offences relating to the President

The criminal law creates some offences which relate to the protection of the President both in his person and in his office. S.8 of the *Offences*

Against the State Act, 1939 provides that a person who prevents or obstructs by force of arms or other violent means, or by intimidation, the exercise by the President of any of his functions is guilty of a felony. If a person murders the President to prevent the exercise of his functions he is guilty of capital murder and under the *Criminal Justice Act, 1964* suffers death on conviction.

The Council of State

Purpose and Membership

The Council of State is a body established by Art. 31 to aid and counsel the President in the exercise by him of certain of his functions.[45] The Council consists of three classes of members. The first class are *ex officio* members and consist of the Taoiseach, the Tánaiste, the Chief Justice, the President of the High Court, the Chairmen of Dáil and Seanad Éireann and the Attorney General. The second class are former holders of certain offices, who are willing and able to act. This consists of persons who have held the office of President, or Taoiseach, or Chief Justice. In the third class are not more than seven persons whom the President can in his absolute discretion appoint as members.

Every member at the first meeting he attends must make a declaration of fidelity to carry out his duties as a member of the Council of State. The members appointed by the President hold office until his successor enters office. Such members may resign at any time and the President may for sufficient reasons terminate such appointments.

Functions

The meetings of the Council of State are convened by the President at such times and places as he determines. Art. 32 declares that the President must convene the Council of State where the Constitution expressly so provides and the members must 'have been heard by him'. The President has a duty to explain why he has called the meeting, which must entail a duty to outline his proposed action. There is no constitutional right of the members to express an opinion or to be heard. The President is not obliged to accept any advice offered even if that advice is unanimous.

The President must convene the Council of State if he intends to do any of the following: (1) to convene a meeting of either or both Houses of the Oireachtas (Art. 13.2.3°); (2) to communicate with the Houses of the Oireachtas by message or address on a matter of national or public importance (Art. 13.7.1°); (3) to address a message to the nation on a matter of national or public importance (Art. 13.7.2°); (4) when considering a request of Seanad Éireann to refer the question of whether a Bill is or is not a Money Bill to a Committee (Art. 22.2); (5) concur in abridging the time for the consideration by Seanad Éireann of a Bill certified by the Taoiseach to be urgent (Art. 24.1); (6) refer a Bill to the Supreme Court for a decision on its constitutionality (Art. 26.1.1°); and (7) pronounce a decision on a petition from the members of Dáil and Seanad Éireann which requested that a Bill be submitted to the People in a Referendum (Art. 27.4.1°). This list is exhaustive and the Constitution does not empower statute law to authorise additional functions.

While the Council of State may have the appearance of being a constitutional trimming it can, under Art. 14.4, make provision for the exercise of the powers and functions of the President in any contingency which is not provided for in the Constitution.

The Presidential Commission

Ireland, unlike the United States, has no office of Vice-President, to act when the President has died, is absent, has resigned or is incapacitated. Because government must continue in these situations, Art. 14 provides for the establishment of a Presidential Commission which performs the functions of a President in his absence, on his death, following his resignation, removal, incapacity or his wilful refusal to act.

The Commission consists of the Chief Justice, or in his place the President of the High Court; and the Chairman of Dáil Éireann or in his place the Deputy Chairman; and the Chairman of Seanad Éireann, or in his place the Deputy Chairman. The Commission may act by majority.

The most usual function the Commission performs is the signing of Bills into law. The Commission has never had to dissolve Dáil Éireann or perform any of the duties coupled with a power which the President has. For example they have never referred a Bill to the Supreme Court.

Chapter 6

DÁIL ÉIREANN

The Nature of and Eligibility for Membership

A forum of persons elected by popular franchise with certain powers and functions has become an integral part of government in modern democracies. In this country Dáil Éireann is such a forum. Our Constitution emphasises the idea of elected government in two ways: any citizen may offer himself for election, and every citizen has the right to vote in such elections. It is mistakenly thought that the Constitution only acknowledges certain personal rights such as the right to liberty and freedom of expression. Political rights are also acknowledged and these are as fundamental to the well-being of our society as are personal rights.

Every citizen over the age of 21 years and not placed under disability by the Constitution or by law is eligible for membership of Dáil Éireann.

Persons holding specified constitutional offices are disqualified: these are the President (Art. 12.6.1°); a member of the Seanad (Art. 15.14); the Comptroller and Auditor General (Art. 33.3); and a judge (Art. 35.3). Persons holding these offices may run for election and on election must decide which office they wish to keep: duality of office is prohibited. While the Oireachtas may impose further disabilities, the Constitution prohibits such law from discriminating on the ground of sex. The *Electoral Act, 1923* categorises the persons disqualified by law from election. These are: (1) persons serving a six-month prison term or a sentence of penal servitude imposed by a court within the State; (2) a person of unsound mind; (3) an undischarged bankrupt; (4) a member of the Defence Forces or police force of the State on full pay; (5) a temporary or permanent civil servant of the State; and (6) a person convicted of an electoral offence by a court within the State. A number of statutes prohibit the directors of various semi-state bodies from membership.

There are obvious anomalies in this list. Persons convicted outside the State can be members, those serving in foreign armies can be elected, members of foreign legislatures can stand for election, and an ex-director of a liquidated company, which may owe more in debts than any bankrupt, is under no disability. Clearly some classes of persons must be disqualified though there is a danger that the categories could be so extended as to negative the idea of representative government.

Number of Members of Dáil Éireann

It was open to the People when enacting the Constitution to provide for a Dáil with a static number of members as they did for the Seanad. Instead the Constitution provides a system of flexible numbers which is periodically reviewed. The number of members is to be fixed by law but the total number must not be less than one member for 30,000 of the population and not more than one member for each 20,000 of the population (Art. 16.2). The relevant figures are those of population and not merely the total eligible electorate. The Oireachtas must cause a census to be carried out every 12 years. This duty might be enforced by court injunction because a failure may injure the political rights of the citizen in that shifts in the distribution of the population might result in one citizen's vote being devalued at the expense of another citizen's vote. Consequently the total number of members of the Dáil will change as the population increases or decreases.[46]

The Supreme Court in *Art. 26 and the Electoral (Amendment) Bill, 1961* considered the meaning to be given to 'population' and 'census'. It was argued that the Oireachtas ought to have relied on the more accurate, if not precise, figures provided by either the electoral lists or the most recent population estimates rather than on the precise, but no longer accurate, figures provided by the census of 1956. The Court rejected this argument and held that the population must be taken to mean the population as ascertained at the last preceding census. 'Census' meant the last completed census because in no other way could the population be calculated with the degree of certainty required to comply with the provisions limiting the total membership of the Dáil by reference to the total population of the State.

Uniformity of Representation

It is a principle inherent in the concept of democracy that equal weight attaches to the vote of each citizen; a system of weighted voting cannot be regarded as democratic. If this equality were not maintained it would mean that the vote of a citizen in one part of the country had a greater say in securing parliamentary representation than the vote of another citizen in a different part of the country. The slogan 'one man one vote' means more than the obvious that every man should have a vote: it implies that each man's vote should have equal value in an election.

The ratio between the number of members to be elected for each constituency must, as far as is practicable, be the same throughout the country (Art. 16.2.3°). Here is the principle of uniformity of representation. It is not a rigid principle and how far the Oireachtas can stray from it was considered in *O'Donovan v. Attorney General* (Case No. 70). The plaintiff* claimed that the *Electoral (Amendment) Act, 1959* did not maintain the required ratio. To prove his case a great volume of figures was produced: some will illustrate the case. The constituency of Galway South had one member per 16,575 of the population whereas the Dublin South West constituency had one member per 23,128 of the population. Dún Laoghaire and Rathdown had a population of 69,071 while Galway South had 49,726: both returned three members though the difference in population was 19,345. The State defended these variations on the ground that members representing western constituencies had large geographical areas with sparse populations and difficult communications problems and time was spent travelling to and from Dublin. These difficulties were not faced by the members representing constituencies on the eastern seaboard. It was admitted by the State that from the purely administrative point of view a closer approximation to equality of ratio of members to population could have been obtained by grouping and planning the areas and boundaries differently.

The High Court held the Act unconstitutional because it contained substantial departures from the stipulated ratio thus causing grave inequalities of parliamentary representation, and because there was present no circumstances that justified these departures. The Supreme Court, in *Art. 26 and the Electoral (Amendment) Act, 1961* (Case No. 4) agreed with this decision though it refused to lay down a figure above or below which a deviation would be permitted.

In 1968 the Third Amendment to the Constitution Bill was introduced in Dáil Éireann, authorising a tolerance of up to 16 per cent of the national

48

average in drawing the constituencies. A plea was made for more latitude for the under-populated west. The High Court in *O'Donovan v. Attorney General* (Case No. 70) had rejected a tolerance of 19 per cent. The Bill was put before the People and was rejected.[47]

Constituencies

Dáil Éireann is composed of members who represent constituencies determined by law.[48] We have already looked at the constitutional requirement of uniformity of representation. In relation to constituencies the other requirement is that the number of members to be returned for a constituency must at least be three (Art. 16.2.6°). The constituencies must be multi-member seated. There is no maximum number so in theory the usual upper limit of five members could be exceeded. There must be more than one constituency because the Constitution speaks in the plural. The minimum is two, and in theory the country could be divided into two large constituencies. The Constitution gives no direction as to how the constituencies should be drawn. The High Court in *O'Donovan v. Attorney General* (Case No. 70) rejected the notion that they must be based on geographical and administrative counties. 'The Constitution', said Budd J. 'does not say that in forming the constituencies according to the required ratio, that shall be done so far as is practicable having regard to county boundaries. Even if it did, the Oireachtas or the appropriate Minister could alter county boundaries.'

Until 1979 the work of drawing constituencies was in the hands of the Minister for Local Government with the resulting criticism that decisions were made according to party politicial dictates. In that year the Government established a non-statutory *ad hoc* electoral Commission to advise and report on the formation of constituencies for the election of members to Dáil Éireann.[49] Their terms of reference provided that account be taken of geographical considerations, in that the breaching of county boundaries should be avoided. The Commission reported in 1980 and their submissions were accepted for the subsequent revision of Dáil constituencies. The Commission will probably become the permanent method of revising constituencies.

Registration of Political Parties

A candidate for election to the Dáil is not required to be a member of a political party. Such a requirement would offend the democratic concept of every citizen being able to offer himself as a candidate to the electorate. Would it be possible to curtail eligibility to political party members or, more sinisterly, to confine eligibility to one particular political party only? There is nothing in the Constitution expressly prohibiting such a proposal though the courts would probably invalidate it as offending Art. 5 which proclaims the country to be a democratic state.

The *Electoral Act, 1963*, s.13 established a Register of Political Parties.

The Registrar is the Clerk of Dáil Éireann whose duty it is to prepare and maintain the Register in which he registers political parties. Two methods of registration were permitted; one is discontinued. When the Register was first established the Registrar had to include all the parties then represented in the Dáil. Other parties have had to apply for registration in the course of time. Registration will only be effected if the Registrar is of opinion that the applicant is a genuine political party and is organised to contest Dáil or local government elections. If the application is refused an appeal may be made to an Appeal Board consisting of a judge of the High Court, the Chairman of the Dáil and the Chairman of the Seanad.

The constitutionality of s.13 was challenged in *Loftus v. Attorney General* (Case No. 44) where it was claimed that this procedure discriminated against a *bona fide* political party which had failed to secure registration and in favour of a registered political party because it permitted the latter's candidates to have the party affiliation stated on the ballot paper. To adopt instead the misleading description of 'Non-Party' or to remain undescribed imposed an unconstitutional curb on the freedom of political action. The Supreme Court upheld the section. It was reasonable for the Oireachtas to regulate such matters. The purpose of the section was to permit genuine political parties to be distinguished from the feigned and the spurious. 'If some control and regulation were not provided,' said O'Higgins C.J., 'genuine political action might be destroyed by a proliferation of bogus front organisations calling themselves political parties but with aims and objects far removed from the political sphere.' This rather subjective reasoning can be used to justify restrictions on future political actions. Limitations imposed in this area by those practising the art of politics must be resisted because the natural dislike of the newcomer may result in a monopoly by those currently hogging the stage. Could the reasoning of the Chief Justice be used to support a one-party state or at least to limit the badge of orthodoxy to existing political parties on the ground that the electorate have a sufficiency of choice?

How are we to distinguish between the genuine and the bogus? According to the Supreme Court, the existing political parties can legitimately do so. The electorate are ideally placed to draw this distinction. They have the right to elect whom they wish. This is both the legal and the political theory of the Constitution. The expression 'genuine political party' was seen to need interpretation in this case. The Court rejected the test, used on previous occasions, of 'an existing party or group which has a sizeable public image and which has a visible organisation'. Finlay P. said this expression meant that the group should be 'bound together by the cohesion of common political beliefs or aims, and by being organised for electoral purposes into an entity to such an extent and with such distinctiveness as to justify its claim to be truly a political party in its own right'.

The Register of Political Parties contains the name of the party, the address of its headquarters and details of the officers authorised to sign certificates authenticating the candidature of its candidates at elections. The Registrar annually inquires whether the party desires to remain registered and unless he receives an affirmative reply within twenty-one days to his inquiry he cancels the registration.

The Right to Vote

Every citizen on reaching his 18th year is entitled to vote at an election of members to the Dáil provided he has not been disqualified by law and has complied with electoral law (Art. 16.1.2°). There is currently no disqualification on the right to vote. A person convicted of corrupt practices under the *Prevention of Electoral Abuses Act, 1923* was disqualified from voting for 7 years, but this has been repealed.

In order to vote a person must be registered as a Dáil elector in a constituency, and to be entitled to be registered he must be a citizen, be over 18 years and be ordinarily resident in that constituency. It is the duty of each local authority to prepare and publish the register of electors each year. A period of time for corrections is allowed and an appeal can be made to the Circuit Court. No person can be entered more than once in a register and a postal voters' list may be compiled. Currently postal votes are confined to members of the Defence Forces and the Gárda Síochána. This provision recognises the distinction between the right to vote and the ability to vote. It is implicit in the Constitution that a citizen has the opportunity to vote. This right would be denied if a Dublin citizen could only exercise his vote in a polling station in Kerry. Polling stations must be convenient to the voters. Prisoners, long-term hospital patients, merchant seamen abroad and Irish diplomats serving abroad all have the right to vote but do not, because of the general absence of postal voting, have the ability to exercise that right. This issue was raised by a disabled person in *Draper v. Attorney General*. The High Court held that the present law did not infringe the Constitution because, as McMahon J. explained: 'Postal voting necessarily involves some risk of abuse and it is for the legislature to strike a balance between the right to vote of the physically disabled and the risks of abuse of postal voting.'

The Election Process

When the President accepts the advice of the Taoiseach and dissolves the Dáil he issues a proclamation to that effect and declares the date on which the new Dáil must meet which must not be later than thirty days after the election, which itself must be held not later than thirty days after the dissolution. The maximum permitted period between governments is thus sixty days. Under the state of emergency then in operation the *General Elections (Emergency Provisions) Act, 1943* postponed the dissolution of the Dáil until after the members of Dáil Éireann which succeeded it had been elected. Dáil Éireann is dissolved completely: there is no provision for a partial general election. Under the Constitution of the

51

United States the Houses of Congress are never fully dissolved: elections are held in rotation with each member serving a set period in office.

The Constitution declares that the election should be regulated by law and in this regard the *Electoral Act, 1923* and the *Electoral Act, 1963* are relevant. On dissolution the Clerk of the Dáil issues a writ to each returning officer of a constituency directing him to cause an election to be held for the full number of members of the Dáil to serve for that constituency. The returning officer is usually the sheriff, the under-sheriff or the county registrar, and it is his responsibility to properly conduct the election.

In order to contest an election the person must be nominated in writing and the nomination must be delivered to the returning officer before 12 noon on the last day for receiving nominations. A person may nominate himself or be nominated by a person registered as a Dáil elector in the constituency for which he intends to stand as a candidate. The returning officer rules on the validity of a nomination paper within one hour of its delivery in the presence of the candidate, his proposer, if he has one, and one other person selected by the candidate. The paper can only be declared invalid if improperly made out. Objection may be taken to the description of the candidate if it is incorrect, insufficient or unnecessarily long. The candidate must be allowed to alter it or the returning officer may, if the alteration is unsatisfactory, amend it himself. The nomination paper must contain the name, address and description of the candidate. It may contain the name of a registered political party if appropriate.

The *Electoral Act, 1963,* s.20 requires a candidate to deposit £100 with the returning officer which is returned provided the candidate receives a number of votes equivalent to one-third of the quota at the election. If he fails to achieve this figure the deposit is forfeited to the State. This statutory requirement of a deposit is another restriction on the citizen's constitutional right to stand for election. Is this permissible under the Constitution? If the principle of a deposit is accepted, then justification can be found for raising it to any amount, thus depriving many citizens from exercising this right. The amount of £100 is not large by today's standards but it must have been in 1923[50] when it was set and even when the Constitution was enacted in 1937. The requirement of a deposit would be another way of distinguishing the genuine from the bogus, first adopted by the Supreme Court in *Loftus v. Attorney General* (Case No. 44). Whether the courts would uphold as constitutional the requirement of a deposit can only be guessed at by analogy. In *Finnegan v. An Bord Pleanála* it was contended that a £10 deposit required to be lodged by s.15 of the *Local Government (Planning and Development) Act, 1976* by a person appealing a planning decision was a restriction contrary to the democratic nature of the Constitution and a discrimination between those who had money and those who had not. The Supreme Court rejected this argument by holding that the purpose of requiring a deposit was to prevent appeals without substance and that the amount was not so high as to prevent

52

genuine appeals. In addition the deposit was returnable when the appeal was heard, withdrawn or determined. 'A similar provision is made', according to O'Higgins C.J., 'under the Electoral Acts in relation to candidates standing for Dáil and other elections.' This seems an implied recognition that deposits are constitutionally permitted in Dáil elections.

But there are important differences between standing for a Dáil election and lodging a planning appeal. To stand for Dáil election is a constitutional right whereas to lodge a planning appeal is merely a legal right. A deposit is not always returned in Dáil elections whereas in planning appeals it always is. The requirement of a deposit does not prevent the bogus candidate: it merely prevents the bogus candidate with no money from indulging his whims. The bogus candidate with a fortune can indulge himself to his heart's delight. Surely it is the electorate who should decide between the bogus and the genuine and not some administrative method, arbitrary in all events, which smacks of legal high-handedness. The bogus candidate can offer himself for election as President or as a Senator because in both these cases no deposit is required. In favour of the unconstitutionality of deposits stands the decision in *de Búrca v. Attorney General* (Case No. 32). In that case the Supreme Court struck down a statute which favoured persons with particular types of property over both persons with no property and persons with other types of property. A cash deposit discriminates against persons with no property and persons with other types of property such as land, shares and personal possessions. A possible solution is to return the deposit of every candidate, a system favoured by the Supreme Court in the Finnegan case.

If no more candidates stand nominated than there are vacancies, the returning officer declares these candidates elected and returns their names to the Clerk of Dáil Éireann. If more candidates stand nominated the election stands adjourned in order to conduct a poll.

Because the Constitution requires an election to take place not later than thirty days after a Dáil dissolution there is by implication the notion that a campaign takes place. This enables the candidates to canvass the electorate. A candidate may under the *Prevention of Electoral Abuses Act, 1923* send free of charge to each citizen on the register of electors one postal communication containing matter not exceeding two ounces in weight. A specimen copy of the communication must be deposited in advance with the Department of Posts and Telegraphs. This statutory right came up for interpretation in *Dillon v. The Minister for Posts and Telegraphs* where a candidate's communication was rejected as ineligible because the sentence 'Today's politicians are dishonest because they are political and must please the largest number of people' was considered offensive. The Supreme Court ordered the Department to accept this communication for free postage. 'I venture', said Henchy J., 'to think that those who practise what is often dubbed the art of the possible would not feel grossly offended by such an expression of opinion which, denigratory and cynical though it may be thought by some, is no more than the small coinage of the currency of political controversy.' A second objection was made to the communication because it contained a list of issues on which the voter was invited to propound a view in order of preference and return this to the candidate. It was argued that the inclusion of this material was not a matter relating to the election. It was held by the Supreme Court that a consultative canvas, which this was, was a matter relating to the election.

A candidate is not entitled as of right to broadcast on Radio Telefís Éireann, the State-owned and controlled broadcasting station. This topic was explored in *The State (Lynch) v. Cooney* (Case No. 93) when the Minister for Posts and Telegraphs made an order prohibiting broadcasts of a certain political party because they would be likely to incite to crime or would tend to undermine the authority of the State. The foolishness of this tactic is demonstrated daily by reportage on foreign television and radio of the activities of the same political party together with fair coverage in Irish newspapers. Objection was taken by the Minister to the organisation and not to what the candidates had to say. The strange irony was that the same Minister had to afford the same candidates the customary free postage. While RTE broadcast political party messages at election time they are not bound to do so.

The *Prevention of Electoral Abuses Act, 1923* creates a number of criminal offences and prohibits various activities in relation to elections.

The poll at a general election must as far as is practicable take place on the same day throughout the country (Art. 16.4.1°). The *Electoral Act, 1963*, s.34 permits advanced polling on islands. Each constituency is divided into polling districts and the poll is conducted by presiding officers and poll clerks appointed by the returning officer. The presiding officer keeps order at his polling station, regulates the number of electors to be admitted at one time and excludes all other persons except the agents of the candidate, companions of infirm electors and members of the Gárda Síochána on duty. The poll is taken on the day nominated by the Minister for the Environment and must continue for a period of not less than twelve hours between 8.30 a.m. and 10.30 p.m. At the close of the poll the presiding officer must return the ballot boxes, the unused ballot papers, the marked copies of the register of electors and the counterfoils of the ballot papers to the returning officer.

The voting at a Dáil election must be by secret ballot (Art. 16.1.4°). The ballot of each voter consists of a paper which shows the names in alphabetical order, address, description and political parties if appropriate of the candidates. Immediately before a ballot paper is delivered to a voter it must be marked with an official embossed or perforated mark which must be visible on both sides of the paper. The name and address of the voter is called out and his details are crossed out in the register to denote that he has applied for a ballot paper. The voter goes to a compartment in

54

the polling station, marks his paper, folds it and places it in the appropriate ballot box. This process ensures privacy to the voter and it is sufficient to fulfil the constitutional requirement of a 'secret ballot'. This point was considered in *McMahon v. Attorney General* (Case No. 52) where it was claimed that by reassociating the ballot paper and the counterfoil through the identical number printed on both and then associating these with the voter through his number on the register which had been marked on the counterfoil, how the voter voted could be revealed. The State argued the necessity of such a method in order to trace votes cast illegally: for example the vote cast by a person convicted of personation could be traced and eliminated. This reason for these procedures did not impress the Supreme Court. Ó Dálaigh C.J. explained: 'The fundamental question is: *Secret to whom?* In my opinion there can be only one plain and logical answer to that question. The answer is: *secret to the voter.* It is an unshared secret. It ceases to be a secret if it is disclosed. In my opinion the Constitution therefore requires that nothing shall be done which would make it possible to violate that secrecy.' The problem of votes cast by personators could be dealt with by a limited re-poll, which was already possible if the votes in a polling station should be destroyed. The procedure has since been altered. The *Electoral Act, 1923*, s.38. provides that in legal proceedings to question an election no voter can be required to state for whom he voted.

The presiding officer may, and must if so requested on behalf of a candidate, put certain questions to a person applying for a ballot paper in order to ascertain his identity, whether he is of voting age and whether he has already voted. To fulfil this duty the presiding officer may administer an oath to that person. It is a criminal offence for a person to be registered if he is not so entitled and to vote if he is not properly registered. It is an offence to apply for a voting paper if a person has already voted. An incapacitated voter is allowed the assistance, under certain conditions, of a companion.

Proportional Representation

Members of Dáil Éireann must be elected on the system of proportional representation by means of the single transferable vote (Art. 16.2.5°). This method allows the voter to give some measure of support to all the candidates by marking his ballot paper in the order of his preference. The single transferable voting method had been in operation for many years and was continued by the Constitution though it is not the only proportional representation method. To operate this voting system it is necessary to have multi-seat constituencies. When counting the votes a quota is fixed: this is the number of votes that can be obtained by as many candidates as there are seats to be filled but not by more. The formula for ascertaining the quota is $\frac{\text{Total valid votes}}{\text{Total seats} + 1} + 1 = \text{Quota}$.[51] The logic of this formula can be seen by applying it to a case where there are 1000 valid votes cast for 4 seats. The quota is then $\dfrac{1,000}{4+1} + 1 = 201$. If 4 candidates get 201 votes each, there can only be a total of 196 left for all the other candidates. Only 4 quotas are obtainable under the formula. Any candidate who on the first count of the votes has reached the quota is elected.

If that candidate has obtained more first preference votes than the quota his surplus votes are redistributed among the other candidates in proportion to the respective second preferences shown on all his ballot papers. These distributed votes count as first preference for the candidates benefitting from the transfer of the surplus. This may bring the total of votes cast for one or more of the other candidates above the quota. If so each such candidate gets a seat on the second count. Should no candidate exceed the quota, then the candidate with the lowest number of votes is eliminated and each of these votes is credited to the candidate marked by the voter as his next preference among the candidates still remaining in the count. This process is continued until all the seats are filled.

That the Irish electorate like this system of voting is shown from the fact that on the two occasions when proposals to amend the Constitution in this regard were submitted to the People, both were rejected, the second time more heavily than the first.[52]

Term of Office

The returning officer as soon as is possible gives public notice of the names of the candidates elected. He must give the total of votes cast for each candidate together with details of transfers. The returning officer returns the writ to the Clerk of Dáil Éireann containing the names of the elected members.

A newly elected member is notified by the Clerk of the Dáil to attend and sign the roll of members, and at the first meeting of the House on the date set by the President when he dissolved the previous Dáil, the Clerk announces to the House the names and constituencies of the members returned to serve in it. The same Dáil must not continue for a period longer than seven years though a shorter period may be fixed by law (Art. 16.5). The *Electoral Act, 1963,* s.10 prescribes the maximum period of five years. In times of emergency the lifetime of a Dáil could be extended though it is worthy of note that during the Second World War two general elections were held.[53]

An elected candidate is a member of the Dáil from the moment of his election to the moment that Dáil is dissolved. On signing the roll he is entitled to take his seat and to other privileges attaching to membership. A member ceases to be a member if he dies, resigns or is disqualified. A member may voluntarily resign his seat by notice in writing to the Ceann Comhairle which resignation takes effect from the moment it is announced to the Dáil. A member is disqualified from sitting on the same grounds as those which make him ineligible for election. The disqualification is not automatic: it must be done by the proper procedures.

Casual Vacancies

Casual vacancies are to be filled in accordance with law (Art. 16.7). *The Electoral Act, 1963*, s.12 provides that where a vacancy occurs the Ceann Comhairle on the direction of the Dáil instructs the Clerk to issue a writ to the appropriate returning officer. The procedures are then the same at those at a general election. The decision as to when a by-election is to be held is a matter for Dáil Éireann alone. There have been occasions, because it was politically inopportune to have a by-election, when vacancies were not filled, or were left vacant for very long periods. This has the effect of reducing the voters' representation. The aid of the courts might be sought if a constituency was left without any representation. This situation would clearly be a denial of the citizens' right to representation.

Disputed Election

The *Parliamentary Elections Act, 1868*, as amended, permits a person who has (a) voted or had the right to vote, or (b) claimed to have had a right to have been returned or elected at an election, to petition the High Court within twenty-one days claiming that irregularities have taken place which render the election void. Two judges of the High Court constitute an election court and should they differ the election stands though if they agree then the election can be declared void. The problem is that this statute was passed in the time of the single-seat constituency and any declaration seems to mean that a new election for the constituency would have to be held.

Chapter 7

SEANAD ÉIREANN

Nature of and Eligibility for Membership

The Seanad unlike Dáil Éireann is not elected directly by popular franchise. Nomination for membership is also restricted. This absence of popular involvement has led the Constitution to limit both the membership and powers of the Seanad. The extent of these limitations was discussed in Chapter 4. The Seanad is a debating chamber which exercises limited powers over Dáil Éireann.

The Constitution declares that to be eligible for membership of the Seanad a person must be eligible for Dáil Éireann (Art. 18.2). No deposit is required and there is no provision for having the political party of the candidate included on the ballot paper.

57

Number of Members

The Seanad is composed of the static number of sixty members (Art. 18.1). It bears no relationship to the shifts in population, and an alteration in this static number requires a constitutional amendment.

Membership can be acquired in three ways. A person can be nominated a member by the Taoiseach; secondly, a person can be elected by the universities; and thirdly a person can be elected from panels. In general the public are excluded from this process and may even be forgiven for not knowing that a Seanad election is in progress. It is not in keeping with the concepts of democracy that public office-holders should be appointed or elected to office by elite groups. The basis on which the Seanad electorate is composed is arbitrary and unrepresentative. Even the wider scheme permitted in Art. 19 which empowers direct election by functional groups and associations has never been tried.

Membership by Appointment

The Constitution confers on the Taoiseach who is appointed next after the re-assembly of the Dáil the absolute discretion to nominate eleven persons to be members of the new Seanad. These members hold office as long as the Seanad continues, even though the Taoiseach who has appointed them has died or resigned as Taoiseach. Casual vacancies are filled by the Taoiseach. An appointed member could have his membership challenged on the ground of disqualification.

Election by the Universities

Six members are elected by two named universities: three members are elected for Trinity College and three members are elected for the National University of Ireland. This theory that university graduates have some particular insight into the selection of the ideal public representative might have some credence if there was not an unanswerable discrimination against graduates of other third-level educational institutions. An example will illustrate how incongruous the whole scheme is. A person with a law degree from a university which does not entitle the holder to practise law can vote in a Seanad election whereas a member of the Incorporated Law Society who can practise law without a university degree has no vote. In 1979 the Seventh Amendment to the Constitution was passed which permitted a redistribution by law of these six seats among the existing universities and other institutions of higher education. No such legislation has since been passed.

The *Seanad Electoral (University Members) Act, 1937* establishes the franchise and the method of election. Every citizen of Ireland who has attained 18 years and has received a degree, other than an honorary degree, is entitled to vote. The governing body of each university must keep a register of electors. This contains the name and address at which the voter is ordinarily resident and may contain another address to which the ballot paper should be sent. An appeal from the refusal to register can be made to the Circuit Court.

The Minister for the Environment appoints the last day for receiving nominations, the day for the issue of the ballot papers and the day and time of the poll. The returning officers are the Provost of Trinity College for the Trinity College constituency and the Vice-Chancellor of the National University of Ireland for the National University constituency. It is the duty of the returning officers to hold the election, count the votes and ascertain the results.

Each candidate must be nominated in writing by two registered voters as proposer and seconder and eight other registered voters who assent to the nomination. A candidate does not have to be a graduate of the university. A voter may subscribe to as many nomination papers as there are vacancies. The returning officer rules on the nomination papers which must contain the name, address and description of the candidate. If at one o'clock in the afternoon on the last day for receiving nomination papers no more candidates stand nominated than there are vacancies, the returning officer declares those candidates elected and returns their names to the Clerk of Seanad Éireann. If there are more candidates than vacancies the returning officer adjourns the election in order to take a poll.

On the day appointed for the issue of the ballot papers the returning officer sends by post to each voter a ballot paper with a form of declaration of identity. The voter marks the ballot paper and completes the declaration of identity and returns both by post. The Constitution declares that the poll must be by secret postal ballot (Art. 18.5).

The members must be elected on the system of proportional representation by means of the single transferable vote. As soon as the returning officer ascertains the result he declares the candidates elected and sends to both the Clerk of the Dáil and the Clerk of the Seanad a certificate setting out details of the votes cast and the transfers.

Whenever the Clerk of the Seanad by direction of the Seanad informs the Minister for the Environment that a vacancy has occurred in the membership of a university constituency the Minister must, not later than six months after, direct a by-election to be held. A member for a university constituency may resign by notice in writing to the Chairman of the Seanad, which resignation becomes effective when an announcement is made to the Seanad. No member of the Seanad can be a candidate at a Seanad by-election: he must resign in advance of lodging his nomination papers.

Election to the Panels

The Constitution declares that before a general election for panel members five panels of candidates must be formed in accordance with law (Art. 18.7). The panels demonstrate the idea of having representation from functional or vocational groups. The remaining forty-three seats are drawn from persons with knowledge and practical experience of various professions or trades. The five panels, while themselves enumerated in Art. 18.7, need further regulation by law. This is contained in the *Seanad Electoral (Panel Members) Acts 1947 and 1954.* It is s.52 of the 1947 Act which sets the number of members to be elected for which panel. The guidelines in Art. 18.7.2° prohibit more than eleven and less than five members from any one panel. The panels are divided into two sections with some members being elected from different sub-panels which are considered later. The panels and the numbers to be elected from each are as follows:

1. Five members from the Cultural and Educational panel which includes persons having knowledge and practical experience of the national language and culture, literature, art, education, law and medicine including surgery, dentistry, veterinary medicine and pharmaceutical chemistry. Two members at least to be elected from each sub-panel.
2. Eleven members from the Agricultural panel which includes persons having knowledge and practical experience of agriculture and allied interests and fisheries.
   Four members at least to be elected from each sub-panel.
3. Eleven members from the Labour panel which includes persons having knowledge and practical experience of labour, either organised or unorganised.
   Four members at least to be elected from each sub-panel.
4. Nine members from the Industrial and Commercial panel which includes persons having knowledge and practical experience of industry and commerce, banking, finance, accountancy, engineering and architecture.
   Three members at least to be elected from each sub-panel.
5. Seven members from the Administrative panel which includes persons having knowledge and practical experience of public administration, social services and voluntary social activities.
   Three members at least to be elected from each sub-panel.

Each of the five panels enumerated above is divided into two sub-panels and nominating procedures for each sub-panel are different.

A person to be eligible for nomination must, apart from the constitutional and legal requirements, satisfy the returning officer that he has the knowledge and practical experience to be on the panel to which he seeks election. There are two methods of nomination: the first is by a nominating body. All the candidates nominated by nominating bodies form one sub-panel. The second method of nomination is on the nomination of members of the Oireachtas and all candidates thus nominated form another panel, known as the Oireachtas sub-panel.

A register of bodies known as nominating bodies, entitled to nominate persons to the panels, must be established and maintained. To qualify for registration the body must have objects which relate to the interests and services mentioned in Art. 18.7 of the Constitution or represent persons who have knowledge and practical experience of such interests and services. Certain types of organisations are excluded from registration: any body formed to carry on trade or business for profit is excluded as are bodies composed of persons in the employment of the State or a local authority whose objects include the advancement or protection of employment. Two bodies must be included in the register: the Irish County Councils General Council and the Association of Municipal Authorities of Ireland. An application to be registered must be made in writing and an appeal is permitted if the application is refused. The register must be revised annually. The bodies included in the existing register include professional, academic and charitable bodies together with bodies representing commercial groups and bodies representing trade unions.

Within ten days of the dissolution of the Dáil the Clerk of Seanad Éireann, who is the Seanad returning officer, sends by post to every registered nominating body a nomination paper and a notice informing it of the number of candidates it may nominate, which number fluctuates depending on the number of nominating bodies then registered. The nomination paper must contain the name and qualifications of the candidate and must be sealed if the nominating body is a corporate body, or signed by the proper persons if the body is unincorporated.

A nomination by members of the Oireachtas must be in writing, contain the name and qualifications of the candidate and be signed by not less than four members of the Oireachtas. An Oireachtas member can join in the nomination of only one candidate and members of the outgoing Seanad may nominate persons.

The Seanad returning officer rules on the nomination papers, and issues of dispute are decided by a judicial assessor who is a judge of the High Court. The returning officer then prepares the panels of candidates. Each panel is divided into the sub-panels: one list contains the names nominated by the members of the Oireachtas, and the other the names nominated by the nominating bodies.

The electorate consists, according to the *Seanad Electoral (Panel Members) Act, 1947,* s.44 of the members of the new Dáil, members of the outgoing Seanad and members of every county and borough council. The Clerk of the Dáil within three days of receiving the returns to the writs for a Dáil election sends to the Seanad returning officer a list of the names and addresses of the Dáil members who are entitled to be members of the Seanad electorate.

The secretary of a county council, or the town clerk of a county borough, must, within fifteen days of a dissolution of the Dáil, send to the Seanad returning officer a list of the names and addresses of the council members. If a person can qualify because of Dáil or Seanad membership and council membership he can only be entered once in a register.

The Seanad returning officer sends by post to each person on the

Seanad electoral register a copy of the five panels for his information. Later he sends by registered post to each voter a ballot paper for each of the five panels. A voter marks his papers in the order of preference in which he favours the candidates and returns them by registered post. There is a unique privilege given to Seanad voters: they may in certain circumstances obtain duplicate ballot papers. A postal vote is required by Art. 18.5. The voting system is proportional representation by means of the single transferable vote. The Seanad returning officer ascertains separately the results in respect of each panel and makes the declaration of election.

Where a casual vacancy occurs in the membership of the panels, the Clerk of the Seanad informs the Minister for the Environment in writing of the vacancy and a by-election takes place. Should a person be elected to a university constituency and also to a panel, he must before taking his seat deliver to the Clerk of the Seanad in writing a declaration as to whether he sits as a university or a panel member. If he neglects to make this choice within a month after the first sitting of the Seanad he is deemed to sit as a university member and to have resigned his seat as a panel member.

Term of Office

When the President dissolves Dáil Éireann he does not dissolve the Seanad. One Seanad continues in existence until the day before the polling day of the general election for a new Seanad. While the Dáil stands dissolved the Seanad exists. Constitutionally it seems to mean that a new Dáil and an old Seanad could constitute the Houses of the Oireachtas. The first meeting of Seanad Éireann after a Seanad general election takes place on a date fixed by the President on the advice of the Taoiseach.

Chapter 8

THE GOVERNMENT

Nature of the Executive

The Oireachtas is the law-maker and not the administrator. The executive power of the State is vested in and exercised by the Government (Art. 28.2). The constitutional powers of the Government are few though far-reaching and, like other organs of government, must act *intra vires* the Constitution and the law. The Government is controlled by the Oireachtas.

The executive or administrative function is the general and detailed carrying out of government according to the Constitution and the law. It includes the framing of policy and the choice and manner in which the law may be enacted to render the policy possible. Today it involves the provision and administration of a vast system of social services such as public health, housing, social welfare and education. The supervision of defence and internal order, which function spreads from the provision of legal aid to the building and maintenance of prisons, is within their domain. The State also plays a part in industry by creating and controlling semi-state companies and by assisting the private sector. The financing of government has become a complex and intricate art within the province of the exeuctive. The executive is responsible for the international relations of the State. Many of the functions of the executive are outside the ambit of constitutional law though the last two, financial matters and international relations, are considered later.

Membership of the Government

The Taoiseach, the head of the Government, is appointed by the President on the nomination of the Dáil. The other members of the Government, not less than seven and not more than fifteen, are appointed by the President on the nomination of the Taoiseach with the approval of the Dáil. Members of the Government must be members of either House of the Oireachtas, but the Taoiseach, the Tánaiste* and the Minister for Finance must be members of the Dáil. A maximum of two Senators may be members of the Government.

The Tánaiste, a member of the Government nominated by the Taoiseach, acts in place of the Taoiseach if the latter should die, became permanently incapacitated, or be temporarily absent. It is constitutionally improper for both the Taoiseach and Tánaiste to be absent from the State at the same time.

The Taoiseach continues in office from the moment of his appointment until he dies, resigns, advises the President to dissolve the Dáil or until he has ceased to retain the support of the majority of the Dáil. In any event he continues in office until his successor is appointed. There is no formal procedure for deciding upon the permanent incapacity of the Taoiseach unlike the role given to the Supreme Court in deciding this question about the President. Presumably the Tánaiste would anounce the fact to the Dáil and the appointment by the President of his successor would be sufficient to remove the incapacitated Taoiseach from office.

Other members of the Government may resign by placing their resignation in the hands of the Taoiseach for submission to the President. The Taoiseach may dismiss a Government member at any time for reasons which to him seem sufficient and should that member fail to resign, his appointment is terminated by the President on the Taoiseach's advice. Dáil Éireann cannot remove a Government member from office; this can be done only by the Taoiseach. When the Taoiseach resigns from office the other Government members are deemed to have resigned though all remain in office until their successors are appointed. The same situation obtains if the Dáil is dissolved.

Collective Responsibility

The Constitution is silent as to who summons meetings of the Government and how regular these must be. Presumably this is the responsibility of the Taoiseach and, in his absence, the Tánaiste. The only constitutional direction given to the Government is that it meets and acts as a collective authority (Art. 28.4.2°). The individual members must act in co-operation in reaching and implementing its policy. They must appear unified even though decisions are taken by majority. Each must accept the responsibility for all, and all must accept the responsibility for each. There is one constitutional exception to collective responsibility: the Taoiseach alone advises the President to dissolve Dáil Éireann. The Government is collectively responsible for the Departments of State. While an individual Minister may be the head of a particular Department all the members of the Government are responsible for all Departments.

A legal challenge to the Government must name all the members of Government. In *Boland v. An Taoiseach* (Case No. 14) the plaintiff was required to include all the Government members as defendants when he challenged as unconstitutional an executive policy. It was not sufficient to sue the Taoiseach as representing the Government: success against him might not have bound the other Government members.

Responsibility to Dáil Éireann

The scheme of the Constitution is that Dáil Éireann, because it is directly elected by popular franchise, has the greater prerogative powers. The Government must, with two exceptions, be drawn from Dáil members and since the Dáil nominates the Taoiseach and approves the other members of the Government, this control of the Government by Dáil Éireann is completed by Art. 28.4.1° declaring that the Government is responsible to Dáil Éireann. Of course the Taoiseach, and his Government, must resign when they cease to retain the support of the majority of the Dáil. The Government is not responsible to the Seanad, and votes of no confidence or the withdrawal of majority support by that House cannot force the resignation of the Taoiseach.

This constitutional requirement that the Government is responsible to Dáil Éireann is how the legislature checks the executive under the doctrine of the separation of powers. While the political reality and the legal theory may not always coalesce, the Taoiseach and his Government have on occasion been forced to resign. The control is real.

The Government and Financial Affairs of the State

One of the executive duties of the Government is to manage the financial affairs of the State. The Government must prepare Estimates of the Receipts and Estimates of the Expenditure of the State for each financial year and present them to the Dáil for consideration (Art. 28.4.3°). The Dáil can only consider them and not necessarily vote on them. The Dáil and each member must be given adequate time to consider these Estimates.

The Constitution declares that all State revenues from whatever source arising must, subject to such exceptions as may be provided by law, form one fund (Art. 11). This is known as the Central Fund and the Dáil must not pass any vote or resolution, and no law can be enacted, for the appropriation of revenue or other public monies unless the purpose of the appropriation has been recommended to the Dáil by a message from the Government signed by the Taoiseach (Art. 17.2).

When the Estimates have been debated and agreed to, a Bill is introduced to appropriate the total sum mentioned in the schedule to the Bill. The Seanad has only twenty-one days to consider it and the President cannot refer it to the Supreme Court because it is a Money Bill. Should there be any delay in preparing, debating or enacting into law the Estimates, there is provision in the *Central Fund (Permanent Provisions) Act, 1965* to authorise the Minister for Finance to issue from the Central Fund an amount not exceeding four-fifths of the amount appropriated for each particular service during the preceding financial year.

There is no constitutional requirement for an annual budget but the practice has been to have one or even two. The annual statement of the Minister for Finance outlines proposals for new taxation and indicates the proposed changes to the existing tax structure. Some of these proposals are reduced into financial resolutions because some taxation measures come into effect on budget day. These resolutions contain declarations that it is expedient that they should have statutory effect under the *Provisional Collection of Taxes Act, 1927*, normally for a period not exceeding four months. The Finance Bill for the year which is based upon the financial resolutions is introduced as soon as possible. This gives legislative effect to the budget.

There are three paramount features in the management of State finances. The executive initiates action, the legislature controls these actions and finally there is inspection and audit by an independent official. We have considered the first two stages in the procedure; now we examine the third.

The Constitution creates the office of the Comptroller and Auditor General (Art. 33). He is appointed by the President on the nomination of the Dáil, cannot be a member of the Oireachtas and cannot hold another position of emolument. His removal from office for stated misbehaviour requires a resolution of both Houses of the Oireachtas. The President, on receipt of copies of the resolutions from the Taoiseach, removes the Comptroller and Auditor General from office under his hand and seal.

As the title implies, the Comptroller and Auditor General has two tasks. As Comptroller he sees that no money leaves the Central Fund without statutory authority and that such money is properly applied. As Auditor he audits the accounts of income. He reports annually to the Dáil and may raise questions on which he has doubts. He has never resorted to law because this may be inappropriate: his function is to raise irregularities in order to allow the Dáil to take action if it chooses.

The Preamble to the Constitution directs that concord be established with other nations. One of the criteria of statehood is the ability to enter into relations with other states. Ireland declares its devotion to the ideal of peace and friendly co-operation amongst nations, founded on international justice and morality and affirms its adherence to the principle of the pacific settlement of international disputes by international arbitration or judicial determination (Art. 29).

The executive power of the State with regard to external relations is exercised by the Government and is an area of policy into which the courts cannot stray except when its exercise is *ultra vires* the Constitution. This was amply illustrated in *Boland v. An Taoiseach* (Case No. 14) where the Supreme Court refused to injunct the Government from entering into an agreement which the plaintiff claimed was unconstitutional though some members of the Court hinted that should the agreement be incorporated into legislation it might then be open to challenge.

Every international agreement to which the State becomes a party must be laid before the Dáil. Ireland has become a party to many international agreements though no international agreement becomes part of the domestic law of the State 'save as may be determined by the Oireachtas' (Art. 29.6). Legislation has enacted many international agreements into domestic law.[54] Can the citizen avail of an international agreement to which the State is a party but which has not been enacted into domestic law? This question arose in *In re Ó Láighléis* (Case No. 72) where the applicant was interned and could not challenge the constitutionality of internment without trial because this process had been declared constitutional by the Supreme Court in *Art. 26 and the Offences Against the State (Amendment) Bill, 1940* (Case No. 7) and consequently its constitutionality could never again be questioned. Instead the applicant argued that internment offended the European Convention on Human Rights, which Ireland adopted in Rome on 4 November 1950 and which came into force on 3 September 1953. The non-enactment of the Convention into domestic law was fatal to the applicant's case. According to Davitt P. in the High Court: 'Where there is an irreconcilable conflict between a domestic statute and the principles of international law or the provisions of an international agreement, the Courts administering the domestic law must give effect to the statute. If this principle were not to be observed it would follow that the Executive Government by means of an international agreement might, in certain circumstances, be able to exercise powers of legislation contrary to the letter and spirit of the Constitution. The right of the citizens of this State to be bound by no other laws than those enacted by their elected representatives in the Oireachtas assembled is one to be carefully preserved and jealously guarded.'

Ireland accepts the generally recognised principles of international law as its rule of conduct in its relations with other states (Art. 29.3). This direction was felt to conflict with part of the *Extradition Act, 1965* in *The State (Sumers Jennings) v. Furlong* because the Act did not contain the rule of speciality which it was claimed was a recognised principle of international law. Rejecting this contention in the High Court, Henchy J. said that Art. 29.3 was not to be interpreted 'as a statement of the absolute restriction of the legislative powers of the State by the generally recognised principles of international law. As the Irish version makes clear, the section merely provides that Ireland accepts the generally recognised principles of international law as a guide *(ina dtreoir)* in its relations with other states.' Since the rule of speciality was not in the statute it was not part of the domestic law and could not be implied.

In *Bourke v. Attorney General* the Supreme Court looked for assistance in interpreting the phrase 'a political offence or an offence connected with a political offence', contained in the *Extradition Act, 1965*, s.50, to the European Convention on Extradition which was signed by Ireland in Paris in 1957. In this case the plaintiff had aided a convicted spy to escape from a British prison and claimed he could not be extradited because the offence was political. The Supreme Court accepted the proposition that extradition was not possible for political offences or offences connected with political offences in international law. The Court held that the plaintiff's offence of escaping from prison was not a political offence but that the convicted spy's escape was a political offence and therefore the plaintiff, because of his connection with the spy, could not be extradited. The principle that there is no extradition under international law for political offences was accepted by the Irish members of the Law Enforcement Commission.[55] 'For so long as these generally recognised principles forbid extradition of persons charged with or convicted of political offences these members cannot advise that any agreement or legislation designed to produce this result would be valid' (paragraph 68). The British members concurred: 'There is a widespread and well-accepted practice, usually embodied in multilateral or bilateral agreements and in the domestic law of each State, according to which persons are not extradited in respect of political crimes' (paragraph 77).

Chapter 9

THE COURTS

The Administration of Justice

In most modern states the judicial function is the third arm of government. The judicial function consists in the interpretation of the law and its application by rule or discretion to disputes which arise between individual and individual, and between the State and the individual. The

Constitution establishes courts of law or courts of justice to exercise the judicial function. Under the doctrine of the separation of powers the courts must be independent and be capable of exercising some control over the other organs of government. The courts exercise a fundamental control over the legislature by being empowered to declare statutes invalid if they infringe any provision of the Constitution. In matters of policy the courts refuse to interfere with the executive power but where legal powers are given, the courts insist that these are exercised *intra vires.*

Justice shall be administered in courts established under the Constitution (Art. 34). The administering of justice and the administering of the law may at first glance appear to be the same, though on reflection it can be seen that the two, while related, are not synonymous. Justice is pursued through the law but there are many injustices because the law has not developed to grant a remedy though the general idea of law without justice is repugnant. The purpose of law is to achieve justice: justice without law is an impossibility. Leaving aside the *moral* concept of justice our society, by the use of law, attempts to secure fairness for all. This is known as the rule of law. This concept has a number of meanings which all attempt to explain the one idea that justice is attainable by using the law. The first meaning given is that everything must be done according to law or that an action done without legal justification is illegal. This is known as the principle of legality. The second meaning given is that law must, by recognised rules and principles, restrict unlimited power. Often a discretion given can be abused, so the law forces it to be exercised within certain boundaries. A third meaning of the rule of law is that tribunals before which disputes are heard must be independent of the other organs of government. A fourth meaning is that the law should apply to all persons and, while this is impossible, some effort must be made to ensure some equality of treatment, because otherwise some persons may believe they are immune from the law while others will feel oppressed.

Defining the administration of justice has defied many leading authorities though Kennedy C.J. in *Lynham v. Butler* (No. 2) mapped out its scope admirably when he explained that: 'The controversies which fall to it for determination may be divided into two classes, criminal and civil. In relation to the former ... the judicial power is exercised in determining the guilt or innocence of persons charged with offences against the State itself and in determining the punishments to be inflicted upon persons found guilty of offences charged against them, which punishments it then becomes the obligation of the Executive Department of Government to carry into effect. In relation to justiciable controversies of the civil class, the judicial power is exercised in a final manner, by definitive adjudication according to law, rights or obligations in disputes between citizen and citizen or between citizens and the State ... and in binding the parties by such determination which will be enforced if necessary with the authority of the State. Its characteristic public good in its civil aspect is finality and authority, the decisive ending of disputes and quarrels, and the avoidance of private methods of violence in asserting or resisting claims alleged or denied.' It would be dangerous to draw the conclusion that in Irish law justice is administered only in courts. It may be administered elsewhere under Art. 37 of the Constitution. This is discussed later in the chapter.

Justice must be administered in public. Courts open to the public gaze and the scrutiny of a free press are less likely to abuse their powers than a system of courts in secret. Apart from this, there are advantages in open courts. The citizen is aware of the law, how it is applied and the relevant punishment for its infringement. The citizen is protected from unsustainable accusation because his accusers under our accusatorial system must give evidence in public and be subject to cross-examination. The disadvantage may be that a wronged party, because of the glare of possible publicity, may not seek redress. Justice in public identifies the anti-social citizens. The courts themselves have recognised and welcomed the necessity for publicity. In *Beamish and Crawford Ltd. v. Crowley* (Case No. 11) Ó Dálaigh C.J. said: 'But publicity, deserved or otherwise, is inseparable from the administration of justice in public; this is a principle which, as the Constitution declares, may not be departed from except in such special and limited cases as may be prescribed by law.' There are many instances permitted by statute where justice is administered totally in private or where some aspects of the case may not be disclosed. Each instance should be examined carefully to see whether it is in the best interests of society. Some clearly are not. For example, all our family law is now heard in private and this has given rise to the false impression that there are no disputes in this vital area. Surely it is possible for the facts of the cases to be disclosed without identifying the parties. The public would have a better way of knowing the prevailing state of matrimonial relations, particularly when attempting to decide whether the constitutional ban on divorce should remain.

The Judiciary

A judge can be defined as a person vested with authority to decide questions in dispute between parties and to award the appropriate remedy. Together with judicial functions a judge may be entrusted with administrative functions.[56] The Constitution declares that justice shall be administered in courts established by judges appointed in the manner provided in the Constitution (Art. 34). Judges appointed under Art. 34 of the Constitution must be appointed by the President (Art. 35.1). This does not mean that all judges must be appointed by the President, because special courts may be established under Art. 38 and in these latter courts the judges may be appointed in a different manner. This is the distinction between the ordinary and special courts which is considered more fully later. The Constitution is silent as to who recommends to the President which persons are to be appointed judges. This is done, at present, by the Government, though the task could be given elsewhere. Criticism is often made that many of the persons appointed are politically aligned to the Government making those appointments. This is valid though the appointees are not subject to executive direction in their judicial functions. Appointments are not made on merit or ability but on political affiliation and those with different allegiance, and with none, are blandly ignored. This method not alone debases politics but denies to the judicial system and to the public the best legal talent. Other methods of appointment should be considered.

Provisions relating to the terms of appointment, the number of judges, their remuneration, age of retirement and pensions, shall be regulated by statute. Many of these matters have been regulated by law and the effect of their non-observance was considered in *The State (Walshe) v. Murphy* where a conviction was challenged on the ground that the District Justice had not been validly appointed because he had not practised as a barrister for the requisite period and was not practising as a barrister on the date of his appointment, which were qualifications for the appointment. The High Court quashed the conviction, and by this decision indirectly removed the District Justice from office. The same principle could be invoked to invalidate decisions of a judge who had continued to serve after the date of his retirement.

The Constitution provides a number of ways in which the independence of the judiciary can be ensured and the common law complements these. No judge must be a member of either House of the Oireachtas and by implication of the Government. This preserves the basis for the separation of powers. Nor must a judge hold any other office or position of emolument. This prevents a judge from placing himself in a position where his personal interest would clash with his judicial function or even where this would seem to happen. It permits a judge to give all his talents to his profession. A judge who heard a case in which he had a pecuniary interest, such as being a shareholder in a defendant company, offends the rule of natural justice, *nemo judex in sua causa* (no one should judge in his own cause), and the other party could have the decision set aside. A judge must be seen to approach a case without bias though there are occasions when a judge may have a preconceived attitude towards a case. For example the Chief Justice is *ex officio* a member of the Council of State and may be called to advise the President who is considering whether to refer a Bill to the Supreme Court for a decision as to its constitutionality. If the President refers the Bill then the Chief Justice may sit and may appear to approach the question with some preconceived ideas. The second way by which the Constitution ensures judicial independence is by making it difficult to remove a judge from office. Art. 35.4 declares that a judge of the Supreme or High Court can only be removed for stated misbehaviour and on resolution passed by both Houses of the Oireachtas. The Taoiseach notifies the President and forwards to him copies of each resolution. On receipt of these the President removes the judge from office. From the inception of the State this has not happened. It is a drastic step though one which could not be evaded if circumstances demanded it.

The third constitutional guarantee of judicial independence is contained in Art. 35.5 which declares that the remuneration of a judge cannot be reduced during his continuance in office because the impartiality of the judiciary could be attacked if reductions in their incomes were threatened by a Government displeased at their decisions. A novel point was taken under this Article in *O'Byrne v. The Minister for Finance* (Case No. 69) where the widow of a deceased judge claimed that taxation payments deducted from his salary while in office were a breach of the constitutional guarantee. Dixon J. in the High Court rejected the argument but warned: 'However unlikely in practice, it is still conceivable that the Legislature might at some time discriminate unduly in its taxation as regards some particular group ... If judicial remuneration were involved, the Courts would also have to determine whether there was not, in the guise of taxation, a prohibited attack on the independence of the judiciary.' On appeal this decision was affirmed only by a majority of the Supreme Court. At the conclusion of his judgment Maguire C.J. explained: 'The purpose of the Article is to safeguard the independence of judges. To require a judge to pay taxes on his income on the same basis as other citizens and thus to contribute to the expenses of Government cannot be said to be an attack upon his independence.' Art. 34.5.1° of the Constitution provides the fourth guarantee. Every judge must make a declaration that he will faithfully and to the best of his knowledge and power execute his office without fear or favour, affection or ill-will towards any man, and that he will uphold the Constitution and the laws. This declaration must be made by the Chief Justice in the presence of the President, and every other judge must make it before the Chief Justice in open court. It must be made before taking up office and not later than ten days after appointment. Failure to do this results in the office being deemed vacated.

The common law developed two further protections which complement the constitutional guarantees just explained. The first is the law of contempt. This contempt is of two kinds. Civil contempt consists in disobedience to the judgments, orders or other processes of the superior courts. Criminal contempt consists of acts tending to obstruct the due process of justice. It includes contempt in the face of the court, consisting of words or actions in the presence of the court that interfere or tend to interfere with the course of justice. A physical attack on a judge, jury, lawyer or witness or the use of threatening language against them is contempt. Even when proceedings have terminated, it may be contempt to scandalise the court by publishing scurrilous personal abuse of a judge's conduct of the case. This was the allegation in *The State (DPP) v. Walsh* (Case No. 90) where, after a conviction for capital murder, a newspaper published an item drafted by the defendant which referred to the verdict 'as particularly reprehensible because it was passed by the Special Criminal

71

Court, a court composed of Government-appointed judges having no judicial independence, which sat without a jury and which so abused the rules of evidence as to make the court akin to a sentencing tribunal.' The Supreme Court, per Henchy J., found this statement 'calculated to undermine the reputation of the Special Criminal Court as a source of justice'. The purpose of the law of contempt is not to buttress the dignity of the judges by protecting them from insult but to protect the rights of the public by ensuring that the administration of justice is not obstructed.

The second protection granted by the common law is that judges enjoy immunity from action when performing their judicial functions. The object of this is to uphold judicial independence in that decisions may not be warped by fear of personal liability. This protection extends to acts done or things said maliciously and corruptly, as hardly seems appropriate. In *Macaulay & Co. Ltd v. Wyse-Power* the plaintiff sued a Circuit Court judge for slander arising out of remarks made by the judge during a case that seriously assailed the character and reputation of the company. The action was unsustainable because, as Maguire J. explained in the High Court, 'There was a long line of authority which establishes the proposition that no action would lie against a Judge of a Court of Record. It was better that an individual should suffer than the course of justice be hindered and fettered by apprehensions on the part of the judge that his own words might be made the subject of an action. That was generally called judicial privilege ...' Since this immunity is claimed it behoves judges to be circumspect in their remarks. A judge can sue if he is defamed while performing his office.

The System of Courts

A court can be defined as a tribunal having power to adjudicate in a civil, criminal or military matter and must be distinguished from a courthouse which is the building in which justice is administered (where the law courts are held). The Constitution envisages a hierarchical system of courts which has many of the characteristics of the system in force prior to 1922. The Constitution declares that there must be a Supreme Court and a High Court and other courts of limited and local jurisdiction.

While the Constitution was enacted in 1937 the system of courts it envisaged was not established until the *Courts (Establishment and Constitution) Act, 1961* was passed and, though the system in force until that year is similar to the present system, it is not identical. For example there was no similar provision to Art. 26 in the 1922 Constitution and it is doubtful whether the Supreme Court of Justice which continued until 1961 had the jurisdiction to advise the President. Thus a question hangs over the validity of the three references of Bills to the old Supreme Court prior to 1961. If they possess no constitutional validity, the question whether internment without trial permitted under the *Offences Against the State (Amendment) Act, 1940* is or is not constitutional is open for consideration by the new Supreme Court.

72

The court of final appeal is called the Supreme Court (Art. 34.4.1°). The Constitution grants certain jurisdictions some of which cannot be curtailed without constitutional amendment and others of which may be curtailed by law. The Supreme Court must advise the President whether any Bill he refers to is or is not constitutional and the Supreme Court has appellate jurisdiction from decisions of the High Court in cases which involve the validity of any law, having regard to the provisions of the Constitution. These jurisdictions granted by the Constitution cannot be curtailed by law though its appellate jurisdiction from all other decisions of the High Court can be regulated by law. The extent of this appellate jurisdiction has been considered a number of times. It was held by the old Supreme Court in 1939 that an appeal could not be made against the granting of an order of *habeas corpus**** by the High Court in *The State (Burke) v. Lennon* (Case No. 86) though by 1967 the new Supreme Court in *The State (Browne) v. Feran* refused to adopt this curtailment of its appellate jurisdiction and permitted such an appeal. In *The People (A. G.) v. Conmey* (Case No. 73) the Supreme Court decided that an appeal could be made against a conviction of the Central Criminal Court, which is the High Court exercising its criminal jurisdiction, though statute permitted only an appeal to the Court of Criminal Appeal. The Supreme Court held that to exclude its appellate jurisdiction the language of the statute must be, according to O'Higgins C.J., 'clearly intended to have this effect'. This decision has had the effect of giving a person convicted in the Central Criminal Court an option of where he will appeal. This appellate jurisdiction of the Supreme Court could be curtailed by statute. The question was raised, following Conmey's case, whether the State could appeal an acquittal which at common law it could not do. In *The People (DPP) v. O'Shea* (Case No. 80) the question came a little closer to being answered. In this case the Supreme Court decided it had jurisdiction to hear an appeal where the trial judge in the Central Criminal Court had directed the jury to acquit an accused. It can hardly be doubted that, in the absence of statutory probhibition, the Supreme Court will in an appropriate case hear an appeal from a jury acquittal. It may not be a welcome development. At present an acquittal by a jury is the only instance of a decision within the judicial system which is outside the scope of review by a higher court. In civil cases the Supreme Court has adopted the same stance of protecting its appellate jurisdiction. In *In re Morelli* the High Court in a probate matter made no order as to costs and the party affected appealed. The other party's argument that it was the practice not to appeal such decisions was rejected by the Supreme Court which heard the appeal.

The Supreme Court may be given extra appellate jurisdiction by law. At present it hears appeals from the Court of Criminal Appeal though the right of appeal is not automatic. Some statutes confer a consultative jurisdiction**** on the Supreme Court but whether this is constitutionally permissible is doubtful because the only kind of extra jurisdiction which can be conferred is appellate. In a consultative case only a point of law is raised for consideration while the verdict of the lower court cannot be reviewed. The only original jurisdiction* possessed by the Supreme Court is under Art. 26 and it is also doubtful whether it can be endowed with other original jurisdiction simply because the Supreme Court is a court of appeal.

The Supreme Court has appellate jurisdiction from the High Court in cases which involve the validity of any law having regard to the provisions of the Constitution (Art. 34.4.4°), a jurisdiction which cannot be modified by law. The exercise of this jurisdiction depends on the willingness of the parties to appeal. The State usually appeals, though not always, and the private individual, probably because of the expense, is more likely not to. Because it is desirable that the views of the Supreme Court be obtained, some method of alleviating the problem of costs must be found. It seems peculiar that an individual who by his action gives the Supreme Court the opportunity to state or clarify the law for the benefit of society should be penalised for his efforts. The judges should remember that the status and standing of the Supreme Court has been achieved and will be maintained by pronouncements and not by silence. In this type of constitutional case the decision of the Court should be pronounced by one of the judges as the Court directs and no other opinion should be pronounced or its existence disclosed (Art. 34.4.5°). The Supreme Court has given this sub-article a restrictive meaning in that it is only applied to a statute of the Oireachtas established under the Constitution. A pre-Constitution statute is likely to suffer as many judgments as there are judges because the Court does not consider the question under Art. 34.4.5° but under Art. 50 which declares that the laws in force in Saorstát Éireann continued in force provided they are not inconsistent with the Constitution, and this Article does not contain any direction as to how many judgments can be pronounced.

The courts of first instance must include a High Court invested with full original jurisdiction in all matters and questions whether of law or fact, civil or criminal (Art. 34.3.1°). It is difficult to determine the scope of this jurisdiction though it appears literally to mean unlimited jurisdiction in the civil and criminal fields. The Constitution limits this jurisdiction by permitting the exercise of limited functions and powers of a judicial nature in civil matters by those other than courts or judges (Art. 37) and offences may be tried summarily, in special courts and by military tribunals (Art. 38). It is undeniable that the Oireachtas could limit the existing jurisdiction of the High Court, with one important exception. The Constitution declares that the High Court has jurisdiction to question the validity of any law having regard to the provisions of the Constitution (Art. 34.3.2°). This is the power which the American Supreme Court implied in *Marbury v. Madison* in 1803. Judicial review of an Act of the Oireachtas as to its constitutionality is firmly and clearly stated to reside in the High Court, and, on appeal, in the Supreme Court. There is one exception to this review in that no court has the jurisdiction to question the validity of a law the Bill of which is referred by the President to the Supreme Court. This was considered fully in Chapter 4.

In exercising judicial review the courts have adopted a number of rules of interpretation. The first of these was formulated in the *Pigs Marketing Board v. Donnelly (Dublin) Ltd.* (Case No. 82) by Hanna J. when he said: 'When the Court has to consider the constitutionality of a law it must ... be accepted as an axiom that a law passed by the Oireachtas, the elected representatives of the people, is presumed to be constitutional unless and until the contrary is clearly established.' The onus of proof is on the plaintiff. The second rule was explained in *The State (Sheerin) v. Kennedy* (Case No. 100) by Walsh J. thus: 'All law in force on the date immediately prior to the coming into operation of the Constitution ... enjoy no such presumption in respect of the present Constitution ...' The third rule is that the courts will only exercise this jurisdiction if it is unavoidable. As explained by O'Higgins C.J. in *M. v. An Bord Uchtála:* 'Where the relief which a plaintiff seeks rests on two distinct grounds, as a general rule the court should consider first whether the relief sought can be granted on the ground which does not raise a question of constitutional validity. If it can, then the court ought not to rule on the larger question of the constitutional validity of the law in question.' The fourth rule was explained in *East Donegal Co-operative v. Attorney General* (Case No. 35) by Walsh J.: 'An Act of the Oireachtas ... will not be declared to be invalid where it is possible to construe it in accordance with the Constitution; and it is not only a question of preferring a constitutional construction to one which would be unconstitutional where they both may appear to be open but it also means that an interpretation favouring the validity of an Act should be given in cases of doubt.'

Because there is no constitutional procedure for ensuring that proposed legislation is constitutional, apart from the limited provisions of Art. 26, a decision as to a statute's constitutionality must be made in hindsight. By what procedure should a challenge be made? The courts themselves will not initiate such an inquiry, which looks like a failure by the judges to honour their declaration of upholding the Constitution. Since the Oireachtas has the duty not to pass unconstitutional laws, surely the courts have the corresponding duty not to apply such laws. The courts will not act until an individual seeks their assistance. Why should the onus of proving a statute unconstitutional rest on an individual? Surely he should be able to rest assured that the Oireachtas will not enact, and if it does, that the courts will not apply, unconstitutional laws.

The challenge to a statute may be *direct* or *collateral.** It is direct if the originating proceedings seek a declaration that the statute is invalid having regard to the provisions of the Constitution, a claim made where the statute is post-1937. If the statute is a pre-1937 one, it is claimed that it is inconsistent with the provisions of the Constitution. The essence of

75

a declaratory judgment is that it states the rights or legal position of the parties and if the court declares the statute unconstitutional that settles the point. The declaratory action is a common method of attacking legislation on constitutional grounds: it was used in *McGee v. Attorney General* (Case No. 50) where a pre-1937 statute was successfully challenged, and in *O'Donovan v. Attorney General* (Case No. 70), a post-1937 statute was successfully challenged. The second type of direct action is one for damages which attempts to compensate a citizen who has suffered a breach of his constitutional rights at the hands of another. In two cases, *Meskell v. CIE* (Case No. 56) and *Crowley v. Ireland* (Case No. 29), damages were awarded for conspiracy to breach constitutional rights, in the first case against a semi-state body and in the second case against a teachers' union. In the successful cases to date no claim for damages or a declaration has been sought though there is no reason why they should not be. It might in some cases be difficult to prove that the plaintiff suffered. For example what damage did the plaintiff in *de Búrca v. Attorney General* (Case No. 32) suffer because the jury would not have been drawn in accordance with the Constitution. On the other hand, in some cases, such as *McGee v. Attorney General* (Case No. 50) where artificial contraceptives were not available to a married woman, damage might be suffered. A question not considered by the courts is whether damages could be awarded in lieu of a declaration. For example the result in *Blake v. Attorney General* (Case No. 13) effectively put an end to rent control in an action taken by landlords who were not getting a fair return in rent from their properties. New legislation was enacted and referred by the President to the Supreme Court, which rejected it: *Art. 26 and the Housing (Private Rented Dwellings) Bill, 1981.* Further legislation was enacted providing new procedures for assessing rents which may in certain cases be subsidised by the State. Might it not have been administratively easier to have financially compensated the landlords, and left the legislation intact?

Statutes may be indirectly challenged as to their constitutionality in collateral proceedings by assaulting a decision based on the statute. *Certiorari,* * which is commonly used, is issued to quash a decision already made, on the ground that the deciding authority acted *ultra vires* the Constitution though it may have acted *intra vires* the statute. In *The State (Nicolaou) v. An Bord Uchtála* (Case No. 96) it was sought to quash an adoption order made under the *Adoption Act, 1952,* on the ground that the statute was unconstitutional. The injunction has been used in a similar way. In the *Educational Co. of Ireland v. Fitzpatrick* (Case No. 36) an injunction was used to prevent picketing undertaken in order to prevent employees from exercising their constitutional right to dissociate. The commonest method of challenging statutes in collateral proceedings is by an application under Art. 40 of the Constitution which obliges the High Court to inquire into a detention, and if it is unlawful a release is ordered. If the detention is unlawful but the High Court is of opinion that the law itself is unconstitutional it must refer the question to the Supreme Court. It was decided in *The State (Sheerin) v. Kennedy* (Case No. 100) that this necessity of referral applied to post-1937 statutes only, and in other cases it was open to the High Court to decide the issue itself. In that case the prosecutor was released because the 1908 statute under which he was detained was unconstitutional, and in *The State (Quinn) v. Ryan* (Case No. 97) an 1851 statute was held to be inconsistent with Art. 50.

What is the effect on a statute of declaring it unconstitutional? Prospectively the statute, or at least the impugned section, is null and void: it is without legal effect. Should the Oireachtas wish to continue with the impugned statute as law, it must initiate a constitutional amendment because an ordinary statute cannot negative such a decision. One attempt has been made to do this where it was proposed that a tolerance of up to 16 per cent of the national average be permitted in drawing up constituencies after the High Court in *O'Donovan v. Attorney General* (Case No. 70) had rejected a tolerance of 19 per cent. The People rejected the proposal. The more difficult question is from what date is impugned legislation null and void? In *Murphy v. Attorney General* (Case No. 61) the question arose whether income tax paid under impugned sections of the *Income Tax Act, 1967* could be recovered. The Supreme Court drew the distinction between pre- and post-1937 legislation and held that, in the former, inconsistency dated from the coming into operation of the Constitution. As regards post-1937 legislation it was void *ab initio,* that is retrospectively from its enactment and not from the date of the court's judgment. Does this mean that all actions done under the impugned legislation are null and void? This thorny problem was explained and answered by Henchy J.: 'For a variety of reasons, the law recognises that in certain circumstances, no matter how unfounded in law certain conduct may have been, no matter how unwarranted its operation in a particular case, what has happened has happened, and cannot or should not be undone. The irreversible progressions and bye-products of time, the compulsion of public order and of the common good, the aversion of the law from giving a hearing to those who have slept on their rights, the quality of legality — even irreversibility — that tends to attach to what has become inveterate or has been widely accepted or acted upon, the recognition that even in the short term the accomplished facts may sometimes acquire an inviolable sacredness, these and other factors may convert what has been done under an unconstitutional, or otherwise void, law into an acceptable part of the *corpus juris.* This trend represents an inexorable process that is not peculiar to the law, for in a wide variety of other contexts it is either foolish or impossible to attempt to turn back the hands of the clock.' The Supreme Court permitted a reclaim of tax from the year the proceedings were instituted and confined this benefit to the individuals who had taken the action.

A dilemma facing the courts when impugning legislation is not to stray into the domain of the legislator. The courts in deleting the offending sections, expressions or words must be careful not to change what remains into something not intended by the Oireachtas. The removal of the one offending word in *Maher v. Attorney General* (Case No. 53) would have left a section never intended. The Supreme Court refused to remove the word and impugned the whole section.

Courts of Limited and Local Jurisdiction

The courts of first instance must include courts of limited and local jurisdiction with a right of appeal as determined by law (Art. 34.3.4°). *Local* must be given some geographical meaning so that justice is readily available locally, and *limited* must mean that a court established will have a lesser jurisdiction than the High Court. Statute has established the Circuit and District Courts which are both local and limited. The Court of Criminal Appeal has also been established and while it is limited it is not local. The Constitution envisages a system of appeals from courts of limited and local jurisdiction. Must there be the availability of an appeal in every instance? This question arose in *The State (Hunt) v. O'Donovan* where the prosecutor* having signed a plea of guilty in the District Court was sent forward for sentence to the Circuit Court and then could not appeal to the Court of Criminal Appeal because he had not been convicted on indictment. His argument that the absence of a right of appeal was unconstitutional was rejected. Finlay J. explained: 'I have no difficulty in interpreting Art. 34.3.4° as prohibiting the constitution of a court of local and limited jurisdiction from which there is no appeal at all, but there is a very large gap between that interpretation and one which excludes the right of the law to determine from which precise decision an appeal should lie.'

Our System of Laws

It would have been impossible to invent a new system of laws for the State on the day the Constitution came into force. Apart from the question of desirability it would have been impossible to achieve without great turmoil and anarchy. The simple solution of continuing the same system of laws then in force was adopted. The enactment of the Constitution while important politically and legally went almost unnoticed in the courts. Art. 50 declares that the laws in force in Saorstát Éireann were to continue to have full force and effect until amended or repealed by the Oireachtas provided they were not inconsistent with the Constitution. There have been many instances of statutes and the common law being declared inconsistent. While it is not a crucial issue in constitutional law, it is a useful exercise to consider the nature of our legal system. It is not an indigenous one but imported and has all the characteristics of the common law. Essentially it is judge-made law complemented by legislative intervention by the Westminster parliament of the mid-nineteenth century. With the coming of independence it was almost fifty years before the judiciary,

78

and the legislature, felt competent to follow a unique direction. Except in constitutional law, and then only because our basic legal document has no counterpart in the law of our nearest neighbour, our legal system has little to show for sixty years of independence. Despairingly our legislators plagiarised British statutes, our judges slavishly applied British precedents, our academic lawyers failed miserably to produce a written jurisprudence and our law reform was instigated by changes in British law and the fear that we would be out of step. Admittedly there are hopeful signs that this dependence is weakening with the realisation that independence means legal independence as much as political independence.

The Trial of Offences

Due Process on a Criminal Charge

The Constitution declares that no person shall be tried on any criminal charge save in due course of law (Art. 38). Four methods of trial are provided, namely summary trial, trial by jury, trial by special court and trial by military tribunal, and the courts claim an inherent jurisdiction to try certain types of contempt summarily. Each is considered in turn later but some consideration must be given to the nature of a criminal charge and the meaning of *due process*. Any person, and not merely a citizen, can be tried and *person* includes both natural and artificial persons.*

What is a criminal charge? In *Melling v. Ó Mathghamhna* (Case No. 55) the question arose whether smuggling was criminal or civil in nature with the Supreme Court opting for the former. For an action to be criminal Kingsmill Moore J. enumerated the *indicia* of a crime: (1) it is an offence against the community at large; (2) the sanction to be imposed is punitive; (3) failure to pay involves imprisonment; and (4) *mens rea* is a requirement. While not strictly accurate, it is a useful guideline. Lavery J. looked to procedure in search of a definition. He thought that a proceeding 'which permits the detention of the person concerned, the bringing of him in custody to a Gárda Station, the entry of a charge . . . the searching of the person detained and the examination of papers and other things found upon him, the bringing of him before a District Justice in custody, the admission to bail to stand his trial and the detention in custody if bail is not granted or is not forthcoming, the imposition of a pecuniary penalty with the liability to imprisonment if the penalty is not paid has all the *indicia* of a criminal charge.' Many proceedings are commenced by summons and these are equally criminal. In *The State (McFadden) v. The Governor of Mountjoy* (Case No. 94) the High Court held that extradition proceedings are ancillary to criminal proceedings because the procedures for executing an extradition warrant were identical to those used when arresting for an offence.

The expression 'due course of law' means that there must be a basic fairness of procedures provided. It would be impossible to give a comprehensive list of these and to discuss in detail many matters which are more relevant to a textbook on the law of evidence. It includes the right to be adequately informed of the nature and substance of the charge, to hear and test the evidence offered by cross-examination, to be allowed to give and call evidence in rebuttal, to have the case heard by an impartial and independent tribunal, to have legal aid available if needed, the right to bail, the presumption of innocence, the burden and standard of proof, the right not to be put in double jeopardy, and the right of appeal. In *Abbey Films Ltd. v. Attorney General* (Case No. 1) the Supreme Court held that statute could impose on an accused the onus to establish a limited and specified matter in a criminal case whereas in *King v. Attorney General* (Case No. 42) the Supreme Court struck down a statute because it permitted the guilt of an accused person to be proved by reference to his previous convictions.

Classification of Crimes

The common law divided crimes into felonies, misdemeanours and statutory offences. The Constitution has introduced the concept of minor and non-minor offences (Art. 38.2). In the absence of constitutional definition Gannon J. in *The State (Rollinson) v. Kelly* said: 'As the creation of offences is a matter for the legislature the limitations which may classify any offence as being 'minor' may be expressed by the legislature in the enactment. If they are not so expressed they may be declared by the courts following the accepted principles of construction of statutes ...' The principles for deciding whether an offence is minor or non-minor have been laid down and applied in a number of cases. The first of these was *Melling v. Ó Mathghamhna* (Case No. 55) in 1961 where the Supreme Court laid down the criteria for deciding the question (1) how the law stood when the statute was passed; (2) the severity of the penalty; (3) the moral quality of the act; and (4) its relation to common law offences. Punishment, according to Lavery J., 'is the most important consideration'. In *The State (Sheerin) v. Kennedy* (Case No. 100) it was argued that a two-year period in a borstal was not a punishment but training and rehabilitation. This was rejected by the Supreme Court. Walsh J. said: 'It can scarcely be contended that a sentence to a period of detention in St Patrick's Institution is not a punishment even if the punishment may produce more beneficial results by way of reform or rehabilitation in the offender than would an equal period in an ordinary prison. The deprivation of liberty is the real punishment.' In *In re Haughey* (Case No. 41) Ó Dálaigh C.J. explained: 'In ordinary criminal prosecutions, the severity of penalty authorised, not the penalty actually imposed, is the relevant criterion.' From these decided cases some guidelines can be drawn. An offence which carries a six-months' sentence is a minor offence, whereas an offence which carries two years or more is not.

There are other cases where the penalty was monetary and these are considered now. In *Cullen v. Attorney General* (Case No. 30) the imposition of an unlimited fine in lieu of damages for negligent driving was non-minor. In *Kostan v. Ireland* the Bulgarian master of a fishing vessel was convicted of a fishing offence which permitted forfeiture of the catch and fishing gear. In holding the offence non-minor, McWilliam J. said: 'No one can deny that a punishment involving the loss of property to the value of anything in the region of £100,000 is severe.' The penalty for the unlawful possession of salmon of £25 and £2 for each fish was challenged in *O'Sullivan v. Hartnett* because for illegal possession of 900 salmon the penalty would have amounted to £1,825. The High Court held the offence non-minor. McWilliam J. rejected the novel argument that salmon to the value of £7,862, which was in the unlawful possession of a defendant,* should count as part of the penalty. He explained: '... it appears to me that a person who is unlawfully in possession of property ... cannot be said to be penalised in the sense of being fined when it is taken from him in the course of enforcing the law.' In *The State (Rollinson) v. Kelly* a fine of £500 was in issue. The High Court compared the fine, imposed by a 1926 statute, with the salaries of judges in that year. A District Justice earned £1,000, and a judge of the High Court earned £2,500. 'It would seem to follow', concluded Gannon J., 'that a fine of £500 would necessarily have been regarded by the legislature, and must have been regarded by the judiciary, as a very severe penalty.'

Why is it necessary to draw such a classification? It is because the Constitution declares that minor offences may be tried in courts of summary jurisdiction whereas non-minor offences must be tried by jury.

Summary Trial

A court of summary jurisdiction is one which gives judgment forthwith by hearing and disposing of the case. Apart from providing summary trial the Constitution is silent as to how this should be done and the probability is that it must be completed in a court of local and limited jurisdiction. The Constitution leaves procedural matters to statute. At present the only ordinary court exercising summary jurisdiction is the District Court, which is presided over by a District Justice who sits alone and is a full-time lawyer paid from State funds. This court must try minor offences and may in certain circumstances try non-minor offences. The District Court decides all issues of law and fact and its decisions can be appealed to the Circuit Court. Its decisions are open to review by the High Court by way of *certiorari*, prohibition,* *mandamus,** and applications under Art. 40.

Trial by Jury

Apart from minor offences, special courts and military tribunals, no person shall be tried on any criminal charge without a jury (Art. 38.5). A jury is a body of persons sworn to inquire of a matter of fact and to declare the truth on such evidence as is before them. How a jury should be composed was considered in *de Búrca v. Attorney General* (Case No. 32) where Henchy J. explained it thus: '... the jury must be drawn from a pool broadly representative of the community so that its verdict will be stamped with the fairness and acceptability of a genuinely diffused community decision. The particular breadth of choice necessary to satisfy this requirement cannot be laid down in advance. It is left to the discretion of the legislature to formulate a system for the compilation of jury lists and panels from which will be recruited juries which will be competent, impartial and representative.' The *Juries Act, 1976* provides that jury panels are drawn from citizens aged between 18 and 70 years who are registered on the Dáil register of electors with certain persons excluded.

Trial by jury means trial by judge and jury. The judge supervises the conduct of the trial and decides and directs the jury on all questions of law. The jury must decide the verdict and have, at present, no function in the imposition of punishment on a guilty verdict. Jury trials are available in the Circuit and Central Criminal Courts. Appeals from the former go to the Court of Criminal Appeal and from the latter either to the Court of Criminal Appeal or to the Supreme Court at the election of the appellant.*

Special Courts

The Constitution permits the establishment of special courts and their constitution, powers, jurisdiction and procedure have to be prescribed by law (Art. 38.3). The provisions of Art. 34 and Art. 35 do not apply to special courts (Art. 38.6). This means that members of special courts need not be appointed by the President as are the judges of ordinary courts, can be removed from office by methods other than resolutions of both Houses of the Oireachtas, can have their salaries regulated and reduced while in office, and are not required to make a declaration to uphold the Constitution and the law. The traditional protections which ensure judicial independence are not given to members of special courts. The mere possibility of establishing special courts is a dangerous threat to equality of treatment of those accused of crime. Once the concept of special courts is accepted it is impossible to defend the continued existence of the ordinary courts and this is particularly so if it is argued that special courts and ordinary courts administer the same standards of justice. A critical study of special courts is impossible because of the vigorous use of the law of contempt against those venturing to do so.

Special courts are only permitted when the ordinary courts are inadequate to secure the effective administration of justice and the preservation of the public peace and order. This crucial decision is to be made in a manner prescribed by law. The current law on this matter, the *Offences Against the State Act, 1939,* vests this power in the executive arm of government, which was given judical approval in *In re MacCurtain* (Case No. 48) by Gavan Duffy J. when he said: '... the Government, in declaring itself satisfied ... cannot be said to be acting either in a judicial or in a legislative capacity.'

Part V of the 1939 Act which sets out the constitution, powers, jurisdiction and procedure of special courts has been brought into force on numerous occasions, the last in May 1972. The essential feature of such courts is the absence of a jury. Membership of this court may be drawn from existing judges of the High, Circuit and Districts Courts or be barristers or solicitors of seven years' standing or officers of the Defence Forces not below the rank of commandant. Many judges of the ordinary courts serve as members of the Special Criminal Court though resort has been made to lawyers. Members of the court are appointed and removable at the will of the Government and are paid such sums as the Minister for Finance decides. A Special Criminal Court must contain an uneven number of members, never less than three, and a verdict is that of the majority. In order to suffer conviction only two persons need be satisfied as to the guilt of an accused whereas in a trial by jury all twelve jurors must be satisfied. (See Appendix.)

Ordinary criminal courts and special courts operate together so who, and on what basis, decides by which court a person should be tried. The decision rests with the Director of Public Prosecutions and it is impossible to discern any pattern from his decisions. Presumably a decision is made on the basis of Gárda reports and hopefully these are of a better quality than those used to intern persons without trial. In *In re Ó Laighléis* (Case No. 72) the commission reviewing the applicant's continued internment was furnished with a file marked 'Secret and confidential' which contained, *inter alia,* carbon copies of certain documents with no originals, unsigned and anonymous reports from unspecified persons, and at least one report emanating from the 'Special Branch'.

Military Trials

The Constitution provides two kinds of military trials (Art. 38.4). One termed military tribunals, may be established to try offences against military law committed by persons while subject to military law and to deal with a state of war or armed rebellion. The second, termed courts martial, may be established for the enforcement of military discipline to try members of the Defence Forces. The *Defence Act, 1954* sets out the constitution, powers, jurisdiction and procedure of courts martial.

Trial of Contempt

Criminal contempt of court takes three forms. Contempt *in facie curiae* consists of conduct which is obstructive or prejudicial to the course of justice and is committed during court proceedings. Contempts committed outside court, and known as constructive contempt, occur where pending proceedings may be interfered with or prejudiced by something said or done. The third form, scandalising the court, is committed where what is said or done is calculated to endanger public confidence in the administration of justice. Until the *The State (DPP) v. Walsh* (Case No. 90) all these contempts were dealt with summarily. In that case the alleged contempt was that of scandalising a court and it was argued that trial by jury was more appropriate. The Supreme Court divided on the issue. The minority held that justice could only be protected by swift action and that summary disposal was constitutionally permissible. The majority held that there was *prima facie* a right to trial by jury where there were live and real issues of fact to be decided. Where there are none the matter can be disposed of summarily.

Limited Judicial Powers

The Constitution permits the exercise of limited functions and powers of a judicial nature by persons or bodies who are not judges or courts established under the Constitution (Art. 37). There are limitations on the extent of these powers. The first is that only judges and courts can exercise jurisdiction in criminal matters, though what is a criminal matter may cause some difficulty of definition. This occurred in *The State (Murray) v. McRann* (Case No. 95) where an assault was punished as a breach of prison discipline. A criminal offence was defined as an offence against the State or the public, and 'a criminal matter within the meaning of Art. 37' according to Finlay P. 'can be construed as a procedure associated with the prosecution of a person for a crime'. This decision is at variance with the view of Kingsmill Moore J. in *In re O'Farrell* (Case No. 71) when he said: 'A characteristic feature of criminal matters is the infliction of penalties, a consideration which gives weight to the submission that a tribunal which is authorised to inflict a penalty, especially a severe penalty, even in cases where the offence is not strictly criminal, should be regarded as administering justice.'[57]

The second limitation on the administration of justice by persons or bodies other than courts or judges is that the function or power must be limited. How is this direction to be applied? In *In re O'Farrell* (Case No. 71) Kingsmill Moore J. in the Supreme Court suggested 'the test as to whether a power is or is not "limited", in the opinion of the Court, lies in the effect of the assigned powers when exercised. If the exercise of the assigned powers and functions is calculated ordinarily to affect in the most profound and far-reaching way the lives, liberties, fortunes or reputations of those against whom they are exercised, they cannot properly be described as "limited".' The Court held invalid the striking off from the roll of solicitors of two solicitors by the Incorporated Law Society. This test was applied in *Cowan v. Attorney General* (Case No. 28) where it was decided that a local election court presided over by a practising barrister did not have a limited power.

By *McDonald v. Bord na gCon* (Case No. 49) this approach of looking at the effect of the power was departed from. In that case a distinction was made between an administrative power and a judicial power without any great attempt at definition of either these terms. If the power was administrative, then, no matter how prejudicial its effects, it was permitted. If the power was judicial, then the question as to whether it was limited or not would arise. In this case Kenny J. in the High Court held that the power in question was an administration of justice and not limited. This decision was overruled by the Supreme Court. In *O'Brien v. Bord na Mona* (Case No. 66) an examination of the statute in question led to the conclusion that the power of compulsory acquisition, drastic in effect, was administrative rather than judicial.

There are many powers exercisable by persons or bodies who are not judges or courts. Each must be examined in the light of decided cases to determine firstly, whether the power is judicial and secondly, whether it is limited.

Part Two

CONSTITUTIONAL RIGHTS

Chapter 10

CONSTITUTIONAL RIGHTS IN GENERAL

Under the system of laws pertaining in 1922 an individual had legal rights and legal duties. A right, according to Salmond, was an interest recognised and protected by a rule of right, or a principle or rule enforced by the courts.[58] This definition has all the hallmarks of legal positivism which sees law as the command of the sovereign and which excludes moral values from the definition of legal rights. Legal rights are given by man-made laws and can be curtailed in the same manner. The law must be obeyed however iniquitous or unjust. The enactment of two constitutions was in time to change this philosophy. The enumeration of a collection of rights in a document which was given a superior status as a source of law inevitably gave rise to the theory that these rights were of a different character than mere legal rights. Two classes of rights were in existence: *constitutional rights* and *legal rights.*

The courts were slow to grasp this idea probably because the judges of that era had been educated in the positivist school. The clash between the two kinds of rights can be seen in *The State (Ryan) v. Lennon* in 1935 which was concerned with an amendment of the Constitution of Saorstát Éireann. The positivist view, held by the majority of the Supreme Court, was explained by FitzGibbon J.:

> They [counsel for the applicant*] assert that there are certain rights, inherent in every individual, which are so sacred that no Legislature has authority to deprive him of them. It is useless to speculate upon the origin of a doctrine which may be found in the writings of Rousseau, Thomas Paine, William Godwin, and other philosophical writers, but we have not to decide their theories and those of Delolme and Burke, not to mention Bentham and Locke . . . as we are concerned, not with the principles which might or ought to have been adopted by the framers of our Constitution, but with the powers which have actually been entrusted by it to the Legislature and Executive which it set up. When a written Constitution declares that 'the liberty of the person is inviolable' but goes on to provide that 'no person shall be deprived of his liberty except

in accordance with law' then if a law is passed that a citizen may be imprisoned indefinitely upon a *lettre de cachet* signed by a Minister ... the citizen may be deprived of his 'inviolable' liberty, but, as the deprivation will have been 'in accordance with law' he will be as devoid of redress as he would have been under the regime of a French or Neapolitan Bourbon.

But Kennedy C.J., in a minority judgment, looked to some higher source than mere man-made law:

> It follows that every act, whether legislative, executive, or judicial, in order to be lawful under the Constitution, must be capable of being justified under the authority thereby declared to be derived from God. From this it seems clear that, if any legislation of the Oireachtas (including any amendment to the Constitution) were to offend against that acknowledged ultimate Source from which the legislative authority has come through the people to the Oireachtas, as, for instance, if it were repugnant to the Natural Law, such legislation would be necessarily unconstitutional and invalid, and it would be, therefore, absolutely null and void.

Here was the first judicial attempt to mark rights expressed in the fundamental legal document of the State with a characteristic distinctively different from mere legal rights. Kennedy C.J. looked to the natural law for his authority. The natural law is based on judgments which emanate from some absolute source such as God's revealed word. These judgments reflect the essential character of the universe and are immutable and eternally valid and can be grasped and understood by the proper employment of human reason. When perceived they must overrule all positive law.[59]

A further attempt to introduce the idea that the Constitution of 1937 by expressing certain sentiments was laying down ideal propositions against which ordinary law was to be judged was made in *The State (Burke) v. Lennon* (Case No. 86). 'The opinion of FitzGibbon J. in Ryan's case is relied on,' said Gavan Duffy J., 'but it does not apply, in my judgment, to a Constitution in which fundamental rights and constitutional guarantees effectively fill the *lacunae* disclosed in the polity of 1922. The Constitution, with its most impressive Preamble, is the Charter of the Irish People and I will not whittle it away.' But the Supreme Court some months later again paid homage to the supremacy of positive law. In *Art. 26 and the Offences Against the State (Amendment) Bill, 1940* (Case No. 7) Sullivan C.J. reaffirmed: 'The phrase "in accordance with law" is used in several Articles of the Constitution, and we are of opinion that it means in accordance with the law as it exists at the time when the particular Article is invoked and sought to be applied ... A person in custody is detained in accordance with law if he is detained in accordance with the provisions of a statute duly passed by the Oireachtas ...'

The natural law basis for the fundamental rights enumerated in the Constitution had to wait until the mid 1960s before it came into its own and then with a vengeance. A new era in constitutional law dawned. It began with *Ryan v. Attorney General* (Case No. 84) and has fundamentally altered our attitude to the Constitution and constitutional rights and as a consequence our laws and administrative action. The words, by Kenny J., which brought about this transformation were: 'there are many personal rights of the citizen which follow from the Christian and democratic nature of the State which are not mentioned in Article 40 at all.' Not alone were constitutional rights superior to positive law but there were natural rights to which the citizen was entitled which were not expressed in the Constitution. If the Constitution was not their source, then inescapably it must be the natural law. Following this decision the concept of natural law swept across judicial thinking and the consequences were far-reaching. The summit was reached in *McGee v. Attorney General* (Case No. 50) when Walsh J. declared that 'Articles 41, 42, and 43 emphatically reject the theory that there are no rights without laws, no rights contrary to the law and no rights anterior to the law.'

The Constitution is not the source of natural rights because if it were, then by an amendment, fundamental rights enumerated therein could be negatived. 'Natural rights or human rights', according to Walsh J. in the same case, 'are not created by law but the Constitution confirms ... their existence and gives them protection. The individual has natural and human rights over which the State has no authority ...' A novel point was raised by Murnaghan J. in *The State (Ryan) v. Lennon* when he warned that 'the view contended for by the appellants must go to this extreme point, viz., that certain Articles or doctrines of the Constitution are utterly incapable of alteration at any time, even if demanded by an absolute majority of the voters'. Such alteration has occurred but has not been the subject of judicial review. In *G. v. An Bord Uchtála* (Case No. 40) the Supreme Court in December 1978 declared that the mother of an illegitimate child had a constitutional right to the custody of that child. In July of the following year the People added a provision to Art. 37 by the Sixth Amendment to the Constitution, which declared that no adoption order made under legislation enacted after the enactment of the Constitution could be invalidated on the ground that the body making the adoption order was not a judge or court. Effectively this prevents mothers of illegitimate adopted children from asserting their constitutional rights to the custody of their children.

The citizen is also the possessor of legal rights though legal rights may be curtailed or negatived by legislation. Constitutional rights may be regulated but cannot be totally abrogated.

No Absolute Constitutional Right

A man stranded on a desert island has, within environmental limitations, all the rights he likes. He can go where he pleases, say what he wants and do as he likes. In a sense he has absolute rights. But once he is joined on the island by another human he surrenders some of his rights in order to live in community. The obvious needs of society demand that each person's rights are limited for the common good, which is, in simple terms, the needs of others. An absolute right to personal liberty means that a wrongdoer could not be imprisoned, and an absolute right to freedom of expression would mean that another's right to his good name could not exist. According to Kenny J. in *Ryan v. Attorney General* (Case No. 84):

> None of the personal rights of the citizen are unlimited: their exercise may be regulated by the Oireachtas when the common good requires this. When dealing with controversial, social, economic and medical matters on which, it is notorious, views change from generation to generation, the Oireachtas has to reconcile the exercise of personal rights with the claims of the common good, and its decision on the reconciliation should prevail unless it is oppressive to all or some of the citizens or unless there is no reasonable proportion between the benefit which the legislation will confer on the citizens or a substantial body of them and the interference with the personal rights of the citizen.

While regulation is necessary the quality of that regulation must be such as not to infringe constitutional rights, as exemplified by FitzGibbon J. in *The State (Ryan) v. Lennon* and the Supreme Court in *Art. 26 and the Offences Against the State (Amendment) Bill, 1940*. While regulating personal rights with the common good is a matter for the Oireachtas it was accepted in *Abbey Films Ltd. v. Attorney General* (Case No. 1), per Kenny J. that 'there is nothing to prevent the legislature from investing the Courts with the sole jurisdiction to determine whether a particular act is or is not required by the exigencies of the common good'.

The possessor of an absolute right, presuming that such a thing were possible, is under no duty to another as to its exercise. A *duty*, according to Salmond, is an obligatory act, the opposite of which is a wrong.[60] When the law recognises an action as a duty it commonly enforces the performance of it or punishes the disregard of it. Some jurists argue that duties, and not rights, alone exist. A person only sees the benefit of a right when another refrains from acting in a particular way towards him or is punished for such an action. Rights and duties are different sides of the one coin. This concept of duty is another method of limiting the performance of a right. The possessor of a right is limited as to its exercise: it cannot be used to the detriment of others. 'Liberty to exercise a right, it seems to me', said Ó Dálaigh J. in *The Educational Co. of Ireland v. Fitzpatrick* (Case No. 36), *'prima facie* implies a correlative duty on others to abstain from interfering with the exercise of such right.'

A Hierarchy of Rights

Has each constitutional right the same status and value? Taking each one in isolation and judging other conduct against it, the answer is yes. Each constitutional right must be given a quality and consist of characteristics which are neither inferior nor superior to other constitutional rights. The difficulty arises where constitutional rights collide. The advancement of a constitutional right may mean the infringement of another's constitutional right. This problem arose in *The People (DPP) v. Shaw* (Case No. 81) where the constitutional right of one person to personal liberty clashed with the constitutional right of another to life. 'Where such a conflict arises,' said Griffin J., 'a choice must be made and it is the duty of the State to protect what is the more important right, even at the expense of another important, but less important, right. The State must therefore weigh each right for the purpose of evaluating the merits of each, and strike a balance between them, and having done so take such steps as are necessary to protect the more important right.' Clearly each case must be considered on its own merits and it cannot follow that in general any particular right is more important than another right.

The Availability of Implied Rights

A reading of the Articles on fundamental rights quickly establishes the various rights acknowledged. Are these expressed rights exhaustive and can other rights only be acknowledged by constitutional amendment? The rejection of this notion and the acceptance of interpretations which acknowledged the existence of implied constitutional rights were first chartered in *Ryan v. Attorney General* (Case No. 84) where Art. 40.3 was considered. It declares that the State guarantees in its laws to respect, and, as far as practicable, by its laws to defend and vindicate, the personal rights of the citizen, and the State shall, in particular, by its laws protect as best it may from unjust attack and, in the case of injustice done, vindicate the life, person, good name, and property rights of every citizen. Kenny J. in the High Court reasoned that the use of the words 'in particular' related to rights connected with the life and good name of the citizen and, as mere examples, did not exhaust the category of personal rights. 'It follows', he said, 'that the general guarantee ... must extend to rights not specified in Art. 40. Secondly, there are many personal rights of the citizen which follow from the Christian and democratic nature of the State which are not mentioned in Art. 40 at all.'

This view was accepted by the Supreme Court on appeal. Who then should declare these implied constitutional rights? 'In modern times', said Kenny J., 'this would seem to be a function of the legislative rather than of the judicial power but it was done by the Courts in the formative period of the Common Law and there is no reason why they should not do it now.' This function is not exclusive to the courts: it can and should be exercised by the Oireachtas. It is a rather unfortunate consequence of the great development in constitutional rights in recent years that the Oireachtas should, wrongly we feel, be cast as the whittler away of rights. A more positive role in this respect might recover for it some of the ground lost to the courts.

'To attempt to make a list of all the rights which may properly fall within the category of "personal rights" would be difficult,' warned Ó Dálaigh C.J. in the Ryan case on appeal. This difficulty has not deterred the courts from declaring implied constitutional rights when the occasions arise. It has been one of the more spectacular constitutional developments in recent years and one which will continue unabated for the foreseeable future. Because these implied rights form an amorphous group without any clear connection with each other apart from the fact that they are implied rights, and because each of them can be connected, sometimes loosely, to an expressed right, a separate chapter is not given to them. Instead each implied right is examined when considering the expressed right most similar to it.

Can Constitutional Rights be Waived?

Provided an adult is not subjected to duress or undue influence he can in law waive a legal right. The question whether a person can waive a constitutional right has been discussed. 'A person *sui juris** may,' said Murnaghan J. in the High Court in *Murphy v. Stewart* (Case No. 60), 'agree to surrender or to waive all or part of his constitutional right ... Before a court could decide that such a person had in fact made such a surrender or waiver it would have to be satisified that the person involved, with a clear knowledge of what he was doing, deliberately decided to make such a surrender or waiver.' This view was largely accepted by the Supreme Court in *G. v. An Bord Uchtála* (Case No. 40) where the question arose whether the mother of an illegitimate child could abandon her constitutional right to guardianship and custody of her child. 'This requires', said O'Higgins C.J., 'a free consent on the part of the mother given in the full knowledge of the consequences which follow upon her placing her child for adoption.' 'I am satisfied', said Walsh J., 'that, having regard to the natural rights of the mother ... the consent, if given, must be such as to amount to a fully-informed, free and willing surrender or an abandonment of these rights.'

Who Can Avail of Constitutional Rights?

Some fundamental rights are declared to attach to *citizens* while others attach to *persons*. Thus no citizen shall be deprived of his liberty whereas any person can make an application under Art. 40. This distinction between 'citizens' and 'persons' has been further complicated by the addition of two further categories by the Eighth Amendment to the Constitution. The 'unborn' and the 'mother' are acknowledged as possessors of a particular constitutional right. The question of *locus standi** has been canvassed in some cases and ignored in others. *Locus standi* can be considered under four headings; rights confined to citizens, rights available to all, rights available to human persons as distinct from artificial persons, and rights of the unborn.

The first division of the *locus standi* rule is whether rights confined to citizens are available to aliens. In *The State (Nicolaou) v. An Bord Uchtála* (Case No. 96) a British citizen challenged a statute and the three judges of the High Court had differing views on this issue. Murnaghan J. refused to express an opinion, Henchy J. held that Art. 40.3 could not apply though other provisions such as that relating to the family did and Teevan J. held that where there was no conflict between the common good and the right to be asserted by the alien, the court should not refuse to hear the issue. The Supreme Court, according to Walsh J., 'expressly reserved for another and more appropriate case consideration of the effect of non-citizenship upon the interpretation of the Articles in question and also the right of a non-citizen to challenge the validity of an Act of the Oireachtas ...'[61] In *The State (McFadden) v. The Governor of Mountjoy* (Case No. 94) the High Court on procedural grounds granted the right of fair procedures to a British citizen. 'Where the Constitution', according to Barrington J., 'prescribes basic fairness of procedures in the administration of the law it does so, not only because citizens have rights, but also because the courts in the administration of justice are expected to observe certain forms of due process ... Once the courts have seisin of a dispute, it is difficult to see how the standards they should apply in investigating it should, in fairness, be any different in the case of an alien than those to be applied in the case of a citizen.' In *Somjee v. The Minister for Justice* (Case No. 85) where a Pakistani citizen challenged a statute, Keane J. followed the line taken by Walsh J. in *The State (Nicolaou) v. An Bord Uchtála* (Case No. 96) when he said: 'It is, accordingly, not necessary ... for me to express any opinion on the submission advanced on behalf of the defendants that, in any event, the plaintiff was precluded from asserting such rights ...' In *The People (DPP) v. Shaw* (Case No. 81) the Supreme Court ignored the fact that it was a British citizen who was pleading the constitutional right to personal liberty.

The second divison of the *locus standi* rule is to what extent a citizen can challenge a statute on the ground that it infringes constitutional rights. There are two possible avenues that may be followed in this respect, as explained by Walsh J. in *East Donegal Co-operative v. Attorney General* (Case No. 35) when he said:

> With regard to the *locus standi* of the plaintiffs the question raised has been determined in different ways in countries which have constitutional provisions similar to our own ... at one end of the spectrum of opinions on this topic one finds the contention that there exists a right of action akin to an *actio popularis* which will entitle any person, whether he is directly affected by the Act or not, to maintain proceedings and

92

challenge the validity of any Act passed by the parliament of the country of which he is a citizen or to whose laws he is subject by residing in that country. At the other end of the spectrum is the contention that no one can maintain such an action unless he can show that not merely do the provisions of the Act in question apply to activities in which he is currently engaged but that their application has actually affected his activities adversely. The Court rejects the latter contention and does not find it necessary in the circumstances of this case to express any view upon the former.

But the latter contention, rejected by Walsh J. in that case, has now come to be rule in constitutional actions. In *Cahill v. Sutton* (Case No. 20) Henchy J. declared: 'The primary rule as to standing in constitutional matters is that the person challenging the constitutionality of the statute, or some other person for whom he is deemed by the court to be entitled to speak, must be able to assert that, because of the alleged unconstitutionality, his or that other person's interests have been adversely affected, or stand in real or imminent danger of being adversely affected, by the operation of the statute.' This does seem an over-strict rule because the publicity, effort and cost of litigating constitutional actions are deterrents in themselves. The respect for constitutional rights, and thus for the courts which declare them, has been gained in large measure by individuals prepared to run this gauntlet. A study of many of our fundamental cases in constitutional law reveals the fact that had this strict rule been applied, most of them would never have reached decision. The difficulty of enforcing this strict dictum can be seen in two subsequent cases. In *The State (Lynch) v. Cooney* (Case No. 93) it was argued that the prosecutor had no *locus standi* to challenge a prohibition order because it was directed against RTE and that since he had no legal right to broadcast he had no complaint. This was rejected because the Supreme Court held that once RTE had agreed to broadcast, the order prohibiting the broadcast gave the prosecutor sufficient standing. In *Norris v. Attorney General* (Case No. 64) the judges disagreed as to how to apply this strict rule of *locus standi* where a challenge was made to statutes which prohibited certain sexual activities by an individual who had not been prosecuted or convicted of these offences or, it seems, was likely to be prosecuted. Some judges thought he had the standing to challenge the statutes on various grounds while some judges felt he had no standing to challenge the statutes on the ground that they infringed marital privacy because the plaintiff was unmarried. It seems that the decision in *Cahill v. Sutton* has caused unnecessary complications which will take some time to untangle and may act as a disincentive to litigation. A plaintiff might be willing to suffer defeat on the merits of a case but will hardly be likely to proceed if the possibility exists that the action would be dismissed because of lack of standing.

The third division of the *locus standi* rule is whether artifical persons,

93

as distinct from human persons, can claim the protection of fundamental rights. The first consideration of this point was made by O'Keeffe P. in *East Donegal Co-operative v. Attorney General* (Case No. 35): 'Artificial persons may possibly not be entitled to rely on the constitutional guarantees (although they have been held to be so entitled in the United States).' In *Quinn's Supermarket v. Attorney General* (Case No. 83) Walsh J. referring to Art. 40.1 said: '. . . it need scarcely be pointed out that under no possible construction of the constitutional guarantee could a body corporate or any entity but a human person be considered to be a human person for the purposes of this provision.' This view was followed in *Abbey Films Ltd. v. Attorney General* (Case No. 1) where McWilliam J. in the High Court said: 'I am not satisfied . . . that a company is a citizen within the meaning of the Constitution . . . it also appears to me to be very doubtful whether, having regard to the expression "human persons" in Art. 40.1, personal rights can be attributed to a company for the purposes of the application of the Constitution.' On appeal to the Supreme Court the question was left open.

The fourth division of the *locus standi* rule has arisen because of the most recent amendment of the Constitution. A constitutional right to life is now accorded to the unborn though it must of necessity be vindicated by another. It will be interesting to see how the courts apply the *locus standi* rule in this regard. Must the litigant, to use the phraseology of *Cahill v. Sutton* (Case No. 20), stand in real or imminent danger of being adversely affected? If this is so then unless near relatives of the unborn act to vindicate this right, the right guaranteed is meaningless. This may be an instance where the litigious stranger may be admitted to defend and vindicate the right to life of the unborn.

Can the Courts Direct the Oireachtas as to Rights?

In all constitutional cases, until recent times, the claim was made that some statutory provision infringed some express or implied constitutional right. Recently an innovative claim was made which, while not impugning the contents of a statute, suggested that the absence from the statute of some particular provision rendered the statute constitutionally unsound. In *Somjee v. The Minister for Justice* (Case No. 85) the claim was made that a statute which granted citizenship to an alien woman who married a citizen was invalid because it did not grant the same right to an alien male who married a citizen. This was rejected because, as Keane J. explained: 'that would confer no benefit whatever on the plaintiff: it would not redress any injustice . . . or in any sense known to the law vindicate their personal rights'. The judge further explained that: 'The jurisdiction of this Court in a case where the validity of an Act of the Oireachtas is questioned . . . is limited to declaring the Act in question to be invalid, if that indeed be the case. The Court has no jurisdiction to substitute for the impugned enactment a form of enactment which it considers desirable or to indicate to the Oireachtas the appropriate form of enactment which should be substituted for the impugned enactment.' This is an area where scope for development is possible.

Chapter 11

EQUALITY BEFORE THE LAW

Art. 40.1 declares that all citizens shall as human persons be held equal before the law. While this is a statement of high moral content it cannot be taken literally. The law is peppered with inequalities both in its enacted laws and by its failure to legislate. Inequalities are often just. For example it is fair and proper that infants be protected from contractual liability, from certain sexual activity and from certain civil liberties such as the right to vote. Positive inequalities are necessary in a civilised society. So something more than mere inequality must be sought if this Article is to have any substance. The courts in interpreting this constitutional guarantee have suggested that legislation which *invidiously discriminates* is offensive. It has been difficult to formulate some accepted test by which legislation in this regard can be judged because of the subjective nature of each opinion given. But one worthy of consideration was suggested by Walsh J. in *Quinn's Supermarket v. Attorney General* (Case No. 83); 'This provision is not a guarantee of absolute equality for all citizens in all circumstances but it is a guarantee of equality as human persons and ... is a guarantee related to their dignity as human beings and a guarantee against any inequalities grounded upon an assumption, or indeed a belief, that some individual or individuals or classes of individuals, by reason of their human attributes or their ethnic or racial, social or religious background, are to be treated as the inferior or superior of other individuals in the community.'

Art. 40.1 has been considered in many cases and a study of them will give some indication how the courts have interpreted the guarantee. It must be remembered that a decision which favours constitutionality may be impugned in the future and that existing inequalities are likely to fall foul of the guarantee.

Instances of Invidious Discrimination

Art 40.1 was successfully raised in a number of cases, the first of which was the *East Donegal Co-operative v. Attorney General* (Case No. 35) where a section which empowered the Minister for Agriculture to grant exemptions from the application of a statute was impugned because the Oireachtas unconstitutionally delegated this function to a Minister. This judgment is unsatisfactory because the power had never been exercised and the Supreme Court refrained from expressing an opinion as to whether the Oireachtas could exempt individuals from the application of the law. In *de Burca v. Attorney General* (Case No. 32), a law which restricted jury service to persons with certain types of property was struck down. 'This is a discrimination', said O'Higgins C.J., 'based not only on property but necessarily on a particular type of property ... if service [on a jury] be regarded as a right, then this means the exclusion of many thousands of citizens merely because they do not possess a particular type of property ... Without question, this is not holding all citizens as human persons to be equal before the law ...'

In *King v. Attorney General* (Case No. 42) a statute which permitted the proving of current criminal conduct by previous convictions was struck down in the High Court by McWilliam J. because the citizens mentioned in Art. 40.1 must 'include those who have been previously convicted, at any rate when acting in any capacity which is not directly concerned with their previous conviction'. On appeal to the Supreme Court O'Higgins C.J. said: 'Apart from being repelled by the class-conscious and un-Christian philosophy which inspired such legislation, I regard the inconsistency ... as being so clear ...' . The common law rule that where a wife commits a crime in the presence of her husband it is presumed she committed it under his coercion was considered in *The State (DPP) v. Walsh* (Case No. 90) not to have survived the enactment of the 1937 Constitution. 'A legal rule that presumes', explained Henchy J., 'even on a *prima facie* and rebuttable basis that a wife has been coerced by the physical presence of her husband into committing an act prohibited by the criminal law, particularly when a similar presumption does not operate in favour of a husband for acts committed in the presence of his wife, is repugnant to the concept of equality before the law ... therefore, the presumption contended for must be rejected as being a form of unconstitutional discrimination.'

Instances of No Invidious Discrimination

There are more decided cases upholding legislation on the ground that no invidious discrimination exists than cases where such discrimination was acknowledged. In *O'Brien v. Keogh* (Case No. 67) the statutory provision, 'far from effecting inequality', said Ó Dálaigh C.J., 'would appear to attempt to establish equality between the two groups ... Art. 40 does not require identical treatment of all persons without recognition of differences in relevant circumstances. It only forbids invidious discrimination.' In *Landers v. Attorney General* (Case No. 43) Finlay J. in the High Court could not 'be persuaded that to prevent even a boy of unusual musical talent from singing in a dance hall or similar place of public entertainment until he has reached the age of 14 years could fairly be described as invidious discrimination.' In *O'Brien v. Manufacturing Engineering Co. Ltd.* (Case No. 68) a statute which limited the bringing of an action by a workman who had accepted compensation to a period shorter than those who had not accepted compensation was not a discrimination but a diversity of arrangements.

In *Somjee v. The Minister for Justice* (Case No. 85) a statute which conferred citizenship on alien females who married citizens without a reciprocal arrangement for alien males who married citizens was upheld. 'It is only in the case of aliens becoming married to Irish citizens', said Keane J., 'that a distinction is drawn, and, in my view, the distinction is more properly regarded as conferring a form of privilege on female aliens rather than as being invidiously discriminatory against male aliens ... the provisions of the sections in question do not more than provide a diversity of arrangements which is not prohibited by Art. 40.1.' In *Norris v. Attorney General* (Case No. 64) the Supreme Court rejected the argument that because statute prohibited certain sexual conduct between males and did not prohibit the same conduct between females it offended Art. 40.1. 'The legislature', said O'Higgins C.J., 'would be perfectly entitled to have regard to the difference between the sexes and to treat sexual conduct ... between males as requiring prohibition because of the social problem which it creates, while at the same time looking at sexual conduct between females as being not only different but as posing no such social problems.'

Discrimination Constitutionally Permitted

Art. 40.1 declares that the guarantee of equality before the law does not mean that the State shall not in its law have due regard to differences of capacity, physical and moral, and of social function. Here is a clear direction that inequalities are permissible on the grounds of capacity and of social function.

Difference of capacity justified legislation which interfered with a citizen's rights in *In re Philip Clarke* (Case No. 23) because, per O'Byrne J.,

> the impugned legislation is of a paternal character, clearly intended for the care and custody of persons suspected to be suffering from mental infirmity and for the safety and well-being of the public generally. The existence of mental infirmity is too widespread to be overlooked, and was, no doubt, present to the minds of the draughtsmen when it was proclaimed in Art. 40.1 of the Constitution that, though all citizens, as human persons, are to be held equal before the law, the State may, nevertheless, in its enactments, have due regard to differences of capacity, physical and moral, and of social function. We do not see how the common good would be promoted or the dignity and freedom of the individual assured by allowing persons, alleged to be suffering from such infirmity, to remain at large to the possible danger of themselves and others.

In *The State (Nicolaou) v. An Bord Uchtála* (Case No. 96) a provision which excluded the natural father of an illegitimate child from being consulted before an adoption order was made was justified because, said Walsh J., 'when it is considered that an illegitimate child may be begotten by an act of rape, by a callous seduction or by an act of casual commerce

97

by a man with a woman, as well as by the association of a man with a woman in making a common home without marriage ... and that, except in the latter instance, it is rare for a natural father to take any interest in his offspring, it is not difficult to appreciate the difference in moral capacity and social function between the natural father and the several persons described in the sub-section.'

In *Murphy v. Attorney General* (Case No. 61) certain provisions of the income tax code were upheld on the ground of social function. According to Kenny J.,

> In so far as unequal treatment is alleged as between, on the one hand, married couples living together and, on the other, unmarried couples living together, the social function of married couples living together is such as to justify the Legislature in treating them differently from single persons for income tax purposes. Numerous examples could be given from the income tax code of types of income tax payers who are treated differently, either favourably or unfavourably, because of their social function. This particular unfavourable tax treatment of married couples living together, set against the many favourable discriminations made by the law in favour of married couples, does not, in the opinion of the Court, constitute an unequal treatment forbidden by Art. 40.1 particularly having regard to the vital roles under the Constitution of married couples as parents, or potential parents, and as heads of a family.

In *Dillane v. Attorney General* (Case No. 33) the inability of a District Justice to award costs against a Gárda was upheld on the ground of social function. According to O'Higgins C.J., 'when the State, whether directly by statute or mediately through the exercise of a delegated power of subordinate legislation, makes a discrimination in favour of, or against, a person or a category of persons, on the express or implied ground of a difference of social function, the courts will not condemn such discrimination as being in breach of Art. 40.1, if it is not arbitrary, or capricious, or otherwise not reasonably capable, when objectively viewed in the light of the social function involved, of supporting the selection or classification complained of.'

The Right to Fair Procedures

We have examined one meaning to be given to the expression 'equality before the law' and now we turn to a second meaning which while having been expounded in different ways in different types of cases lacks cohesion and this prevents it from taking its place as a particular constitutional right. The subject has surfaced under different titles such as 'constitutional justice', 'natural justice' and 'fair procedures'. It is probably more at home in administrative law, but because it has developed as an implied right under Art. 40 it must be considered in constitutional law. Discretionary power in its exercise may lead to abuse, and to control this likelihood the courts have evolved a number of procedural rules which attempt to balance the scales in favour of the person against whom the power is exercised.

The courts have implemented the common law rules of natural justice which were an implantation of its own standards to those making administrative decisions which affect the welfare of an individual. The first of these common law rules is *audi alteram partem:* hear both sides. It is fundamental to fair procedure that both sides should be heard before a decision is reached. The law is not concerned with the decision but with the method by which it is reached. In *The State (Gleeson) v. The Minister for Defence* the dismissal from the Army of a soldier was invalid because, as Henchy J. explained, 'the requirements of natural justice imposed an inescapable duty on the army authorities ... to give him due notice of the intention to discharge him, of the statutory reason for the proposed discharge, and of the essential facts and findings alleged to constitute that reason; and to give him a reasonable opportunity of presenting his response to that notice'. The second of the common law rules of natural justice is *nemo judex in sua cause:* never be a judge in one's own cause. This is taken to mean that the person making the decision is without bias in relation to the matter at issue. In *O'Donoghue v. The Veterinary Council* a complaint was made against a veterinary surgeon by a colleague who later sat as a member of the committee which heard the complaint. The decision of the committee was quashed. One final and often repeated word on this subject of natural justice. Once the procedural requirements are fulfilled the courts are not concerned with the decision.

Where a person may not be affected by a decision but instead have his good name tarnished, he must be given some opportunity of vindicating his good name. This problem arose in *In re Haughey* (Case No. 41) where the applicant, who was a witness before a public committee, was not allowed to cross-examine another witness who had given prejudicial evidence against him nor was allowed to address the committee in his own defence. The Supreme Court accepted that the applicant's good name was in issue and that the absence of these two requirements amounted to an unfair procedure.

Sometimes the nature of the inquiry may be such that a person summoned before it may of necessity have to be afforded legal aid supplied by the State. Serious criminal charges are an instance where fair procedure demands that the accused be represented at the expense of the State. In *The State (Healy) v. Donoghue* (Case No. 91) Henchy J. explained:

A person who has been convicted and deprived of his liberty as a result of a prosecution which, because of his poverty, he has had to bear without legal aid has reason to complain that he has been meted out less than his constitutional due. This is particularly true if the absence

99

of legal aid is compounded by factors such as a grave or complex charge; or ignorance, illiteracy, immaturity or other conditions rendering the accused incompetent to cope properly with the prosecution; or an inability, because of detentional restraint, to find and produce witnesses; or simply the fumbling incompetence that may occur when an accused is precipitated into the public glare and alien complexity of courtroom procedures, and is confronted with the might of a prosecution backed by the State. As the law stands, a legal aid-certificate is the shield provided against such an unjust attack.

In *The State (McFadden) v. The Governor of Mountjoy* (Case No. 94) it was held that in extradition proceedings, which are akin to criminal proceedings, a person arrested should be given a copy of the warrant and should when brought before the District Court be given the opportunity of a remand in order to prepare a case or to obtain legal advice or representation. Anything less amounted to an unfair procedure.

Discrimination on Religious Grounds

Art. 44.2.3° declares that the State shall not impose any disabilities or make any discrimination on the ground of religious profession, belief or status. This restriction against religious discrimination is on the State and not on other bodies or persons. In an action for wrongful dismissal by laicised members of the teaching staff of a Catholic seminary the allegation was made that because public funds were received the dismissal was unlawful as it discriminated on religious grounds. 'The discrimination complained of', said O'Higgins C.J., in *McGrath v. Trustees of Maynooth*, 'is discrimination not by the State but by the defendants.'

In *Quinn's Supermarket v. Attorney General* (Case No. 83) the Supreme Court held that a statutory order which exempted kosher meat shops from its application was a discrimination on the ground of religious profession, belief or status. In *Mulloy v. The Minister for Education* (Case No. 58), a scheme which excluded certain secondary school teachers because they were members of religious orders was struck down. 'The present case,' according to Walsh J., 'concerns the disposition of public funds on a basis which, if sustainable, enables a person who is not a religious to obtain greater financial rewards than a person who is a religious and is otherwise doing the same work and is of equal status and length of service ... if that were constitutionally possible it would enable the State to prefer religious to lay people, or *vice versa,* in a manner which is in no way concerned with the safeguarding or maintenance of the constitutional right to free practice of religion.' In *M. v. An Bord Uchtála* (Case No. 45) a statute which prohibited adoption where the parties were not of the one religion was struck down as unconstitutional.

Chapter 12

PERSONAL LIBERTY

The sign of a free man is that he can live as he pleases: he can come and go without restraint and without permission from the executive. The citizen is not alone free to move from place to place but free to decide his own destiny. Once an adult he can live where he chooses, he can marry, he can work, he can change his occupation and do many things that are the badge of the free man. The Constitution in Art. 40.4.1° expresses this right to liberty in a negative form. It declares that no citizen shall be deprived of his liberty save in accordance with law. Most of the legal restrictions and of necessity the case law are concerned with the narrow aspect of arrest for a criminal offence. While this is important, it must not be allowed to overshadow the wide extent and scope of the right to personal liberty. Not alone is liberty guaranteed but the quality of that liberty has been explained by the courts on occasion. The right to bodily integrity and the right to travel outside the State are examples of this wider meaning of personal liberty.

The most likely interference with the citizen's right to personal liberty will be at the hands of the police. This is because the police are charged with the task of detecting those suspected of crime in order that the courts can exercise their constitutional function. Two public interests must be balanced: the necessity to ensure that those who commit crime are apprehended and the right of the citizen to conduct his affairs without undue interference. This chapter will attempt to outline the occasions on which a citizen's liberty may be infringed lawfully: it cannot be exhaustive for reasons of space. Examples will be given to illustrate each occasion and it can be assumed that other similar restrictions apply.

Demands of Various Sorts

In general the police can *ask* a citizen anything they like and with a few exceptions the citizen does not have to answer. Under various statutes a police officer can demand a person's name and address and a refusal to furnish these is an offence and may lead to the arrest of the person. Under the *Road Traffic Act, 1961*, s.107 a member of the Gárda Síochána may demand the name and address of a person whom he suspects of having committed a specified offence while using a motor vehicle. Under the *Misuse of Drugs Act, 1977* a Gárda officer may arrest without warrant if he has reasonable doubts as to a person's identity or place of abode where he has reasonable suspicion that that person has committed an offence under the Act. Where members of the Gárdaí or the Defence Forces are acting under a search warrant by virtue of the *Offences Against the State Act, 1939*, s.29, as amended, they may demand the name and address of any person found where the search takes place. From these three examples it can be seen that a demand can only be made in particular circumstances. Usually the Gárda officer must have formed the prior opinion on reasonable grounds that some criminal offence has been committed.

Statutes permit other demands to be made. Where a Gárda officer has reasonable grounds for believing that a motor vehicle has been used in a public place on a particular occasion he may, under the *Road Traffic Act, 1961,* s.69, demand of the person using the vehicle the production of a certificate of insurance. S.40 permits a Gárda to demand the production of a driving licence from a person driving in a public place or who is accompanying the holder of a provisional licence while the latter is driving in a public place. Under s.42 a Gárda may request a specimen of signature from a person driving in a public place or when that person produces his driving licence at a Gárda station. Where a Gárda has reasonable grounds for believing that a road traffic offence has been committed he may demand of the owner of the vehicle whether he was, and (if he was not) who was, driving the vehicle at a material time. This power under the *Road Traffic Act, 1961,* s.107 was curtailed in *The People (A.G.) v. Gilbert* where admissions made after the demand was made were ruled inadmissible on the ground that the answers were not voluntary on a charge unconnected with road traffic offences. Under the *Road Traffic Act, 1978,* s.12, whenever a Gárda is of opinion that a person in charge of a motor vehicle in a public place has consumed alcohol he may require that person to provide a sample of his breath by exhaling into a special apparatus.

Search before Arrest

In general the police have no right to search a citizen. Statute gives this power but again, like demands, it can only be exercised on reasonable suspicion that some specified crime has been or is about to be committed. A refusal to be searched may either be an offence itself or may be the more general offence of obstruction of a police officer in the execution of his duty. An acquittal must result if the Garda does not satisfy the court that he had reasonable grounds of suspicion. The *Misuse of Drugs Act 1977,* s.23 permits a Gárda who has reasonable cause for suspecting that a person is in possession of certain drugs to search that person. The *Criminal Law Act 1976,* s.8 empowers a Gárda who has reasonable suspicion that certain offences have been or are about to be committed to stop a vehicle and search it and its occupants.

Arrest

An arrest is a formal procedure which means that a person is detained usually for the purpose of being brought before a court. For an arrest to be effective the Gárda, or other person effecting the arrest, must make clear that the person being arrested is compelled to remain and accompany the person making the arrest: a mere request to accompany the person authorised to make the arrest is not sufficient. The mere pronouncing of words of arrest is not sufficient unless the person to be arrested submits to the process. Usually the person making the arrest will touch the arm of the person being arrested and reasonable force is permitted though the use of force cannot be justified where the person to be arrested does not resist or attempt to escape. If he does, the degree of force which can be used is measured by the amount of force used in the resistance or escape. The use of excessive force is unlawful. The resisting of a lawful arrest is an offence and a person is entitled to resist by using reasonable force against an unlawful arrest. Discretion probably requires submission to an unlawful arrest with the availability of both civil and criminal remedies against the culprit. In *The People (A.G.) v. White* armed detectives surrounded a house in which two men were staying. They knew the identity of one man who they wanted to arrest but not of White. A gun battle took place. At the appeal for a conviction for the murder of one of the detectives the Court of Criminal Appeal substituted a conviction of manslaughter. Gavan Duffy P. explained: 'Since there was no lawful authority for the intended arrest it was manslaughter even if White was forearmed to resist an attempted arrest with a lethal weapon.'

At common law a Gárda can arrest a person whom he reasonably suspects of committing a felony without a warrant whether in fact a felony has or has not been committed. He may arrest for a breach of the peace committed in his presence. A collection of statutes authorise arrest without warrant in certain circumstances. Some examples will illustrate the extent of this power. The *Larceny Act, 1916*, s.41 empowers a Gárda to arrest without warrant any person whom he finds lying or loitering in any highway, yard or other place during the day and of whom he has good cause to suspect of having committed or being about to commit an offence under the Act or certain other offences. The *Road Traffic Act, 1961* permits arrest without warrant for a number of offences including drunken driving, dangerous driving, failing to allow a Gárda to read a produced driving licence or certificate of insurance, taking a vehicle without the consent of the owner and interfering with the mechanism of a vehicle. The *Misuse of Drugs Act, 1977* empowers the arrest without warrant of persons suspected of certain drug offences. The *Road Traffic Act, 1978*, s.12 permits arrest without warrant for failure or refusal to give a specimen of breath.

At common law a lay person has powers of arrest. He may arrest without warrant a person whom he suspects of having committed a felony though he may be sued for damages if in fact no felony* has been committed. He may arrest for a breach of the peace. Some statutory powers of arrest are conferred on 'persons' rather than being confined to the Gárdaí. For example the *Criminal Law (Jurisdiction) Act, 1976*, s.19 empowers any person to arrest without warrant anyone whom he, with reasonable cause, suspects of having committed certain offences in Northern Ireland.

An arrest may be made by warrant which is a written document, signed by a judicial officer, which direct a member of the Gárdaí to arrest a suspected offender. It cannot be issued to a lay person. To obtain a warrant the Gárda must give details of the case on sworn evidence to the court, and it is for the court to decide whether or not to issue the warrant. The warrant must include the name of the person and a description of the offence. The person to be arrested should be given an opportunity of perusing the warrant in order to decide whether it is lawful or not. In *The State (McFadden) v. Governor of Mountjoy* (Case No. 94), Barrington J. said: 'it would appear to be appropriate and fair that a Gárda Officer executing a foreign warrant should not only produce and read the warrant to the person being arrested, but should also hand him a copy of the warrant ...' There the court was considering the lack of fair procedures in extradition proceedings and there seems no valid reason why this rule should not apply to domestic warrants.

It is common practice for a person under suspicion of being involved in an offence to be questioned at a Gárda station without being arrested. The person is said to be 'helping the police with their inquiries'. Unless the person voluntarily goes to, and remains in, the Gárda station he is in fact under arrest and the questioning is unlawful. Whether a person is under arrest is a question of fact to be decided by the courts. This conflict arose in *The People (DPP) v. Lynch* (Case No. 77) where the appellant who went to a Gárda station voluntarily remained there for twenty-two hours and was subjected to sustained questioning, never had the opportunity of communicating with his family and was never permitted to rest or sleep until he made an admission of guilt. Speaking on this aspect of the case Walsh J. in the Supreme Court said: 'that the evidence points coercively to the fact that he was under arrest in the sense that he was not at liberty to leave the station'.

Reasons for Arrest to be Given

Since the personal liberty of a citizen is at stake, and in order to decide whether an arrest is lawful or unlawful, a person should be told the reasons for his arrest. From the decided cases a number of rules can be stated. If a police officer arrests without a warrant on reasonable suspicion of felony or of other crime of a sort which does not require a warrant he must in ordinary circumstances inform the person arrested of the true ground of arrest. He is not entitled to keep the reason to himself or to give a reason which is false. This requirement naturally does not exist if the circumstances are such that the person must know the general nature of the alleged offence for which he is arrested. The arrested person cannot complain that he has not been supplied with the above information as and when he should be if he himself produces the situation which makes it practically impossible to inform him, e.g. by immediate counter-attack or by running away. Technical or precise language need not be used once the substance of the offence is stated.

Whether the failure to inform a person of the reasons for his arrest at the moment of arrest amounted to an unlawful arrest was considered in *The People (DPP) v. Walsh* by the Supreme Court. The appellant had been arrested in a crowded pub one evening on suspicion of having committed a burglary five months previously. He was not told the reason for his arrest them but was so informed in the Gárda station. It was held that informing the appellant of the reason within a reasonable time was sufficient and as O'Higgins C.J. explained: 'The appellant's right to be informed was not questioned. It simply was not exercised by him. Since the appellant immediately acquiesced in the arrest no question concerning the authority for the arrest arose.'

The Purpose of Arrest

There. is only one purpose of a lawful arrest and that is to bring the arrested person before a court of law. O'Higgins C.J. in *The People (DPP) v. Walsh* explained, 'an arrest and subsequent detention is only justified at common law if it is exercised for the purpose for which the right exists, which is the bringing of an arrested person to justice before a court. If it Appears that the arresting Gárdaí have no evidence on which to charge the person arrested, or cannot justify the suspicion on which he was arrested, he must be released.' In that case the majority of the Supreme Court held the arrest lawful because the Gárdaí had reasonable suspicion, whereas Walsh J., in his minority judgment, held that the purpose of the arrest was to obtain evidence, namely the appellant's fingerprints.

It is commonly believed that the Gárdaí are entitled to detain a suspect for a reasonable time during which inquiries can be made and that such detention does amount to an arrest. The courts have repeatedly condemned this notion. In the first of these cases, *Dunne v. Clinton,* two brothers, suspected of having committed a felony, went voluntarily to the Gárda station and were detained from Tuesday afternoon to Wednesday night before they were charged before a Peace Commissioner. Later the charges were dismissed, and they sued the Gárdaí for false imprisonment; admittedly their arrest was lawful, but their detention was not. They were awarded damages. Hanna J. in the High Court explained the law:

> In law there can be no half-way house between the liberty of the subject, unfettered by restraint, and an arrest ... a practice has grown up of 'detention', as distinct from arrest. It is, in effect, keeping a suspect in custody, perhaps under as comfortable circumstances as the barracks will permit, without making any definite charge against him, and with the intimation in some form of words or gesture that he is under restraint, and will not be allowed to leave ... this so-called detention amounts to arrest, and the suspect has in law been arrested and in custody during the period of his detention. The expression 'detention' has no justification in law in this connection, and the use of it has in a

sense helped to nurture the idea that it is something different from arrest and that it relieves the guards from the obligation to have the question of the liberty of the suspected person determined by a Peace Commissioner or the Court.

There are occasions when detention is allowed by law. Every person in whose presence a breach of the peace is being, or reasonably appears about to be, committed has the right to take reasonable steps to make the other refrain. Those reasonable steps include detaining the other against his will though the person doing this must release or arrest him once he no longer presents a danger to the peace. A person arrested for drunken driving may be requested by a member of the Gárdaí acting under s.13 of the *Road Traffic Act, 1978* to provide either a specimen of his breath or a blood or urine sample. Here is a statutory exception which allows a period of detention to acquire evidence.

The main statutory exception to the rule that the only purpose of arrest is to bring before a court is s.30 of the *Offences Against the State Act, 1939,* which empowers a Gárda to arrest a person whom he suspects of having committed, or being about to commit, certain offences and detain that person for a period of twenty-four hours. This period can be extended for a further twenty-four hours. This section is commonly used and is frequently abused. While the courts accept this statutory exception, they are not powerless in curtailing its abuse. 'A statutory provision of this nature', according to O'Higgins C.J. in *Art. 26 and the Emergency Powers Bill, 1976* (Case No. 5), 'which makes such inroads upon the liberty of the person, must be strictly construed. Any arrest sought to be justified by the section must be in strict conformity with it. No such arrest may be justified by importing into the section incidents or characteristics of an arrest which are not expressly or by necessary implication authorised by the section.' He was speaking of a statutory provision permitting seven-day detention but the principle is the same. And strictly interpreted it was in *The State (Hoey) v. Garvey* where a person having been arrested and detained for seven days was released and re-arrested some days later on the same suspicion. The High Court ordered his release. 'If this arrest is to be justified by the section,' said Finlay P., 'it seems to me that every further or repeated arrest would also be justified so long as suspicion remained in the minds of the Gárda Síochána . . .' The common practice of detaining a person for forty-eight hours under s.30, and on release re-arresting him for a further forty-eight hours, has ceased since this decision.

The courts have policed this section in another way. They refuse to admit into evidence statements obtained in breach of the section. In *The People (DPP) v. Madden* (Case No. 78), a person was arrested under s.30 which permitted detention for twenty-four hours. Shortly before this period was due to expire he began to make an incriminatory statement which was not finished until three hours after this period expired. The conviction for murder was quashed. In *The People (DPP) v. Farrell* (Case No. 76), a person arrested under s.30 made an incriminatory statement during the extended period which had not been extended properly in accordance with the Act. The conviction was quashed. Both these cases will be considered again later when examing the rules relating to unconstitutionally obtained evidence.

Hanna J. in *Dunne v. Clinton* said that 'if it is necessary or advisable for the investigation of crime that there should be some intermediate period ... it must be authorised by the Legislature.' S.30 is such an authorisation but it is not available to all crimes. Whether some period of detention should be available is a hotly debated subject. In the *Report of the Committee to Recommend Certain Safeguards for Persons in Custody and for Members of An Gárda Síochána*, most members felt the question was outside its terms of reference though the Chairman in an addendum suggested that six hours' detention should be available.[62] (see Appendix).

Procedure after Arrest

On arrest a suspect may be searched and certain property seized. The law was explained by O'Keeffe J. in *Jennings v. Quinn:* '... the public interest requires that the police, when effecting a lawful arrest, may seize, without a search warrant, property in the possession or custody of the person arrested when they believe it necessary to do so to avoid the abstraction or destruction of that property and when that property is (a) evidence in support of the criminal charge upon which the arrest is made, or (b) evidence in support of any other criminal charge against that person then in contemplation, or (c) reasonably believed to be stolen property or to be property unlawfully in the possession of that person ...'

In general there is no obligation on a suspect to give his fingerprints. He may if he wishes though a person arrested under s.30 of the *Offences Against the State Act, 1939* must give his fingerprints and palm prints if demanded. In general there is no legal restriction at present on the taking of another person's photograph. The Gárdaí have no particular power to compel suspects to be photographed though a person arrested under s.30 may be photographed. There is no legal obligation on a suspect to take part in an identification parade though he may do so if he agrees. There are internal Gárda guidelines for the holding of identification parades in order to ensure fairness.[63] A person whom it is proposed to put on parade should be informed: (1) that the person will be placed among a number of other persons who are, as far as possible, of similar height, age and general appearance as the person; (2) that the person may have a solicitor or a friend present at the parade; (3) that the person may take up any position he may choose in the parade and that, after a witness has left, he may change his position in the parade before the next witness is called; (4) that the person may object to any of the persons on the parade or the arrangements and that such objection be made to the Gárda conducting the parade.

A person arrested under s.30 of the *Offences Against the State Act, 1939* must submit to any test designed for the purpose of ascertaining whether he has been in contact with firearms or any explosive substance and for that purpose may have swabs from his skin and samples of his hair taken. For these tests to be taken in other cases consent must be given. (see Appendix).

A suspect cannot be ill-treated while in custody and according to O'Higgins C.J. in *The People (DPP) v. Madden* (Case No. 78), 'a person held in detention by the Gárda Síochána, whether under the provisions of the Act of 1939 or otherwise, has got a right of reasonable access to his legal advisers and . . . a refusal of a request to give such reasonable access would render his detention illegal. Of course, in this context the word 'reasonable' must be construed having regard to all the circumstances of each individual case and, in particular, to the time at which access is requested and the availability of the legal adviser or advisers sought. However, the Court is not satisfied that there is any obligation on the Gárda Síochána when detaining a person . . . to proffer to such person the assistance of a legal adviser without request.' This latter statement was dissented from by Walsh J. in *The People (DPP) v. Shaw* (Case No. 81) when he said: 'It is not too much to expect that every Gárda station should have a list of all local solicitors to supply to prisoners when a request for a solicitor is made to enable the prisoner to make a choice, particularly if he is a stranger in the area or has not already the name of a particular solicitor whom he wishes to contact.'

The Right to Silence

A person in custody in general is under no legal obligation to answer any question. At present under our law a person in custody on suspicion of having committed a crime may remain silent though he may if he chooses answer questions or make a written statement. Various legal rules have been formulated to protect the suspect for a collection of reasons. The atmosphere of a Gárda station may make it difficult to give a coherent explanation and it has been proven that persons do confess to crimes they could not have committed. One of the sets of rules laid down, known as the *Judges' Rules,* was first formulated in 1912 by the judges in England at the request of the Home Secretary and was added to in 1922. These rules have been applied in our courts since then, though they do not have the status of rules of law.[64] They are administrative directions, though statements obtained in breach of the Rules *may* be rejected as evidence. The trial judge is given a discretion whether to accept or reject statements obtained in breach of the *Judges' Rules*, which are as follows: (1) When a police officer is endeavouring to discover the author of a crime there is no objection to his putting questions in respect thereof to any person or persons, whether suspected or not, from whom he thinks that useful information may be obtained; (2) Whenever a police officer has made up his mind to charge a person with a crime, he should first caution such person before asking him any questions, or any further questions as the case may be; (3) Persons in custody should not be questioned without the usual caution being first administered; (4) If the prisoner wishes to volunteer any statement, the usual caution should be administered. It is desirable that the last two words of such caution should be omitted, and that the caution should end with the words 'be given in evidence'; (5) The caution to be administered to a prisoner when he is formally charged should therefore be in the following words: 'Do you wish to say anything in answer to the charge? You are not obliged to say anything unless you wish to do so, but whatever you say will be taken down in writing and may be given in evidence.' Care should be taken to avoid the suggestion that his answers can only be used in evidence against him, as this may prevent an innocent person making a statement which might help to clear him of the charge; (6) A statement made by a prisoner before there is time to caution him is not rendered inadmissible in evidence merely because no caution has been given, but in such a case he should be cautioned as soon as possible; (7) A prisoner making a voluntary statement must not be cross-examined, and no questions should be put to him about it except for the purpose of removing ambiguity in what he has actually said; (8) When two or more persons are charged with the same offence and their statements are taken separately, the police should not read these statements to the other persons charged, but each of such persons should be given by the police a copy of such statements and nothing should be said or done by the police to invite a reply. If the person charged desires to make a statement in reply the usual caution should be administered; (9) Any statement made in accordance with these rules should, whenever possible, be taken down in writing and signed by the person making it after it has been read to him and he has been invited to make any corrections he may wish. (see Appendix).

There are a number of occasions when statute excludes this right to silence. Some we have mentioned when examining what demands a Gárda can make of a person. Another is worthy of mention. The *Offences Against the State Act, 1939*, s.52 empowers a Gárda to demand of a person detained under the Act a full account of that person's movement and actions during any specified period. Failure to give such an account is an offence.

Unconstitutionally and Illegally Obtained Evidence

The courts must strive to reconcile two highly important interests which are liable to come into conflict: the interest of the citizen in being protected from unconstitutional and illegal invasions of his liberties by the authorities, and the interest of the State in securing evidence bearing upon the commission of crime. Neither of these objects can be insisted upon to the uttermost. The protection of the citizen is primarily protection for the innocent citizen against unwarranted and perhaps high-handed interference. The protection is not intended as a protection for the guilty citizen against the efforts to vindicate the law. On the other hand the interest of the State cannot be magnified to the point of causing all the safeguards for the protection of the citizen to vanish and of offering a positive inducement to the authorities to proceed by irregular methods.

We have already seen that evidence obtained in breach of the *Judges' Rules* may be excluded from evidence. How should the courts treat unconstitutionally and illegally obtained evidence? There are three possible solutions currently obtaining in other jurisdictions. The courts could, as in England, admit all illegally obtained evidence except confessions so obtained: *R. v. Sang.* Or the other extreme could be adopted, as in the United States, where evidence obtained unconstitutionally and illegally is excluded: *Mapp v. Ohio.* Or some measure between both these extremes could be found, as in Scotland, where some discretion, is given to admit illegally obtained evidence: *Lawrie v. Muir.* Our courts have adopted the last proposition which was stated by Walsh J. in *The People (A.G.) v. O'Brien* (Case No. 74) thus: 'evidence obtained in deliberate conscious breach of the constitutional rights of an accused person should, save in excusable circumstances ... be absolutely inadmissible'. In that case the breach of constitutional rights was not deliberate and conscious because the error in the search warrant was an inadvertent one. So there are three stages to the test that the courts must apply: (a) was there a breach of constitutional rights? (b) if there was, was it a deliberate and conscious violation? (c) if it was, then *prima facie* the evidence must be excluded unless there are extraordinary excusing circumstances which render the evidence admissible?

The courts have applied this test in many cases. In *The People (DPP) v. Madden* (Case No. 78) an incriminatory statement admitted at the trial should have been excluded because, as O'Higgins C.J. explained, it 'was taken by a senior Gárda officer who must have been aware of the lawful period of detention which applied in this defendant's case: it was taken in circumstances which suggest that he deliberately and consciously regarded the taking and completion of the statement as being of more importance than according to the defendant his right to liberty'. In *The People (DPP) v. Farrell* (Case No. 76) an incriminatory statement admitted at the trial should have been excluded because, according to O'Higgins C.J., it was 'made at a time when he [the appellant] was being detained in a Gárda station without any authorisation. This was in breach of his rights ... this is a case in which evidence has been obtained in circumstances in which the rights of the person concerned have been frustrated'. In *The People (DPP) v. O'Loughlin* (Case No. 79) an incriminatory statement was also admitted in evidence at the trial which resulted in conviction. On appeal the conviction was quashed because, according to O'Higgins C.J., '... the Gardaí chose not to charge the applicant when the ought to have done so. Instead, in effect they held him further for questioning for many hours. This could not have been due to either inadvertence or oversight. It was done by experienced Gárda officers who must have had a special knowledge of citizens' rights in such circumstances. It could only have been the result of a deliberate decision by these officers who were aware of the applicant's rights. These rights were disregarded and swept aside ...'

In the three cases discussed so far there was no extraordinary excusing circumstance which permitted the unconstitutionally obtained evidence to be admitted. In these cases the interest of the individual prevailed over the public interest. But in *The People (DPP) v. Shaw* (Case No. 81) there was a real dilemma, and the appellant was kept in custody longer than was legally permitted because it was believed by the Gárdaí that the victim of the crime was alive. The Supreme Court accepted that an extraordinary excusing circumstance existed. 'In my opinion', said Griffin J., 'where such a conflict arises, a choice must be made and it is the duty of the State to protect what is the more important right, even at the expense of another important, but less important, right. The State must therefore weight each right for the purpose of evaluating the merits of each, and strike a balance between them, and having done so take such steps as are necessary to protect the more important right. Although the right to personal liberty is one of the fundamental rights, in my view, in any civilised society, if a balance is to be struck between the right to personal liberty, for some hours or even days, of one person, and the right to protection against danger to the life of another, the latter right must ... prevail.'

Where the breach is merely of a legal right as distinct from a constitutional right the courts, according to the decision in *The People (A.G.) v. O'Brien* (Case No. 74), have a discretion to admit or exclude such evidence.

The Right to Bail

Once the judicial process begins on the preferring of a charge the question of bail arises. In *The People (A.G.) v. O'Callaghan* (Case No. 75) the High Court enumerated certain matters which should be considered by a court when considering the question of bail: the seriousness of the charge and the nature of the evidence; the likely sentence; the likelihood of the commission of other offences while on bail; the possibility of disposing of evidence and of interfering with witnesses and jurors; the failure to answer to bail in the past; the fact that the defendant was caught red-handed; the objections of the police; and the possibility of a speedy trial. The Supreme Court held that the fundamental test in deciding whether to allow bail or not was the probability of the defendant evading justice. Many of the matters raised by the High Court went to deciding this central issue except the one which allowed the consideration that further offences might be committed if bail was granted. 'The reasoning underlying this submission', was, in the opinion of Ó Dálaigh C.J., 'a denial of the whole basis of our legal system. It transcends respect for the requirement that a man shall be considered innocent until he is found guilty and seeks to punish him in

111

respect of offences neither completed nor attempted. I say "punish", for the deprivation of liberty must be considered a punishment unless it can be required to ensure that an accused person will stand his trial when called upon.' 'This', according to Walsh J., 'is a form of preventative justice which has no place in our legal system and is quite alien to the true purpose of bail'.

Bail is usually set by the court before which the defendant appears though this jurisdiction is reserved to the High Court under the *Criminal Procedure Act, 1967*, s.29 in cases of treason, usurping the functions of government, obstruction of government, obstruction of the President, certain offences under the *Official Secrets Act, 1963* and murder, attempt to murder, conspiracy to murder or piracy. The same Act, s.31, permits a person brought in custody to a Gárda station to be released on bail. 'Bail must not', according to Walsh J. in O'Callaghan's case, 'be fixed at a figure so large as would in effect amount to a denial of bail and in consequence lead to inevitable imprisonment.'

Other Forms of Detention

Apart from arrest on suspicion of having committed a crime, a person may lawfully be detained on other occasions. The most common is detention while undergoing a lawful sentence of imprisonment or penal servitude. But a person convicted and sentenced does not have all his constitutional rights stripped from him. 'While so held as a prisoner, pursuant to a lawful warrant,' explained O'Higgins C.J. in *The State (McDonagh) v. Frawley*, 'many of the prosecutor's normal constitutional rights are abrogated or suspended.' What rights are unimpaired? 'When the Executive', said Finlay P. in *The State (C.) v. Frawley* (Case No. 87), 'in exercise of what I take to be its constitutional right and duty, imprisons an individual in pursuance of a lawful warrant of a court, then it seems to me to be a logical extension of the principle laid down in *Ryan v. Attorney General* that it may not, without justification or necessity, expose the health of that person to risk or danger.' In both these cases prisoners unsuccessfully complained of medical facilities in prisons, but in *The State (Richardson) v. The Governor of Mountjoy* (Case No. 98) a prisoner was successful because the toilet facilities were a danger to her health. How far other constitutional rights, such as the right to vote, freedom of expression and property rights, are affected by imprisonment has yet to be decided.

A person may be arrested for the purpose of extradition. In *The State (Quinn) v. Ryan* (Case No. 97) the Supreme Court struck down a statute which permitted the removal out of the jurisdiction of a person wanted for a crime in Britain without recourse to the courts in this country. To remedy this lacuna, the *Extradition Act, 1965* was passed. In general a person wanted in another country must be given a judicial hearing here before an extradition order can be made. There are restrictions on the power to extradite; the offence must carry at least one year's imprisonment; the offence must not be political or connected with a political offence; the offence must not be a military or revenue offence; the offence must not carry the death penalty unless the country requesting the extradition agrees not to carry it out; the requesting country must not try the person for any other offence; and the extradition request must contain details of the offence.

It was held in *The State (McFadden) v. The Governor of Mountjoy* (Case No. 94) that because extradition proceedings were akin to criminal proceedings, the constitutional right to fair procedures must be afforded to the person to be extradited.

A once common form of deprivation of liberty was internment without trial, found unconstitutional in *The State (Burke) v. Lennon* (Case No. 86). An amendment to the law was upheld by the Supreme Court in *Art. 26 and the Offences Against the State (Amendment) Bill, 1940* (Case No. 7). Internment without trial is a form of preventive punishment so disliked by the Supreme Court in *The People (A.G.) v. O'Callaghan* (Case No. 75) that Walsh J. thought it could only be used 'in the most extraordinary circumstances carefully spelled out by the Oireachtas and then only to secure the preservation of the State in a time of national emergency or in some situation akin to that'. For reasons explained in Chapter 4 the Supreme Court may not feel bound by its own previous decision regarding internment and may, if the opportunity should arise, consider its constitutionality afresh. Apart from objections to internment without trial on principle, its administration may be difficult following a change of judicial opinion on the scope of judicial review of administrative action. In earlier times the courts refused to look behind the exercise of administrative powers. In *Art. 26 and the Offences Against the State (Amendment) Bill, 1940* (Case No. 7) Sullivan C.J., explained the rule thus: 'The only essential preliminary to the exercise by a Minister of the powers contained in s.4 is that he should have formed opinions on the matters specifically mentioned in the section. The validity of such opinions is not a matter that could be questioned in any Court.' The same conclusion was reached in *In re Ó Láighléis* (Case No. 72) by the Supreme Court, but *The State (Lynch) v. Cooney* (Case No. 93) showed a big change. O'Higgins C.J., speaking of the relevant statute said: 'The Court is satisfied that the subsection does not exclude review by the courts and that any opinion formed by the Minister thereunder must be one which is *bona fide* held and factually sustainable and not unreasonable.' Henchy J. explained: 'It is to be presumed that when Parliament conferred the power, it intended it to be exercised only in a manner that would be in conformity with the Constitution and within the limitations of the power as it is to be gathered from the statutory scheme or design. This means, amongst other things, not only that the power must be exercised in good faith, but that the opinion or other subjective conclusion set as a precondition for the valid exercise of the power must be reached by a route that does not make the exercise unlawful — such as by misinterpreting the law, or by misapplying it through taking into consideration irrelevant matters of fact, or through ignoring relevant matters. Otherwise, the exercise of the power will be held to be invalid for being *ultra vires.'* To justify a particular internment in the future the Minister might in legal proceedings be called upon to expose the evidence on which he based his opinion. This may act as some stop on the abuse of the power of internment.

Another form of detention is that whereby persons of unsound mind can be kept in preventive custody. The necessity for having some judicial determination before such a person can be detained was rejected by the Supreme Court in *In re Philip Clarke* (Case No. 23).

Imprisonment for debt still exists. Under the *Enforcement of Court Orders Act, 1926,* as amended, a procedure whereby a debtor against whom judgment has been given and who has no goods to be seized in execution may be examined by a District Justice and ordered to pay by instalment. If default is made in the instalments an application for the arrest and imprisonment of the debtor may be sought which can only be granted for a period up to three months if the District Justice is satisfied that the failure to pay was due not to inability but to wilful refusal or culpable neglect.

An Application under Art. 40 of the Constitution

At common law a detention was tested as to its lawfulness by the writ of *habeas corpus*. A similar type of procedure is contained in Art. 40.4.2° of the Constitution. Upon complaint being made by or on behalf of any person to the High Court, and any and every judge thereof, that such person is unlawfully detained, the High Court, and any judge to whom such complaint is made, must inquire into the complaint and *may* order the person in whose custody such person is detained to produce the body of such person before the High Court and to certify in writing the grounds of his detention. The High Court must, after the body of such person has been produced, and after giving the person in whose custody he is detained an opportunity of justifying the detention, order the release of such person unless satisfied that he is being detained in accordance with law. This procedure has been used in many different types of situation: suspects in police custody, prisoners in custody, patients in hospitals, children in residential care and in the custody of parents and others, and persons about to be deported.

The usual procedure is that the party complaining of unlawful detention applies *ex parte* for a conditional order directing the person detaining him to justify the detention. If that person fails to justify the detention, the conditional order is made absolute and the person is released. From the wording of the Article, could a person, having obtained a conditional order which was not made absolute, go from judge to judge of the High Court until he found a judge to uphold his complaint or until he exhausted the list of judges? This point was decided in *The State (Dowling) v. Kingston* (No. 2) where a person, being refused an absolute order by the majority of a three-judge High Court, later renewed his application to the judge who had favoured his case. This judge refused to reconsider the matter, and on appeal the Supreme Court held that once the law had been declared by a competent court the decision was binding on the individual members of that Court. Murnaghan J. drew an important distinction when he said: 'there is no right to apply to a Judge after the High Court has pronounced the detention to be legal. It is quite a different matter ... to say that the refusal of a Judge to grant the first *ex parte* application prevents an application to another Judge. In such a case the detention has not been declared to be in accordance with law.' But if new grounds were advanced after a determination was made, the Supreme Court held, in the *Application of Woods,* that the High Court was under a constitutional obligation to consider the matter anew.

It is rare in law for one person to be allowed to bring proceedings on behalf of another. An application under Art. 40 is one of the exceptions. In *The State (Burke) v. Lennon* (Case No. 86) a brother of the person detained brought the application, and in *The State (Quinn) v. Ryan* (Case No. 97) the solicitor of a person released was allowed to bring a fresh application after the person was again detained and removed out of the jurisdiction.

Because the word 'may' is used, there is no obligation on the High Court to order the production of the person in court. It was held by the Supreme Court in *The State (M. Woods) v. Kelly* that this was merely an enabling power and that an order for release can be made where the person is not in court.

Art. 40.4.2° provides a two-stage procedure in that firstly an inquiry must be made and secondly the person in whose custody the individual is alleged to be must be given an opportunity to be heard. It was held in the *Application of Zwann* that an absolute order cannot issue in the first instance: '... this provision expressly provides that *before* ordering the release of such person', said Griffin J., 'an opportunity must be given to the person in whose custody he is detained to justify the detention'.

If the High Court rules that the person is detained in accordance with law but that such law is invalid having regard to the provisions of the Constitution, it must state a case for the opinion of the Supreme Court and may allow the person bail (Art. 40.4.3°). The Supreme Court held in *The State (Sheerin) v. Kennedy* (Case No. 100) that this provision applied only to post-1937 statutes.

This was done in accordance with the Constitution as it then stood.

Art. 40.4.6° declares that the procedure for testing the validity of a detention cannot be invoked to prohibit, control, or interfere with any act of the Defence Forces during the existence of a state of war or armed rebellion.

The Right to Life

Probably the greatest right of all is the right to be born. Without it all other rights are superfluous. It had been hinted that the right to life was one of the unspecified constitutional rights. In *Conroy v. Attorney General* (Case No. 25) Kenny J. said that 'every individual, as an individual, has certain inherent rights of which the right of life is the most fundamental ...' The right to life of the unborn has now been expressly acknowledged by the Eighth Amendment to the Constitution. The equal right to life of the mother is also acknowledged. Which right prevails when the two conflict, and in what type of situations, remains to be decided by the courts in the appropriate cases.

The Right to Bodily Integrity

Having examined the right to personal liberty we now look at a right that is a corollary to it: the right to bodily integrity. This was first expounded as an implied constitutional right in *Ryan v. Attorney General* (Case No. 84). Kenny J. thought it extended to 'no mutilation of the body or any of its members may be carried out on any citizen under authority of the law except for the good of the whole body and that no process which is or may, as a matter of probability, be dangerous or harmful to the life or health of the citizens or any of them may be imposed (in the sense of being made compulsory) by an Act of the Oireachtas'. On the evidence then presented, it was held in that case that the fluoridation of the public water supply was not an interference with that right. The existence of the right was accepted in *The State (C.) v. Frawley* (Case No. 87) and *The State (McDonagh) v. Frawley,* though in neither case was it breached. In *The State (Richardson) v. The Governor of Mountjoy* (Case No. 98) this right was extended to include the right of a person in custody not to have his health endangered.

Freedom to Travel

The right to personal liberty would be meaningless if there was no corollary of freedom to travel. It was suggested by Kenny J. in *Ryan v. Attorney General* (Case No. 84) that one of the unspecified constitutional rights was 'the right to free movement within the State ...' In *The State (K.M.) v. The Minister for Foreign Affairs* (Case No. 92) the right to travel outside the State was firmly established. 'It appears to me', said Finlay P., 'that the citizens of the State may have a right (arising from the Christian and democratic nature of the State—though not enumerated in the Constitution) to avail of such facilities without arbitrary or unjustified interference by

116

the State. To put the matter more simply and more bluntly, it appears to me that, subject to the obvious conditions which may be required by public order and the common good of the State, a citizen has the right to a passport ...' Obvious exceptions would be in time of war, or a debtor fleeing his creditors, or a criminal fleeing from justice.

The existence of this constitutional right was affirmed by the High Court in *Lennon v. Ganley* where an injunction to restrain the Irish Rugby Football Union who were organising a rugby tour of South Africa from associating themselves with Ireland was refused. 'The defendants,' said O'Hanlon J., 'and the players who are participating in the tour, have a *prima facie* constitutional right to travel abroad for the purpose of taking part in sporting fixtures in other countries as well as in Ireland if they wish to do so. They should only be restrained from exercising such right if it was in some way unlawful for them to act in the manner in which they seek to act.'

Chapter 13

FREEDOM OF ASSOCIATION

That man is a social animal is acknowledged in Art. 40.6.1° of the Constitution where the State guarantees to the citizen, subject to public order and morality, the right to form associations and unions. Ordinary social intercourse, which man finds so essential, is a constitutional right. The citizen can associate for an infinite number of reasons. Personal relationships not often considered under the freedom of association are central to society. The right to marry, have children and form a family are examples of this personal right of association. Political, social, charitable, sporting, educational, religious and economic clubs, groups and associations can be formed without permission or interference from the State.

The Right of Dissociation
The right of association must imply the complementary right to dissociate. This was decided in two trade union cases but the principle applies to all associations. In the *Educational Co. of Ireland v. Fitzpatrick* (Case No. 36) Budd J. declared this right thus: 'I hold ... that under the Constitution a citizen is free to join or not to join an association or union as he pleases. Further, that he cannot be deprived of the right to join or not to join such association as he pleases ... is tantamount to saying that he may not be compelled to join any association or union against his will.' This view was upheld by the Supreme Court and an attempt by some employees using a picket to compel their employer to dismiss other

117

employees who refused to join a union failed. An attempt by an employer to impose union membership on an existing employee is also an infringement of this right of dissociation. This was decided by the Supreme Court in *Meskell v. C.I.E.* (Case No. 56) where a grand scheme by the employer and unions whereby employees would be dismissed and re-employed on condition that they joined and remained members of a particular union was held to be a conspiracy to deprive a citizen of his constitutional right to dissociate.

A point not decided by the courts is whether a condition in a new employee's contract of employment that he must belong to a union, or indeed that he cannot join a union, is constitutional. This is a different point than Meskell's case because there the employee was dismissed under a contract which contained no compulsory union membership clause. An attempt to impose one failed but in order to gain employment a citizen may accept terms he might not otherwise accept. This type of situation arose in *Becton, Dickinson v. Lee* but the employees pre-empted dismissal by withdrawing their labour leaving the courts only to decide whether a trade dispute existed. In this case the employer agreed with a union that all craft employees would join it and remain members of that union. Craft employees on entering employment signed an agreement to this effect, but once in employment refused to honour the commitment because they already belonged to a union. When the employer refused to negotiate with the employees' existing union, they went on strike and the employer sought an injunction to prevent the picketing. The constitutional point was not relevant but the differing views of two judges may give some indication of the answer to the question when it arises. Walsh J. said: 'I have assumed that the term in the contract of employment with regard to trade-union membership is not one which would be held void. It is not necessary to express any opinion upon the question of how far, or in what circumstances, a person can contract out of a constitutional right; or to what extent such an agreement would be enforced.' Henchy J. was inclined to the view that such a term in the contract was possible. He said: 'The question whether it is permissible under the Constitution to ensure by contract that a man must remain indefinitely a member of a particular union does not arise for decision in this case. All I find necessary to decide is that Art. 40.6 is no impediment to providing by contract that membership of a particular union is to be a prerequisite for a particular employment.'

A citizen cannot be compelled to associate, but the question whether an organisation can be compelled to accept a person it does not want arose in *Tierney v. Amalgamated Society of Woodworkers* where a union refused an application for membership. In refusing assistance to the person concerned, Budd J. said: 'It has heretofore been of the essence of a voluntary organisation that the members, and they alone, should decide who should be their fellow-members.' In *Murphy v. Stewart* (Case No. 60) one union would accept the plaintiff's membership only if the union to which he

118

tence on conviction on indictment is seven years' imprisonment.

already belonged gave its consent, which it would not do, and the Supreme Court in an unsatisfactory decision held that it was not the refusal to agree to the transfer that was the real issue but the refusal of the new union to accept membership.

It was held in *Abbott v. Irish Transport & General Workers Union* (Case No. 2) that there was no constitutional right of negotiation and that the High Court could not order an employer to negotiate with a union of the employees' choice.

Public Order

The Constitution permits a limitation on the freedom of association on the ground of public order. There are statutory limitations imposed on associations which threaten to undermine the authority or security of the State. The *Offences Against the State Act, 1939* defines an unlawful organisation as one which promotes treason, or which advocates by force the alteration of the Constitution, or which maintains an armed force without constitutional authority, or encourages the commission of criminal offences, or promotes the attainment of any particular object by violent or unlawful means, or encourages the non-payment of taxation. The Government may by order declare an organisation to be an unlawful one and while this suppression order does not have to be laid before the Houses of the Oireachtas a person who claims to be a member of an organisation suppressed has thirty days to apply to the High Court for a declaration, known as a declaration of legality, that such organisation is not an unlawful organisation. The applicant must give evidence and submit to cross-examination. Once the High Court makes a declaration of legality the suppression order becomes null and void.

It is an offence to belong to an unlawful organisation, and s.3 of the *Offences Against the State (Amendment) Act, 1972* provides a special method of proof. Where a Gárda officer not below the rank of chief superintendent, in giving evidence on such a charge, states that he believes the accused at the material time was a member of an unlawful organisation, that statement shall be evidence of that fact. This section only operates when Special Criminal Courts exist. The practice has been to acquit the person charged if he denies membership. The maximum sentence on conviction on indictment is 7 years imprisonment.

The law of conspiracy is another limitation on the freedom of association. It is a common law misdemeanour for two or more persons to do an unlawful act or to do a lawful act by unlawful means. It is a civil wrong if two or more persons combine together for the purpose of damaging another's trade or business or if they agree to perform an unlawful act and that other person is damaged by that unlawful act. The law of conspiracy has been extended to include a conspiracy to deprive a citizen of his constitutional rights. It first surfaced in *Meskell v. C.I.E.* (Case No. 56) and again in *Crowley v. Ireland* (Case No. 29). In the latter case the High

Court held that a directive issued by a teachers' union to its members not to enrol pupils from a school in which a trade dispute existed into neighbouring schools was a conspiracy to deprive those children of their constitutional right to primary education.

Much of the sting of the law of conspiracy was removed when trade unions were given statutory protections. How far, if at all, can the Oireachtas regulate the growth in the number of trade unions? Some attempt was made to do this in the *Trade Union Act, 1941* which was litigated on constitutional grounds in the *National Union of Railwaymen v. Sullivan* (Case No. 63). The High Court upheld the legislation on the ground that it merely regulated and controlled trade union membership: it did not prohibit membership. On appeal the Supreme Court struck down the legislation. Murnaghan J. explained: 'it purports to limit the right of the citizen to join one or more prescribed organisations ... any such limitation does undoubtedly deprive the citizen of a free choice of the persons with whom he shall associate. Both logically and practically, to deprive a person of the choice of the persons with whom he will associate, is not a control of the exercise of the right of association, but a denial of the right altogether.' The scheme underlying the 1941 Act could have been adopted to provide for one or more State-established trade unions.

The *Defence Act, 1954* prohibits members of the permanent Defence Forces from joining, remaining in, or subscribing to any political organisation or society or any secret society whatsoever. The *Gárda Síochána Act, 1924,* as amended, prohibits members of the Gárda Síochána from being members of a trade union though a representative body may be established to promote the welfare and efficiency of its members but must not concern itself with discipline and promotion.

In the commercial field there are some restrictions on the right to associate. S.376 of the *Companies Act, 1963,* as amended, provides that no partnership of more than twenty persons can be formed for the purpose of any business that has for its object the acquisition of gain except in the cases of solicitors, accountants and bankers. A private limited company must at least have two members and not more than fifty whereas a public limited company must at least have seven members. A challenge was made in the *Private Motorists Provident Society Ltd. v Attorney General* (Case No. 82a) to the provisions of a statute that prohibited the plaintiffs from carrying on a banking business, as they had done prior to the enactment of the statute, on the ground that it infringed the right of association. 'The exercise of such a right', said O'Higgins C.J., in the Supreme Court when rejecting the claim, 'is not prevented by a law limiting and controlling in the public interest what such an association may do.'

There are not many instances where statutes attempt to impose association. The *Unfair Dismissals Act, 1977* empowers the Employment Appeals Tribunal to order the reinstatement or re-engagement of an employee who has been unfairly dismissed. An employer is thus restricted in his freedom to dissociate, and this may be unlawful. Other proposed restrictions may be unconstitutional. Would compulsory military service be a breach of the right to dissociate or could it be justified on the ground that the common good required such activity?

Morality

There are a number of instances where the law restricts freedom of association on the ground of morality. Certain blood relations cannot marry: such marriage is void. Sexual relations are forbidden between different classes of persons. Incest is forbidden as is intercourse with females under the age of 17 years. A distinction must be drawn between association and certain types of activity. This was emphasised in *Norris v. Attorney General* (Case No. 64) where the criminalisation of certain sexual activity was alleged to infringe the right to freedom of association. This claim was rejected by the Supreme Court. To associate with others who have the same attitude to sexual morals is not an offence though to associate with others for the purpose of engaging in forbidden sexual activities would be.

Chapter 14

FREEDOM OF ASSEMBLY

Man as a social animal needs the company of other humans. The Constitution in Art. 40.6.1° acknowledges this human necessity by providing that the citizen has the right to assemble peaceably and without arms. The obvious assembly is man within the family. Art. 41 acknowledges the family as the natural primary and fundamental unit group of society and as a moral institution, the possessor of inalienable and imprescriptible rights antecedent and superior to all positive law. Often when enumerating constitutional rights the most obvious are neglected. Man is thus constitutionally entitled to form families and other personal relationships. Freedom of assembly is usually considered in a different light, and the remainder of this chapter concentrates on this aspect.

Meetings can broadly be divided into three types. Into the first go private meetings in private places, and the law rarely attempts to regulate such assemblies. But on occasion it does. For example meetings of limited companies must be in accordance with the *Companies Act, 1963* and the meetings of other bodies may be regulated by their rules which may be judicially enforced in appropriate circumstances. Apart from the law of nuisance and planning regulations, a person can use his property as he wishes. The holding of meetings therein is not the concern of any public authority.

121

Into the second category of meetings go public meetings in private places. Here again there are very few legal controls. Provided the other legal rules about trespass, defamation and proper behaviour are adhered to, the holders of the meetings and those attending are subject to no legal restraints and need no permission.

The third category of meetings are processions and meetings held in public places. It is in this category that the legal restraints are felt. A public place is an open space to which the public have access for the time being whether on payment or not. Many of the restraints are of common law origin and probably survive the enactment of the Constitution. The Constitution limits freedom of assembly subject to public order and morality. We will look at the restraints under these two broad headings, though under the second there will be very little to say.

Public Order

Most processions are lawful because they simply consist of people exercising their legal right to move along the highway. The common law permits on public highways that activity alone for which they were built, namely the movement from one premises to another. But a procession may be an obstruction of the highway, which is a criminal offence, and the practical test is whether an unreasonable use is being made of the highway. The police have a long-established right to regulate traffic on the highway and this, it seems, may include processions. In order to hold a procession Gárda permission, or any other permission, is not necessary but notice of the route facilitates the Gárdaí, those taking part in the procession and the public.

The holding of a meeting on the public highway is not in itself a criminal offence though there is no unlimited right to hold such meetings. It may constitute an obstruction of the highway or it may be conduct likely to lead to a breach of the peace: this means that there must be a reasonable belief that the behaviour in question would lead to a disturbance involving physical force. It is an offence under the *Public Meeting Act, 1908* to attempt to break up a public meeting.

But a meeting on a public highway which is not initially unlawful may become so in a number of ways. An *unlawful assembly* means an assembly of three or more persons in order to commit a crime or in order to do something, legal or illegal, together, which endangers public peace or makes firm and courageous people fear a breach of the peace. *Riot* is defined as a tumultuous disturbance by three or more persons who have assembled in order to carry out some common purpose and to help one another by force if necessary against anyone who opposes them and then to do what they have planned using enough force or violence to alarm at least one person of reasonable firmness. The difference between unlawful and riotous assembly is that the moment persons in a crowd, however peaceful their original intentions, come together to act for some common purpose in such a way as to make reasonable citizens fear a breach of the peace the assembly becomes unlawful. It becomes riotous when alarming force or violence begins to be used and anyone who actively encourages such an assembly by words, signs or actions or by participating in it is guilty of riotous assembly.

A *rout* is a disturbance of the peace by persons who intend to do something which if they had would amount to riot but who failed to achieve their purpose. An *affray* is a fight between two or more persons who fight in the presence of others who were neither encouraging nor participating and some of whom were frightened by the fighting.

In dispersing an unlawful assembly no more force than is necessary must be used. In *Lynch v. Fitzgerald,* the father of a youth killed by a bullet fired by a Gárda in suppressing a riot sued for damages. The classical explanation of the law was given by Hanna J.:

> It is an invariable rule that the degree of force to be used must always be moderate and proportioned to the circumstances of the case, and the end to be attained. Hence it is that arms ... must be used with the greatest of care, and the greatest pains must be exercised to avoid the infliction of fatal injuries ... a gun should never be used, or used with any specified degree of force, if there is any doubt as to the necessity.

It is an offence under s.27 of the *Offences Against the State Act, 1939* to hold a public meeting for the purpose of supporting, aiding, abetting, or encouraging an unlawful organisation. If a member of the Gárda Síochána not below the rank of chief superintendent is of opinion that such a meeting is to be held he may, either by notice to the organisers or by publishing in a manner reasonably calculated to come to the knowledge of the organisers, prohibit that meeting. An aggrieved party may apply to the High Court for an order annulling such prohibition and, following the principles established in *The State (Lynch) v. Cooney* (Case No. 93), such administrative decision must be *bona fide* and made on factual grounds that are sustainable and reasonable.

It is an offence under s.28 of the *Offences Against the State Act, 1939* for any public meeting or procession to be held in any public street or unenclosed place within one-half mile of any building in which either or both Houses of the Oireachtas are sitting or about to sit. This offence is only committed if the procession or meeting has been prohibited by a member of the Gárdaí not below the rank of chief superintendent and a Gárda calls on the people taking part to disperse. Presumably the Gárda making the order of prohibition must not act unreasonably or capriciously.

Under s.4 of the *Offences Against the State (Amendment) Act, 1972* any meeting, procession or demonstration intended or likely, directly or indirectly, to influence any court, person or authority concerned with the institution, conduct or defence of any civil or criminal proceedings, including a party or witness, as to whether or how the proceedings should be instituted, conducted, continued or defended or as to what should be their outcome, constitutes an interference with the course of justice and is unlawful.

Picketing is in law a 'watching and besetting' and is a criminal offence under the *Conspiracy and Protection of Property Act, 1875*. But picketing in furtherance of a trade dispute is exempt from criminal and civil liability under s.2 of the *Trade Disputes Act, 1906*. The immunity conferred by this statute depends on two factors: the existence of a trade dispute and that the picketing is solely for the purpose of peacefully obtaining or communicating information or of peacefully persuading any person to work or to abstain from working. In *Brendan Dunne Ltd. v. Fitzpatrick* (Case No. 15) Budd J. explained: 'if citizens in the course of an assembly commit a breach of the peace or some other breach of the law, they thereby disturb public order, and their actions are not protected by the Constitution in respect of the breach of the law committed'.

Morality

Legal interference with the right of assembly on the ground of morality is rare and is connected with the complementary rights of freedom of association and freedom of expression. It is an offence to stage an obscene show, while it is not an offence to attend one. It is an offence to show in public a film not passed by the censor, whereas it is not an offence to attend such a film. Indecent conduct likely to lead to a breach of the peace is unlawful and can be prevented.

Chapter 15

FREEDOM OF EXPRESSION

An individual can express himself in an almost indefinite number of ways. The writing of a song, the wearing of particular clothes, the playing of a sport, the landscaping of a garden, the choosing of a career and the cooking of a meal are different ways of self expression. Art. 40.6.1° of the Constitution guarantees to citizens the right to express freely their convictions and opinions. The tendency to consider this right merely to encompass the freedom of the press is to deny the much wider scope of the guarantee. Convictions and opinions can be expressed in more varied ways than simply the oral or written form. While most of this chapter will concentrate on these forms of communications, sight must not be lost of the wider meanings to be given to this constitutional right.

The right to express convictions and opinions freely contains by implication the complementary right of having those convictions and opinions received by other citizens. This constitutional right would be useless if, for example, the Government, having permitted the citizen to print newspapers, ordered that all such newspapers were to be sold only to the State. The expression of convictions and opinions is only meaningful in the context of the ability to inform and influence. Freedom of expression has as much to do with the freedom to hear the opinions of others as it has with the right to propagate one's own convictions.

The limitations placed by the Constitution on this right are threefold: restrictions are imposed to protect the authority of the State, public order and morality. Difficulties arise in defining these restrictions and further complications are added by the fact that some of the presently accepted legal exceptions do not readily fall within any of the three classifications. Apart from these different reasons for limitation the State imposes different methods of suppressing opinions. Pure or pre-publication censorship operates when the authorities exercise a pre-publication veto. This kind of censorship is rare under our law but it does exist. It is a method of censorship more redolent of war-time conditions. The second method of censorship is commoner. Here the publications or opinions do not require a pre-publication official imprimatur but are banned after publication. A publication may be simply suppressed. Together with suppression, the possibility of prosecution, either criminal or civil, may follow because views are presented which the law declares may not be presented or which the executive power, regardless of the letter of the law, wishes to suppress. The third method of censorship is that of self-censorship. The authorities may create a climate in which it is dangerous to publish certain convictions and opinions. By manufacturing such a situation, the State forces the citizen to perform the task of censor, which the authorities are reluctant to do openly. The State hopes to achieve its repressive aims in this way with a minimum of public odium.

Authority of the State

The Constitution casts on the State a duty to curtail freedom of expression in defence of the State itself. This defence of the existence and integrity of the State is an integral part of the business of government. The process was resorted to in *The State (Lynch) v. Cooney* (Case No. 93). In upholding the legislation in question O'Higgins C.J. explained: 'It follows that the use of such organs of opinion for the purpose of securing or advocating support for organisations which seek by violence to overthrow the State or its institutions is a use which is prohibited by the Constitution. Therefore it is clearly the duty of the State to intervene to prevent broadcasts on radio or television which are aimed at such a result or which in any way would be likely to have the effect of promoting or inciting to crime or endangering the authority of the State.' The Supreme Court upheld the decision of the Minister for Posts and Telegraphs to order RTE to refrain from broadcasting certain electoral broadcasts by members of

Provisional Sinn Féin. This was justified on the ground that other members of the organisation had been convicted of certain offences and others had said certain things on previous occasions. The fact that the broadcast to be made would not have contained any matter which challenged the authority of the State was deemed irrelevant. What was important was that the broadcast was intended to seek and rally support for the Sinn Féin organisation. The danger with this kind of decision is that by attempting to uphold the existence and integrity of the State, ideas or doctrines which are considered essential to its well-being are protected from criticism and views which are declared detrimental are proscribed.

The *Broadcasting Authority Act, 1960,* as amended, permits the Minister for Posts and Telegraphs to prohibit by order broadcasts of a particular matter or any matter of a particular class which in his opinion would be likely to promote, or incite to, crime or would tend to undermine the authority of the State. A number of such orders have been made. One of these was the subject of a challenge in *The State (Lynch) v. Cooney* (Case No. 93). While accepting that such legislation was permissible, the Supreme Court held that the power of the Minister was not unfettered. The exercise of that power was open to judicial review and any opinion formed must be *bona fide* held and factually sustainable and not unreasonable.

The *Offences Against the State Act, 1939* made it unlawful to set up in type, print, publish, send through the post, distribute, sell or offer for sale any document, which includes a book or magazine, which contains anything incriminating, treasonable or seditious. It is unlawful for any person to send or contribute to any newspaper, or for the proprietor of any newspaper to publish, any communication which comes from an unlawful organisation. On conviction the court may order the forfeiture of the offending document and the printing machinery. Foreign newspapers containing such offending material may by order of the Minister for Justice be seized and destroyed or may be prohibited from importation. It is unlawful for any person to have any treasonable, seditious or incriminating document in his possession or on premises or lands owned or occupied by him.

The central issue in the defence of the State is the issue of secrecy. The State has secrets and needs, it feels, to keep them. The *Official Secrets Act, 1963* prohibits the communication of official information by any person unless authorised, or when the communication is made in the course of the duties of a holder of public office, or when it is a duty in the interest of the State to communicate it. It is also unlawful to obtain, record, communicate or publish any matter which would or might be prejudicial to the safety or preservation of the State. There is in general a mania in the public service in favour of secrecy. In recent years this has been dented by judicial review of administrative action. The plea for state secrecy was greatly curtailed in *Murphy v. Dublin Corporation* (Case No. 59)

126

when the Supreme Court refused to allow a Minister of State to hide behind a blanket claim of executive privilege.

According to Art. 40.6 the publication or utterance of seditious matter shall be punishable in accordance with law. *Sedition*, whether by spoken or written words or by conduct, is generally all endeavours which tend to promote public disorder but fall short of treason. It is not a widely used offence because statute has created specific offences from some of its ingredients. It is an offence to cause disaffection in the Defence Forces and in the Gárda Síochána. It is an offence to have a sketch or model of a military establishment or to wear a military uniform when not so entitled.

The *Offences Against the State (Amendment) Act, 1972* makes it an offence to publish a statement orally or in writing which constitutes an interference with the course of justice. The law of contempt, which was explained in Chapter 9, limits the criticism which can be made of courts and judges.

Public Order

It is an offence to use abusive or threatening language calculated to provoke or lead to a breach of the peace. Criminal libel is an offence; the writing or publishing of defamatory words about any living person or words calculated or intended to provoke him to wrath or to expose him to public hatred, contempt or ridicule or to damage his reputation; also the publishing of a picture or effigy. Besides being an offence, a libel is a civil wrong, as is slander. It is difficult to categorise both these civil wrongs under this heading but it can be done because the absence of some remedy might lead to self-help, which the law discourages. Rightly they should be encompassed within the constitutional right to one's good name.

In general a person can carry a poster displaying words or images unless this is likely to lead to a breach of the peace. Some idea of words which may be prevented is contained in the judgment of Walsh J. in *E.I. Co. v. Kennedy*. 'The use of words such as "scab" or "blackleg"', he said, 'is historically so associated with social ostracism and physical violence as to be far beyond anything which might be described as mere rudeness or impoliteness and go begond what is permitted by law. In the present context the references made to the race or nationality of the employers could produce the same disorderly response . . .' Of course a banner which contains defamatory words leaves the bearer open to a civil action and possible injunction to prevent repetition. Flyposting — that is, the sticking up of posters in public places — is now illegal and the offenders can be fined. It is an offence, in general, to use a loudspeaker in a public place. In general it is not an offence to distribute free of charge literature in public, though a person by doing so may obstruct the public highway. The sale of literature in a public street or on a public highway may require a licence from a local authority.

Morality

According to Art. 40.6, the publication or utterance of blasphemous or indecent matter is an offence which shall be punishable in accordance with law. *Blasphemy* and *blasphemous libel* consist of indecent and offensive attacks on Christianity or the Scriptures or sacred persons or objects, calculated to outrage the feelings of the community. The mere denial of Christian teachings is not enough. *Indecency* means any act which offends modesty, causes scandal or injures the morals of the community. Any person who at, or near, or in sight of any place along which the public habitually pass commits any indecent act, commits an offence. It is an offence to show for gain or reward an indecent or profane performance. In the case of the *Attorney General v. Simpson* it was held that there must be an intention to deprave or corrupt those viewing the performance, in that instance *The Rose Tattoo* by Tennessee Williams, whose minds were open to such immoral influences. Any public sale, or exposure for sale, or exposure to public view of any indecent book, picture or print is an offence. Soliciting for prostitution in any public place is an offence.

Censorship of publications was established by the *Censorship of Publications Acts, 1929 to 1967,* which established a Censorship of Publications Board of five persons, appointed by the Minister for Justice, who are entitled to prohibit the sale and distribution of any book which, in their opinion, is indecent or obscene or which advocates the unnatural prevention of conception or the procurement of abortion. They are required to examine any book in respect of which a complaint is made to them by any person or which has been referred to them by a customs officer. They must take into account, in examining a book, the literary, artistic, scientific or historical merit or importance, and the general tenor, of the book, the language in which it is written, the nature and extent of the circulation which, in their opinion, it is likely to have, the class of reader which, in their opinion, may reasonably be expected to read it, and any other matter relating to the book which appears to them to be relevant. An appeal can be brought from an order of this Board to an Appeal Board, also of five persons. The Censorship Board is also entitled to make Prohibition Orders in respect of periodicals which have usually or frequently been indecent or obscene, which advocate the unnatural prevention of of conception or the procurement of abortion, or which have devoted an unduly large proportion of space to the publication of matter relating to crime. The rigorous application of these laws has banned many authors of note, and the 1967 Act places a twelve-year time limit on the life of a Prohibition Order though a publication de-banned in this way might be re-banned. It is an offence to sell or distribute a prohibited publication. Before such a Prohibition Order the Board *may* communicate with its author, editor or publisher.

In *Irish Family Planning v. Ryan* the publishers of a family planning booklet challenged the making of a Prohibition Order on the ground that they should in natural justice have been informed before the Order was made. The Supreme Court held that the direction to communicate was not mandatory but merely discretionary. In order to conclude whether that discretion had been exercised fairly the Court examined the booklet which according to O'Higgins C.J., 'reached out to those who might wish to be informed as to the different methods of contraception which were available ... Far from being pornographic or lewdly commercial or pandering to prurient curiosity, it simply aimed at giving factual information on a delicate topic as to which there is genuine concern. It espoused no cause; it advocated no course of conduct ... In those circumstances it is not possible to hold that this book would have been banned for being "indecent or obscene" ..' Since the Board had not exercised its discretion properly the Order was quashed. It transpired that the Board in eight and a half years had never once communicated with an author, editor or publisher.

The censorship of films was established by the *Censorship of Films Acts 1923 to 1970* under which no film may be shown in public unless the Film Censor has granted a certificate that it is fit for showing. If the censor refuses his certificate, any person affected may appeal to an Appeal Board. The censor may issue a certificate in respect of a film, parts of which he thinks unfit for public exhibition, where the owner of the film consents to the cutting of these parts. The censor may also issue a 'limited certificate' permitting the film to be shown in special places or to special audiences. The Film Censor may only refuse a certificate if he is of the opinion that the film is 'indecent, obscene or blasphemous, or because the exhibition thereof in public would tend to inculcate principles contrary to public morality or would be otherwise subversive of public morality.' The censor's certificate is not required unless the film is being shown in public, so private societies and clubs who confine admission to their members are not obliged to obtain a certificate in respect of the films shown by them.

There is no legislation for the censorship of stage plays though a prosecution may result if it is indecent or obscene. There is no legislation for the censorship of records or video tapes.

Religious Freedom

Art. 44.2.1° declares that freedom of conscience and the free profession and practice of religion are, subject to public order and morality, guaranteed to every citizen. According to Walsh J. in *McGee v. Attorney General* (Case No. 50), 'the meaning of Art. 44.2.1° is that no person shall directly or indirectly be coerced or compelled to act contrary to his conscience in so far as the practice of religion is concerned, and subject to public order and morality, is free to profess and practise the religion of his choice in accordance with his conscience. Correlatively, he is free to have no religious beliefs or to abstain from the practice or profession of any religion.' This guarantee has not been the subject of any constitutional action.

129

Chapter 16

FAMILY RIGHTS

Marriage

Art. 41.3.1° declares that the State pledges to guard with special care the institution of Marriage, on which the Family is founded and to protect it against attack. The Constitution contains no definition of marriage and, while the classical common law definition postulated by Lord Penzance in *Hyde v. Hyde* of 'the voluntary union for life of one man and one woman to the exclusion of all others', is probably acceptable it may in modern circumstances be inadequate. There are religions which permit polygamy and how the courts could cope with a claim by a person charged with bigamy that since religious liberty is guaranteed his marriages must be given constitutional recognition is unclear. An equally interesting question is which of his wives would be his spouse for the purposes of the *Succession Act, 1965.*

The right to marry, which is not expressed, is one of the implied rights suggested by Kenny J. in *Ryan v. Attorney General* (Case No. 84). There are restrictions on the grounds of age and blood relationship and certain formalities must be complied with.

This Article was pleaded in *Murphy v. Attorney General* (Case No. 61) where it was claimed that parts of the income tax code were an attack on marriage because a married couple paid more income tax than two single persons living together with similar incomes. The Supreme Court accepted this contention because, said Kenny J., 'the nature and potentially progressive extent of the burden ... is such that, in the opinion of the Court, it is a breach of the pledge by the State to guard with special care the institution of Marriage.'

Art. 41.3.2° declares that no law shall be enacted providing for the grant of a dissolution of marriage. While 'dissolution of marriage' is not defined it is taken to mean divorce *a vinculo matrimonii* which is a judicial declaration that a valid marriage is at an end. This prohibition does not prevent the courts from granting a decree of nullity which is a declaration that no valid marriage ever existed. The prohibition on divorce presents little difficulty in itself: the difficulty has arisen over how far our courts should recognise foreign divorce decrees and ancillary orders made thereunder. The first case in this category is *Mayo-Perrott v. Mayo-Perrott* (Case No. 54) where an action was brought to recover the costs of a divorce case which had been heard in England. The action was dismised because, as Kingsmill Moore J. explained:

It cannot be doubted that the public policy of this country as reflected in the Constitution does not favour divorce *a vinculo,* and though the law may recognise the change of status effected by it as an accomplished fact, it would fail to carry out public policy if, by a decree of its own courts, it gave assistance to the process of divorce by entertaining a suit for the costs of such proceedings. The debt which it is sought to enforce is one created by proceedings of a nature which could not be instituted in this country, proceedings the institution of which our public policy disapproves.

In the next two cases it was the recognition of the foreign divorce itself that was in issue. In the *Bank of Ireland v. Caffin* (Case No. 10) Kenny J. explained: 'In 1921 the courts of Ireland ... recognised the validity of a decree of divorce *a vinculo* made by the courts of the country where the husband and wife were domiciled ... The National Parliament has not legislated on the matter ... and the law as existing when the Constitution was passed was that a divorce effected by a foreign court of persons domiciled within its jurisdiction was regarded as valid in our jurisdiction.' In a later case of *Gaffney v. Gaffney* this rule was confirmed by the Supreme Court, which refused recognition to a divorce decree because it was granted by a jurisdiction in which the parties were not domiciled.

In *Mahon v. Mahon* the couple divorced in England in 1967 and the ex-wife obtained a maintenance order five years later. Both parties returned to this country and the ex-wife sued for the arrears of maintenance, which the High Court allowed, distinguishing this case from Mayo-Perrott's case on the ground that the maintenance order was severable from the divorce. Hamilton J. said,

I accept unreservedly that if the recognition or enforcement of a Maintenance Order would have the effect of giving active assistance to facilitate in any way the effecting of a dissolution of marriage or to give assistance to the process of divorce that such recognition or enforcement would be contrary to public policy ... In enforcing and recognising this Maintenance Order ... it cannot be said that such enforcement or recognition is giving active or any assistance to facilitate in any way the effecting of a dissolution of marriage or is giving assistance to the process of divorce. It is merely providing for the maintenance of spouses and as such cannot be regarded as contrary to public policy.

Even in events which fall short of divorce the courts may be reluctant to give them recognition. In *Dalton v. Dalton* the High Court refused to make a separation agreement a rule of court because the parties agreed to obtain a decree *a vinculo*. To do so, said O'Hanlon J., 'is to ask the court to lend its support to a course of conduct which is contrary to public policy within this jurisdiction.'

The Family

Art. 41.1 declares that the State recognises the family as the natural, primary and fundamental unit group of society, and as a moral institution possessing inalienable and imprescriptible rights, antecedent and superior to all positive law. The State guarantees to protect the family in its constitution and authority, as the necessary basis of social order and as indispensable to the welfare of the nation and the State. The family is not defined but judicial dicta confine it to family founded on marriage. 'I am satisfied,' said Henchy J., in *The State (Nicolaou) v. An Bord Uchtála* (Case No. 96), 'that no union or grouping of people is entitled to be designated a family for the purposes of the Article if it is founded on any relationship other than that of marriage.' In the Supreme Court Walsh J. said: 'It is quite clear from the provisions of Art. 41 ... that the family referred to in this Art. is the family which is founded on the institution of marriage ... While it is quite true that unmarried persons cohabiting together and the children of their union may often be referred to as a family and have many, if not all, of the outward appearances of a family, and may indeed for the purposes of a particular law be regarded as such, nevertheless so far as Art. 41 is concerned the guarantees ... are confined to families based upon marriage.' A marriage after the birth of a child or children renders the unit a family for the purposes of Art. 41. In *In re J., an infant,* Henchy J. explained:

> In construing Art. 41 ... the first question to be decided is whether the father, mother and child together constitute a family. I am of opinion that they do. It is true that the child was born illegitimate and, therefore, outside a family, but by its parents' marriage it has clearly become a legitimate child of the marriage. I find it impossible to distinguish between the constitutional position of a child whose legitimacy stems from the fact that he was born the day after his parents were married, and that of a child whose legitimacy stems from the fact that his parents were married the day after he was born ... The crucial fact in each case is that the child's legitimacy and consequent membership of the family are founded on the parents' marriage.

The Constitution does not spell out the inalienable and imprescriptible right of the family. It leaves this task to the Oireachtas and the courts. '"Inalienable" means', according to Kenny J. in *Ryan v. Attorney General* (Case No. 84), 'that which cannot be transferred or given away while "imprescriptible" means that which cannot be lost by the passage of time or abandoned by non-exercise.' Before looking at some of these rights we will look at the implied right to marital privacy because, since many of these rights concern the children of a marriage, the fundamental question as to the State's role, if any, in family planning must be considered.

In *McGee v. Attorney General* (Case No. 50), a married woman complained that the prohibition on the importation of artificial contraceptives was a breach of an implied right to marital privacy. In acknowledging such a right, most of the members of Supreme Court held that it rested on Art. 40.3. One judge, Walsh J., based the right on Art. 41: 'It is a matter exclusively for the husband and wife to decide how many children they wish to have; it would be quite outside the competence of the State to dictate or prescribe the number of children which they might have or should have. In my view, the husband and wife have a correlative right to agree to have no children ... It follows that the use of contraceptives by them within that marital privacy is equally guaranteed against such invasion ...'

In attempting to understand family rights it is a mistake to equate these family rights with parental rights. Each member of the family is the possessor of rights: the parents jointly, the parents individually and each of the children. As in other areas of constitutional law, difficulties arise in attempting to reconcile the various rights in cases of dispute. Two broad principles have been developed which now form the corner-stone of the law in this regard. The 'first proposition', said Sullivan C.J. in *In re Frost, infants,* 'was that the court must regard the Family as a unit, the control and management of which is vested in both parents while both are living and, on the death of either of them, in the parent who survives.' The Supreme Court rejected the argument that the rights of parents are absolute rights, the exercise of which cannot in any way be controlled by the courts. The 'second proposition', according to Sullivan C.J., was 'that a child has natural and imprescriptible rights is recognised by the Constitution ... the Court has jurisdiction to control the exercise of parental rights, but in exercising that jurisdiction it must not act upon any principle which is repugnant to the Constitution.' The *Guardianship of Infants Act, 1964* gives statutory expression to these rules by providing that all matters concerning guardianship and custody must be decided on the basis of the welfare of the child and that parents have equal rights to, and are joint guardians of, their children.

In *Cosgrove v. Ireland* (Case No. 27) it was claimed that this legal right to joint guardianship was breached by the Minister for Foreign Affairs in issuing passports for children to a mother despite objections from the father. 'I am of opinion', said McWilliam J., 'that the passports should not have been issued without an application to the court being made by the wife and that this should have been told to the wife. Accordingly, in my view, the Department must share responsibility with the wife for the failure of the wife to obtain the consent of the court to sole custody of the children being had by her.'

In relation to custody of children there are two types of cases: the first is disputes between parents, or a parent, and a stranger though the latter be a relative, and then there are cases involving disputes between parents. In general parents or a parent will be given custody against a stranger or against the State but not in every case. In *In re O'Brien, an infant* a father who through long-term illness gave his daughter to her grandmother, the mother having died, had the daughter restored to him. O'Byrne J. in the Supreme Court said: 'The sanctity of the family and the enduring existence

133

of parental authority seem to me to be guaranteed by these provisions and I consider that I am entitled to say that the framers of the Constitution considered, and enacted, that the best interests and happiness of the child would be served by its being a member of the parental household ... the appellant has failed to show that the father has failed in his duty to his child ...' In *In re Doyle, an infant* a mother deserted the home and the father, unable to support the child, applied to the District Court to have the child taken into care. This was done and, when his circumstances improved, he applied for the return of his daughter. He was met with s.10 of the *Children Act, 1941* which provided that while one parent could commit a child to care it needed the consent of both parents to release the child. This section was ruled unconstitutional by the Supreme Court because, per Maguire C.J., 'it allows a parent in the position of the prosecutor to deprive himself of the control of his child ... It seems that where such a surrender is sanctioned it can only be for a period limited by the parents' inability to provide for the education of a child ... In the view of this Court [Art. 42.5] does not enable the legislature to take away the right of a parent who is in a position to do so to control the education of his child, where there is nothing culpable on the part of either parent or child.' In *P.W. v A.W.* the youngest child of a family of four was, almost from birth, cared for and in the custody of a couple not the parents though with the consent of the parents. The latters' marriage irretrievably broke down and the mother, who suffered from mental illness, sought custody of the child when it was four years old. Ellis J. explained that 'there is no natural or *prima facie* right of a parent to custody of his or her children but that there is a rule of prudence that in most cases the best place for a child is with its parent, but that there can be circumstances varying with each case (not necessarily amounting to intentional misconduct or misbehaviour), to which valid objection can be taken in the interests of the welfare of a child, whereby the parent can lose custody of the child not only to another contending parent but to a stranger.' He left the child with the strangers.

Education and the Family

Art. 42 declares that the primary and natural educator of the child is the family and the State guarantees to respect the inalienable right and duty of parents to provide, according to their means, for the religious and moral, intellectual, physical and social education of their children. Parents are free to provide this education in their homes or in private schools or in schools recognised or established by the State. The State shall not oblige parents in violation of their conscience and lawful preference to send their children to schools established by the State or to any particular type of school designated by the State but, as guardian of the common good, the State may require children to receive a certain minimum education, moral, intellectual and social.

It comes as a surprise to many parents that they are under no obligation

134

to send their children to school. The *School Attendance Acts, 1926 to 1967* are misunderstood and are being misapplied. The State can only interfere when a child is not receiving *'a certain minimum education'*. 'What is the meaning and extent of this provision?' asked the Supreme Court in *Art. 26 and the School Attendance Bill 1940* (Case No. 8). 'We are of opinion', said Sullivan C.J., 'that the State, acting in its legislative capacity through the Oireachtas, has power to define it ... which expression, in the opinion of the Court, indicates a minimum standard of elementary education of general application.' The Supreme Court condemned a section which delegated this power of prescribing a standard to a Minister of State. To the present day the Oireachtas has not laid down a minimum standard of education and it is therefore impossible for the courts to conclude that any child is not receiving such a standard.

Art. 42.4 declares that the State shall provide for free primary education and shall endeavour to supplement and give reasonable aid to private and corporate educational initiative. It was clarified in *Crowley v. Ireland* (Case No. 29) that the State's duty is to provide *for* free primary education and not to provide it. There are, contrary to popular opinion, very few State-owned educational institutions in this country. Art. 44.2.4° provides that legislation providing aid for schools must not discriminate between schools under the management of different denominations nor should such legislation affect prejudicially the right of any child to attend a school receiving public money without attending religious instruction at that school. A scheme providing more advantageous terms to children who wish to attend a boarding school of one religious denomination without providing it for all denominations probably offends this guarantee. A child cannot be compelled to attend the religious instruction at any school which receives public funds, whether directly by way of building or capitation grant, or indirectly by the payment of the teaching staff.

Religion and the Family

Parents have under Art. 42.1 the right to decide the religion of their children and the State cannot interfere in general with such right. Where parents agree there is never a difficulty. It is in cases of disagreement between the parties that the courts must intervene. It is regrettable that this issue of choice of religious instruction was in the earlier cases confused with the right to custody. In these cases, such as Frost and Tilson, it was presumed that the issues were not distinct. It cannot follow that the parent with custody can decide all issues affecting the welfare of the child without the consent of the other party, or, failing that, the consent of the court. Who decides the religion of the child? 'The rule which the courts in this country ... have consistently followed', explained Sullivan C.J. in *In re Frost, infants,* 'is that the father has that legal right, and that when that right has been exercised by him, the children must be educated in the religion which he has chosen, by his wife should she survive him.' In the

135

later case of *In re Tilson, infants* (Case No. 101), Murnaghan J. in the Supreme Court explained that 'the true principle under our Constitution is this. The parents — father and mother — have a joint power and duty in respect of the religious education of their children. If they together make a decision and put it into practice it is not in the power of the father — nor is it in the power of the mother — to revoke such decision against the will of the other party ... if a difference between father and mother leads to a situation in which the child is neglected, the State, through the courts, is to endeavour to supply the place of the parents.'

The State cannot dictate the religion in which parents are to instruct their children, and nor, it seems, can anyone else. In *Burke v. Burke* (Case No. 18) a direction in a will as to the education of a legatee was set aside, because according to Gavan Duffy P., it 'would override the sacred parental authority and defy the parental right and duty of education under Art. 42.' In *In re Blake, deceased* (Case No. 12) the provision in a will that the children to benefit should be brought up as Roman Catholic was void as offending public policy because, per Dixon J., it was 'an attempt to interfere with or fetter the right and duty guaranteed to parents by the Constitution to provide for the education, including the religious education, of their children'.

Adoption and the Family

What has been said up until now about the family could be taken to apply only to the natural family, that is, married parents and children of their blood. The law permits adoption, the purpose of which is to vindicate certain children's rights. The effect of the making of a valid adoption order is that the child acquires the rights of a natural child in relation to its adoptive parents and the adoptive parents acquire the rights of natural parents in relation to the child adopted. The procedure is laid down by statute and is based on the consent of all the parties, except the child if it is under an age to give its consent. At present, only illegitimate and orphan children are in general eligible for adoption. The question has often been posed but never litigated whether legitimate children could be eligible for adoption. Possibly those abandoned or neglected by their parents, or parent, or those whose parents consented might be eligible. In instances such as this a balancing of rights would have to be made, and it seems that the interests of the child favour a steady family environment.

Most of the adoption cases are concerned with the question of consent and do not turn on the constitutionality of adoption itself. One recent case, *Northampton County Council v. A.B.F.* (Case No. 65), is of interest, where the High Court refused to grant custody of a child to an English local authority that originally had custody, because the father objected and because the adoption of legitimate children was not permitted under our law. Hamilton J. refused 'because the effect of granting the order sought ... would have been that the infant child would have been adopted without the consent and in spite of the opposition of his lawful father, a development which is not permissible under the Irish law of adoption'.

Extra-Marital Family

It has been made clear by judicial comments that the family protected under the Constitution is the family founded on marriage. What rights, if any, have extra-marital families? In essence they appear to have the same rights as the constitutional family, though there seems to be some dispute as to whether legitimate children could be given up for adoption whereas it is accepted that illegitimate children can. Where there is no dispute among the parties, the Constitution and the law leave them in peace. Where there are disputes the parties may be treated differently to separated married parties.

Has the natural mother a constitutional right to the custody of her child? In *G. v. An Bord Uchtála* (Case No. 40), Finlay P. in the High Court held that the unmarried mother 'has a constitutional right to the custody and to the control of the upbringing' of her child. In the Supreme Court a majority — O'Higgins C.J., Walsh and Parke JJ. — agreed with him whereas the minority — Henchy and Kenny JJ. — disagreed, holding that the natural mother merely has a legal right to the custody of her child. If the majority are right, then by giving a consent to adoption the mother is alienating permanently a constitutional right.

The natural father has fared much worse. In *The State (Nicolaou) v. An Bord Uchtála* (Case No. 96) the natural father was, in the circumstances existing in that case, denied rights in relation to the child. But it must be stressed that this decision cannot be taken as illustrating a general principle that a natural father has no rights in relation to his illegitimate child. Where he cares for and has custody of that child he may in appropriate circumstances repel the State, a stranger and even the mother because in such a case, as in all cases concerning children, the central and vital question is the best interests of the child.

Constitutional Rights of Children

'All children,' said Henchy J. in *G. v. An Bord Uchtála* (Case No. 40), 'whether legitimate or illegitimate, share the common characteristic that they enter life without responsibility for their status and with an equal claim to what the Constitution expressly or impliedly postulates as the fundamental rights of children. Since Art. 42 recognises the children of a marriage as having a natural and imprescriptible right (as the correlative of their parents' duty) to the provision for them of religion and moral, intellectual, physical and social education, a like personal right should be held to be impliedly accorded to the illegitimate child by Art. 40.3.' In the same case O'Higgins C.J., said: 'Having been born, the child has the right to be fed and to live, to be reared and educated, to have the opportunity of working and of realising his or her full personality and dignity as a human being.' If the parent fails to provide the child with the necessities of life the State must do so (Art. 42.5).

There has been no litigation on when constitutionally a person becomes an adult. The law does not lay down a uniform age to cover every type of situation. A person may take full-time employment at 15, may marry with consent at 16, may vote at 18 and does not have fully contractual capacity until 21 years. There are clearly instances when some of these rules are unconstitutional. To be married and a parent and not to be able to acquire one's family home at, say, 20 years of age, is not a vindication of marriage or the family. Consent of parents must be obtained by a person under the age of 21 years before a passport is issued. How would the courts react to a case of an 18-year-old whose parents refused their consent?

Chapter 17

PROPERTY RIGHTS

Art. 43 declares that the State acknowledges that man, in virtue of his rational being, has the natural right, antecedent to positive law, to the private ownership of external goods and accordingly the State guarantees to pass no law attempting to abolish the right of private ownership or the general right to transfer, bequeath and inherit property. The nature of this Article was considered in *Blake v. Attorney General* (Case No. 13) by O'Higgins C.J.: 'It is an Article directed to the State and to its attitude to these rights, which are declared to be antecedent to positive law. It does not deal with a citizen's right to a particular item of property ... Such rights are dealt with in Art. 40 under the heading 'Personal Rights' ... Under this Art. the State is bound, in its laws, to respect and as far as practicable to defend and vindicate the personal rights of citizens. There exists, therefore, a double protection for the property rights of a citizen. As far as he is concerned, the State cannot abolish or attempt to abolish the right of private ownership as an institution ... In addition he has the further protection under Art. 40 as to the exercise by him of his own property rights in particular items of property.'

The State recognises that the exercise of property rights ought, in civil society, to be regulated by the principles of social justice and accordingly the State may, as occasion requires, delimit by law the exercise of these rights with a view to reconciling their exercise with the exigencies of the common good. There are innumerable instances of the curtailment of private property rights. Examples are the whole range of taxation, price control, planning law, nuisance, trespass, various compulsory purchase procedures, and the necessity to be licensed. How these private rights are reconciled with the common good can be gleaned from the case law. In the

138

first case decided in 1939, the *Pigs Marketing Board v. Donnelly (Dublin) Ltd.* (Case No. 82), the High Court was asked to rule on a measure which interfered with contractual rights. 'The days of *laissez faire* are at an end,' said Hanna J., 'and this is recognised in Art. 43.2.2° ... I am of opinion that the Oireachtas must be the judge of whatever limitation is to be enacted. This law does not abolish private ownership in pigs or bacon, it only delimits the exercise of these rights by the persons in whom they are vested ...' The court had earlier looked at the purpose of the legislation and accepted that the pigs and bacon industry was of great importance to the country, not alone by providing a staple article of food for the citizens but also because it was an industry which both in home consumption and export was of considerable value. In *Foley v. Irish Land Commission* (Case No. 38) the Supreme Court looked at the general nature of the legislation which did, according to O'Byrne J., 'constitute a very important branch of our social legislation ... the object of these Acts is to create a peasant proprietorship of a certain standard.' The plaintiff having been given some land and then built a house on it, the Court was 'of opinion that the imposition of the condition as to residence, with the statutory sanction for failure to comply therewith, is not an abolition of the right of private ownership ... this limitation ... is sanctioned ... as a delimitation of his rights ... with a view to reconciling their exercise with the exigencies of the common good and in accordance with the principles of social justice.'

In *Attorney General v. Southern Industrial Trust* (Case No. 9) the question was whether a statute could be justified which conferred a power to take possession of a particular piece of property and to divest a person, without compensation, of the ownership – a person who had himself committed no breach of the law in relation to that property. In the High Court a consideration of the customs code, which was at issue in this case, was undertaken and found to be for the common good. 'I do not think it can be reasonably contended', said Davitt P., 'that the customs code, severe and unpopular though it may seem to those who have most evidence of it as transgressors, has not been enacted with a view to the promotion of the common good, nor do I think that it can be contended that a person who takes the risk of illegally importing or exporting his own property has any reasonable cause to complain of injustice if it is forfeited in consequence of his offence.' In regard to the seizing of an innocent person's property the Court held that the customs code, by providing a method for the mitigation of penalties, was an attempt to reconcile the rights of innocent owners on the one hand and the exigencies of the common good on the other. In *Central Dublin Development v. Attorney General* (Case No. 21) the nature of the legislation was again examined. 'If there is to be planning development,' said Kenny J., 'someone must decide whether new or altered buildings are to be allowed in a specific place and whether land should be retained as an un-built space. The very nature of town and regional planning requires restriction ... Town and regional planning is an attempt to reconcile the exercise of property rights with the demands of the common good ...'

In the course of his judgment, Kenny J., after an analysis of the Constitution and the decided cases, was led to the following conclusions: (1) The right of private property is a personal right; (2) In virtue of his rational being, man has a natural right to individual or private ownership of worldly wealth; (3) This constitutional right consists of a bundle of rights most of which are founded in contract; (4) The State cannot pass any law which abolishes all the bundle of rights which we call ownership or the general right to transfer, bequeath and inherit property; (5) The exercise of these rights ought to be regulated by the principles of social justice and the State accordingly may by law restrict their exercise with a view to reconciling this with the demands of the common good; (6) The courts have jurisdiction to inquire whether the restriction is in accordance with the principles of social justice and whether the legislation is necessary to reconcile this exercise with the demands of the common good; (7) If any of the rights which together constitute our conception of ownership are abolished or restricted (as distinct from the abolition of all the rights), the absence of compensation for this restriction or abolition will make the Act which does this invalid if it is an unjust attack on the property rights.

This absence of compensation was central in *Blake v. Attorney General* (Case No. 13) where statutes which restricted recovery of premises and prohibited rent increases were challenged successfully. 'It is, therefore, apparent that in this legislation,' said O'Higgins C.J., 'rent control is applied only to some houses and dwellings and not to others, that the basis for the selection is not related to the needs of the tenants, to the financial or economic resources of the landlords, or to any established social necessity and, since the legislation is now not limited in duration, is not associated with any particular temporary or emergency situation. Such legislation, to escape the description of being unfair and unjust, would require some adequate compensatory factor for those whose rights are so arbitrarily and detrimentally affected.' The special security of tenure was also condemned. O'Higgins C.J. explained:

In the view of the court, a restriction to this extent of a landlord's right to obtain possession of rented premises is not in itself constitutionally invalid, provided the restriction is made on a basis that is not unconstitutionally unfair or oppressive, or has not due regard both to the personal property rights of the landlord and the rights that should be accorded to tenants, having regard to the common good. However, the restriction on the right to recover possession contained in Part IV [of the Act] is not distinguishable, or capable of being saved, by such considerations. It is an integral part of the arbitrary and unfair statutory scheme whereby tenants of controlled dwellings are singled out for specially favourable treatment, both as to rent and as to the right to retain possession, regardless of whether they have any social or financial need for such preferential treatment and regardless of whether the landlords have the ability to bear the burden of providing such preferential treatment.

An attempt to soften the effects of this decision was struck down by the Supreme Court in *Art. 26 and Housing (Private Rented Dwellings) Bill, 1981* (Case No. 6) for the same reasons.

If property is taken, for example by compulsory purchase, what form should the compensation take? Must it be money or could it be, as in *Dreher v. Irish Land Commission,* land bonds? The Supreme Court held that the payment in bonds which carried interest, as distinct from monetary compensation, was not an unjust attack on property rights.

In *O'Brien v. Bord na Mona* (Case No. 66) an attack on a statute which permitted compulsory acquisition of bogland (with compensation) failed because 'the purpose of the statute', according to O'Higgins C.J., 'was to make available the considerable natural resource of turf in this State in the best possible fashion for the use of the nation.' In the *Private Motorists' Provident Society Ltd. v. Attorney General* (Case No. 82a) a statute which prohibited certain types of entities from carrying on a banking business was not, according to O'Higgins C.J., 'an expropriation of the business ... it is a regulation and control of the range of business which the Society may lawfully transact. The Oireachtas is bound to legislate having regard to the requirements of the common good. It is clear from the conclusions of the learned trial judge on the evidence she heard that the regulation and control effected by the legislation was reasonable, and was in accordance with the public interest and with the requirements of the common good.'

'Art. 43 of the Constitution', said D'Arcy J. in *O'Brien v. Stoutt* (Case No. 68a), 'does not give an individual right to inherit property. It guarantees that the State will not pass a law attempting to abolish the right to private property or to the *general* right to transfer, bequeath and inherit property. It is the general right to inherit property, not any particular one, that is enshrined and guarded by the Constitution.' The refusal by the Oireachtas to confer inheritance rights on an illegitimate child on the intestacy of his father, was not a constitutional infringement.

The Right to Work

One of the personal rights unspecified in Art. 40.3 is the right to work in certain circumstances. It does not mean that the State must either provide work or provide for work. It seems to mean that where a person is in employment unconstitutional means cannot be used to remove him. In *Education Co. of Ireland v. Fitzpatrick* (Case No. 36) employers prevented picketing which attempted to coerce the employer into dismissing other employees because they refused to join a trade union. In the

141

process the High Court declared the right to dissociate. In *Murtagh Properties Ltd. v. Cleary* (Case No. 62) there was a demand, backed by a threat of a picket, that women should not be employed at all in any capacity solely because they were women. The picket was prevented by injunction because, as Kenny J. explained, 'The purpose of the threat of the picket is to compel the employers to dismiss the bar waitresses solely because they are women, and this is a breach of their constitutional rights.' In *Meskell v. C.I.E.* (Case No. 56) damages were awarded because the employer and the unions had conspired to wrongly dismiss the plaintiff from his employment.

A different type of situation was envisaged by Walsh J. in *Murphy v. Stewart* (Case No. 60) when he said: 'if the right to work was reserved exclusively to members of a trade union which held a monopoly in this field and the trade union was abusing the monopoly in such a way as to effectively prevent the exercise of a person's constitutional right to work, the question of compelling that union to accept the person concerned into membership (or, indeed, of breaking the monopoly) would fall to be considered for the purpose of vindicating the right to work.' This proposition can also be applied to professional bodies.

The Right to Litigate

Like the right to work, the right to litigate is often stated in very broad terms which are not supported by judicial decision. There are two instances where the Constitution acknowledges the right to have recourse to the courts. The first of these is the right to apply to the High Court under Art. 40 to question a particular detention. 'It is quite clear', said Walsh J. in *The State (Quinn) v. Ryan* (Case No. 97), 'that the right to apply to the High Court or any Judge thereof is conferred on every person who wishes to challenge the legality of his detention. It must follow that any law which makes it possible to frustrate that right must necessarily be invalid having regard to that provision of the Constitution.' The second of these constitutional rights to litigate was explained by Kenny J. in *Macauley v. The Minister for Posts and Telegraphs* (Case No. 47): 'That there is a right to have recourse to the High Court to defend and vindicate a legal right and that it is one of the personal rights of the citizen included in the general guarantee in Art 40.3 seems to me to be a necessary inference ... If the High Court has this full original jurisdication to determine all matters and questions ... it must follow that the citizens have a right to have recourse to that Court to question the validity of any law, having regard to the provisions of the Constitution or for the purpose of asserting or defending a right given by the Constitution for if it did not exist, the guarantees and rights in the Constitution would be worthless.'

There is thus no general right to litigate under the Constitution. There are many instances where the law gives no remedy against a wrong. The Oireachtas may abolish causes of action creating a situation in which one person may be able to sue before the Act comes into effect, while another person cannot sue once the Act is in effect. The courts have considered a number of cases in this regard, some where interference occurred after the action had commenced and others where the general right to litigate was curtailed in some respect. In *Buckley v. Attorney General* (Case No. 17) the courts refused to allow the Oireachtas to interfere with a case which was then pending before the courts because it was an unwarrantable intrusion into the judicial domain. The Supreme Court also held that the attempt to divest the plaintiffs of monies lodged in court was an attack on their property rights. 'In the present case,' said O'Byrne J., 'there is no suggestion that any conflict had arisen, or was likely to arise, between the exercise by the plaintiffs of their right of property in the trust moneys and the exigencies of the common good, and, in our opinion, it is only the existence of such a conflict and an attempt by the Legislature to reconcile such conflicting claims that could justify the enactment of the statute under review.' In *O'Brien v. Keogh* (Case No. 67) a statutory provision which gave an infant in the custody of his parents a shorter period of time to bring an action for personal injuries than an infant not in the custody of his parents was rejected by the Supreme Court as an attack on the infant's property rights. This decision has been questioned in *Moynihan v. Greensmyth* (Case No. 57) where the Supreme Court upheld a provision which barred certain claims if not made within a 2-year period. The Supreme Court thought this period reasonable having regard to the defendant's right to have the issue resolved speedily. The failure of the statute to provide a different period for infants was not an unjust attack on the rights of infants. The difference between the two cases is that in *Moynihan v. Greensmyth* the statutory provision applied to all whereas in *O'Brien v. Keogh* more favourable conditions were granted to some infants without any justification.

Property of Religious Denomination or Educational Institution

Art. 44.2.6° declares that the property of any religious denomination or any educational institution shall not be diverted save for necessary works of public utility and on payment of compensation. This Article has not been judicially considered.

Inviolability of the Dwelling

Art. 40.5 declares that the dwelling of every citizen is inviolable and shall not be forcibly entered save in accordance with law. This constitutional guarantee extends only to the dwelling, and not the other property, of the citizen. 'In a case where members of a family live together in the family home,' said Walsh J. in *The People (A.G.) v. O'Brien* (Case No. 74), 'the house as a whole is for the purpose of the Constitution the dwelling of each member of the family. If a member of a family occupies a clearly defined portion of the house apart from the other members of the family, then it may well be that the part not so occupied is no longer his dwelling and that the part he separately occupies is his dwelling as would be the case where a person not a member of the family occupied or was in possession of a clearly defined portion of the house.' A dwelling does not have to be a permanent structure: it can be of a temporary nature such as a caravan, house-boat or a tent.

There are many instances where the law permits the dwelling to be entered. Many statutes provide the issuing of search warrants to search for firearms, explosives, stolen property and drugs. Other officials have limited rights to enter the dwelling. The common law has a rule which provides that where a person under a claim of legality enters premises and then abuses his entry he becomes a trespasser *ab initio.* A consequence of an unconstitutional entry is that evidence obtained as a result of a deliberate and conscious violation must be excluded from evidence unless there are extraordinary circumstances.

Part Three

CASES ON CONSTITUTIONAL LAW

This Part contains in alphabetical order the major cases in constitutional law. Each case contains a statement of the facts and the principle of constitutional law decided. Only the majority decision, which forms the judgment of the appropriate court, is given. Many of these cases decided matters of legal importance and these matters are, for clarity, excluded.

Case No. 1

Abbey Films Ltd. v. Attorney General

The plaintiff was a distributor of films which were rented to exhibitors throughout the country. Two of its directors were directors of a company which owned forty cinemas. The Examiner of Restrictive Practices received complaints that independent cinemas were unable to obtain a fair share of the best films for exhibition. The *Restrictive Practices Act 1972* empowered the Examiner to investigate any aspect of the supply or distribution of goods, or the provision of a service. S.15 of the Act empowered an authorised officer to enter business premises and require the production of documents and such information as the officer might reasonably require. Obstruction of the officer, or non-compliance with a requirement, was an offence. An application could be made within seven days to the High Court for a declaration that the 'exigencies of the common good' did not warrant the exercise of the Examiner's powers. The plaintiff sought a declaration that s.15 was unconstitutional on the grounds that: it made acts infringements of the law which were not so at the date of their commission contrary to Art. 15.5; it imposed an onus of proof on the defendant in a criminal matter which was an infringement of personal rights; it offended Art. 6 in that it entrusted a decision as to the exigencies of the common good to the courts; it empowered the High Court to create a new offence, usurping the function of the Oireachtas; and it was an unjust attack on the right to private property.

The Supreme Court rejected these claims. It held that an offence was committed when the officer was obstructed, or when the information was not given; that the Oireachtas could impose on an accused the onus to establish a limited and specified matter in criminal cases; that while the promotion of the common good is primarily the function of the Oireachtas there was nothing to prevent the Oireachtas from investing the courts with such jurisdiction; that the section, and not the High Court, creates the offence; and that the powers of entry and inspection do not infringe private ownership.

Case No. 2

Abbott v. Irish Transport & General Workers Union

The plaintiff was a member of the I.T.G.W.U. until October 1979 when he resigned and joined the Amalgamated Transport & General Workers Union. By then this union had recruited a sizeable number of the staff in the plaintiff's place of employment though an equal number continued membership with the I.T.G.W.U. A dispute arose which involved the employer and the A.T.G.W.U. The employer decided not to negotiate with the A.T.G.W.U. or any union other than the I.T.G.W.U. in resolving the dispute because of the fear that if he did the I.T.G.W.U. would take industrial action. The plaintiff sought an order to compel his employer to negotiate with the trade union of his choice.

The High Court held that in the absence of a constitutional right of negotiation the employer could not be forced to negotiate with the trade union of the plaintiff's choice.

Case No. 3

Article 26 and the Criminal Law (Jurisdiction) Bill, 1975

The Oireachtas passed the *Criminal Law (Jurisdiction) Bill, 1975*, which proposed, *inter alia,* that a person who commits certain offences outside the jurisdiction of this State could, if apprehended here, be tried and punished in the same way as if the offence had been committed within the jurisdiction. Pursuant to Art. 26.1.1°, the President referred the Bill to the Supreme Court.

The Supreme Court held, in advising the President that the Bill was constitutional, that Ireland, being a sovereign State, had the full power through the Oireachtas to legislate with extra-territorial effect in accordance with the accepted principles of international law.

146

Case No. 4

Article 26 and the Electoral (Amendment) Bill, 1961

The High Court had declared invalid the *Electoral (Amendment) Act, 1959* in *O'Donovan v. The Attorney General* (Case No. 70). The Oireachtas passed the *Electoral (Amendment) Bill, 1961* which revised the constituencies. The 1956 census figures were used notwithstanding that the census of 1961 was nearing completion. Pursuant to Art. 26.1.1°, the President referred the Bill to the Supreme Court.

The Supreme Court held, in advising the President that the Bill was constitutional, that the constitutional requirement that the constituencies must be revised every 12 years having regard to the population as ascertained at the last preceding census means the last preceding completed census. The Constitution recognised that an exact parity in the ratio between members of Dáil Éireann and the population of each constituency is not required. What was practicable was a matter primarily for the Oireachtas. The Court would not lay down a figure above or below which a deviation from the national average would not be permitted but it reserved the right to interfere where the divergences from the national average were such as to indicate that the requirements of the Constitution had been ignored.

Case No. 5

Article 26 and the Emergency Powers Bill, 1976

Invoking Art. 28.3.3° of the Constitution, the Houses of the Oireachtas on 1 September 1976 passed a resolution that arising out of the armed conflict taking place in Northern Ireland a national emergency existed affecting the vital interests of the State. On 16 September the *Emergency Powers Bill, 1976* was passed, which was stated to be 'for the purpose of securing the public safety and the preservation of the State in time of armed conflict'. Its only purpose was to permit detention without charge for a period of seven days. Pursuant to Art. 26.1.1°, the President referred the Bill to the Supreme Court.

The Supreme Court held, in advising the President that the Bill was constitutional, that once it had been established that the procedural requirements affecting a Bill to which Art. 28.3.3° applied had been satisfied the provisions of that sub-article prevented any part of the Constitution being invoked to invalidate such Bill. There was a presumption that the facts stated in the resolution were correct and such presumption had not been displaced. Therefore no part of the Bill could be declared repugnant to the Constitution.

Case No. 6

Article 26 and the Housing (Private Rented Dwellings) Bill, 1981

The *Rent Restrictions Act, 1960* had been declared unconstitutional in *Blake v. The Attorney General* (Case No. 13) and to deal with the resulting situation this Bill was passed. It provided a measure of security for the tenants of certain dwellings, a reasonable return for landlords and for the eventual termination of the tenants' possession of such dwellings. The District Court could determine the gross rent which was defined as the rent which a willing lessee not already in occupation would give and a willing lessor would take for the dwelling. S.9 provided that tenants, from the years 1982 to 1985, would only be required to pay a proportion of the difference between the rent payable when the Act came into operation and the rent fixed by the District Court. Pursuant to Art. 26.1.1°, the President referred the Bill to the Supreme Court.

The Supreme Court held, in advising the President that the Bill was unconstitutional, that the effect of the rebates permitted by s.9, whereby landlords were to receive an amount which was less than the just and proper rent was, in the absence of any constitutionally permitted justification, an unjust attack on property right contrary to Art. 40.3.2° of the Constitution.

Case No. 7

Article 26 and the Offences Against the State (Amendment) Bill, 1940

In *The State (Burke) v. Lennon* (Case No. 86) the High Court declared s.55 of the *Offences Against the State Act, 1939* unconstitutional. Resulting from this decision this Bill was passed. S.4 provided that whenever a Minister of State is of opinion that any particular person is engaged in activities which are prejudicial to the preservation of public peace and order, or to the security of the State, he may by warrant order the arrest and detention of such person. Pursuant to Art. 26.1.1°, the President referred the Bill to the Supreme Court.

The Supreme Court, by a majority, held, in advising the President that the Bill was constitutional, that this power given to a Minister was not a power to administer justice and did not contravene Art. 34 of the Constitution which provides that justice must be administered in courts. This detention is not in the nature of a punishment but of preventive justice, being a precautionary measure taken for the purposes of preserving the public peace and order and security of the State. It did not contravene Art. 38 of the Constitution which provides that no person be tried on any criminal charge save in due course of law.

Article 26 and the School Attendance Bill, 1942

The School Attendance Bill had as its purpose the further and better provision for ensuring school attendance by children to whom the *School Attendance Act, 1926* applied. S.4 provided that a child was not deemed to be receiving suitable education in a manner other than by attending certain schools unless such education, and the manner in which such child is receiving it, had been certified by the Minister for Education to be suitable. Pursuant to Art. 26.1.1°, the President referred s.4 of the Bill to the Supreme Court.

The Supreme Court held, in advising the President that s.4 of the Bill was unconstitutional, that the Minister might require a higher standard of education than could properly be prescribed as a minimum standard under Art. 42.3.2° of the Constitution. The standard contemplated by s.4 might vary from child to child and accordingly was not such a standard of general application as the Constitution contemplated. The requirement as to the manner in which a child was receiving education was not warranted by the Constitution.

Case No. 9

Attorney General v. Southern Industrial Trust
94 I.L.T.R. 161

The defendants financed the purchase of a car on hire-purchase. The hirer exported the car and on re-importation it was seized by the customs. When the Attorney General brought proceedings to forfeit the car it was alleged by the defendant that the *Customs (Temporary Provisions) Act, 1945* was contrary to the Constitution in so far as it purported to authorise the forfeiture of the goods of an innocent party.

It was held by the Supreme Court that the common good at times required that an innocent person's goods or property be forfeited to the State and in such cases the provisions of the Constitution are not violated.

Case No. 10.

Bank of Ireland v. Caffin

The testator married in England in 1928, and in 1956 an English court granted a divorce. The testator came to Ireland and married. He died in 1970 leaving no issue of either marriage. The question arose as to who was the spouse for the purposes of the *Succession Act, 1965* which provides that if a testator leaves a spouse and no children the spouse has a right to one half of the estate.

The High Court held that in 1921 the courts in Ireland applied the common law rule which recognised the validity of a decree of divorce *a vinculo* pronounced by a court of a foreign country in which the parties were domiciled. That rule continued in force, it not being inconsistent with the Constitution of the Irish Free State or the Constitution of Ireland. Accordingly the wife of the marriage celebrated in Ireland was the spouse for the purposes of the Act.

Case No. 11

Beamish and Crawford Ltd. v. Crowley

The plaintiffs were brewers in Cork and owned the defendant's licensed premises. It was a term of the tenancy that the licensee sell only alcohol supplied by the brewers. An injunction was sought to prevent the licensee breaching the tenancy. In his defence he alleged that the alcohol supplied was not of merchantable quality. The plaintiffs served notice that the trial be held in Dublin rather than Cork and the defendant objected.

The Supreme Court held, in directing the trial be held in Cork, that the possibility of adverse publicity was not to be taken into consideration since the Constitution provided, apart from certain exceptions, that publicity was inseparable from the administration of justice.

Case No. 12

In re Blake, deceased

The testator bequeathed a legacy in trust towards the maintenance and education of the children of his daughter provided they were reared as Roman Catholics.

The High Court held that the condition on which the trust legacy was given was void as against the policy of the law. It was an attempt to restrict the right and duty of parents to educate their children as declared in Art. 42 of the Constitution.

Case No. 13

Blake v. Attorney General

The plaintiff was the landlord of premises to which the *Rent Restrictions*

(Amendment) Act, 1960, as amended, applied. These statutes restricted any increase in the rent and restricted the recovery of 'controlled dwellings'. The plaintiff claimed these provisions constituted an unjust attack on his property rights contrary to Art. 40.3.2° of the Constitution.

The Supreme Court, finding these provisions unconstitutional, held that the prohibition on increases in rent was a restriction of the property rights of one group of citizens for the benefit of another group of citizens which was done without compensation and without regard to the financial capacity, or the financial needs, of either group. The legislation gave no opportunity for review and provided no limitation on the period of restriction. The restriction on the landlord's right to recover possession of controlled dwellings was also condemned.

Case No. 14

Boland v. An Taoiseach

In December 1973 a conference was held between the Irish and British Governments. In an issued communiqué the Irish Government fully accepted and solemnly declared that there could be no change in the status of Northern Ireland until a majority of the people of Northern Ireland desired a change in such status. A formal agreement, incorporating this statement, was to be signed later and registered at the United Nations. The plaintiff sought an injunction to restrain the Government from implementing any part of the communiqué and from entering into any agreement which would, he claimed, limit the exercise of sovereignty over any portion of the national territory, or which would prejudice the right of the Oireachtas and Government of Ireland in exercising jurisdiction over the whole of the national territory.

The Supreme Court, in refusing the injunction, held that this declaration of the Government owed its existence to an exercise of the executive power of government and that therefore the Courts had no power under the Constitution to review the conduct or policy of the Government.

Case No. 15

Brendan Dunne Ltd. v. Fitzpatrick

The plaintiffs carried on business and agreed with their staff to open late on occasional evenings. Members of a trade union, objecting to the late openings, picketed the premises and paraded in an adjacent street with placards. An injunction to prevent the picketing was sought. The union members relied on Art. 40.6.1° of the Constitution.

151

The High Court, though deciding the case on other grounds, held that the action in parading around with placards was not protected by Art. 40.6.1° because the rights of expressing freely convictions and opinions could only be exercised subject to there being no risk of a breach of the public peace.

Case No. 16

Brennan v. Attorney General

The plaintiff owned a farm which had a rateable valuation of £73. This valuation was made under the *Valuation Acts 1852-1864* and was made by reference to an estimate of the net annual value which itself was estimated by reference to the average price of certain crops in the years 1849-1852. Once the valuation was made it could not be altered. The amount of the valuation determines the liability for various taxes. The plaintiff claimed this method of valuation was unconstitutional.

The High Court, in upholding the plaintiff's claim, held that the system was hopelessly outdated and unreliable as a guide to the present values of farms, and because there was no method of revaluation these statutes did not respect the plaintiff's property rights under Art. 40.3 or afford him equality before the law guaranteed under Art. 40.1 of the Constitution.

Case No. 17

Buckley v. Attorney General

Unable to determine who were entitled to certain monies, the trustees of Sinn Féin lodged it in the High Court. The plaintiff brought an action seeking payment of these monies. While the action was pending in the High Court, the Oireachtas passed the *Sinn Féin Funds Act, 1947.* S.10 provided that the action should be stayed, and that the High Court, if an application was made on behalf of the Attorney General, should make an order dismissing the action and direct the monies be disposed of in the manner laid down by the Act.

The Supreme Court declared s.10 unconstitutional as being an unwarrantable interference by the Oireachtas with the operation of the Courts in a purely judicial domain. Other sections infringed Art. 43 because they interfered with the right to private property. While the Oireachtas may delimit these rights when the exigencies of the common good so require, it was open to the Courts to review the decision of the Oireachtas in this regard.

Case No. 18

Burke v. Burke

The testatrix left property on trust for the maintenance, education in Ireland and the upbringing as a Roman Catholic of a named infant. The selection of a Roman Catholic school to be attended by the infant was in the absolute discretion of the trustees.

The High Court held that the direction regarding the selection of the school was null and void since it abrogated parental authority and the right and duty of education declared in Art. 42 of the Constitution.

Case No. 19

Byrne v. Ireland

The plaintiff was injured by reason of a subsidence of the footpath where a trench had been excavated and refilled by persons employed in the Department of Posts and Telegraphs. An action was brought against 'Ireland' and the Attorney General alleging negligence.

The Supreme Court by a majority held that the former immunity from action enjoyed by the Crown did not exist in Ireland after 1922 and therefore was not continued by the Constitution of Ireland. The State is a juristic person vicariously liable for the wrongful acts of its servants committed in the course of their employment.

Case No. 20

Cahill v. Sutton

The plaintiff in April 1972 sued the defendant, a medical doctor, for damages for personal injuries that had occurred in March 1968. The defendant pleaded this action was barred by the *Statute of Limitations, 1957* because it had been commenced after the expiration of 3 years from the date on which the action occurred. The plaintiff then challenged the constitutionality of the section on the ground that it contained no exception in favour of an injured person who did not become aware of the facts on which his claim was based until after the expiration of the limitation period or until a short time before its expiration.

The Supreme Court held that the plaintiff failed to establish the *locus standi* necessary to invoke the jurisdiction of the Court since it was admitted that the plaintiff had known all material facts in 1968. The challenge was based solely on the absence of statutory provisions which, if present,

153

would not be applicable. Therefore no right of the plaintiff had been infringed or was threatened by the absence of such provision.

Case No. 21

Central Dublin Development Association v. Attorney General

The *Local Government (Planning and Development) Act, 1963* makes provision, in the interests of the common good, for the proper planning and development of cities, towns and other areas. Planning authorities are obliged to make plans for their areas and permission is necessary for any development. The plaintiffs challenged the Act on the grounds that it constituted an unjust attack on the right to private property and that some of the powers given to the Minister for Local Government were judicial in nature.

The High Court, in finding the Act constitutional, held that there was no attack on property rights because where the planning authority held an opinion the High Court had jurisdiction to inquire whether such opinion was held on reasonable grounds and that the High Court could review the decision of the Minister if he acted on a wrong view of the law or if the rules of natural justice were not observed. The powers given to the Minister were not an administration of justice but decisions of policy in planning matters.

Case No. 22

Cityview Press Ltd. v. An Chomhairle Oiliúna

An Chomhairle Oiliúna was established by the *Industrial Training Authority Act, 1967* for the better training of persons in industry. S.21 empowered the authority, for the purposes of meeting its expenses, to impose a levy on employers in designated industries. A levy, which amounted to £400, was made on the plaintiffs, an employer in the printing industry. The section was challenged because it was a delegation of legislative power to an executive body, which was not permitted by the Constitution.

The Supreme Court held that s.21 was not an unlawful delegation of legislative power in contravention of Art. 15 of the Constitution, because the section contained a clear declaration of the policy of the Oireachtas and provided each House of the Oireachtas with an opportunity to annul a levy order.

Case No. 23

In re Clark, Philip

The *Mental Treatment Act, 1945,* s.165, provides that where a Gárda is of opinion that a person of unsound mind should be placed under care and control, he may take such person into custody and apply to the authorised medical officer for his reception into the appropriate mental hospital. The applicant was taken into custody and detained in a mental hospital. He challenged the section as being contrary to Art. 40 of the Constitution because there was no judicial intervention between his arrest and subsequent detention.

The Supreme Court, in upholding the constitutionality of the section, held that it was of a paternal character designed for the protection of the citizen and the promotion of the common good. The examination by responsible medical officers with the least possible delay satisfied every reasonable requirement.

Case No. 24

Condon v. The Minister for Labour

The plaintiff was a member of an association of bank officials who refused to be bound by the terms of voluntary national wage agreements. The association concluded a separate agreement with the banks. The *Regulations of Banks (Remuneration and Conditions of Employment) (Temporary Provisions) Act, 1975* was passed. This Act could be brought into effect, and expire, by order of the Minister for Labour. When the Minister activated. the Act he made an order prohibiting the payment by the banks of the increases of remuneration. The plaintiff challenged the Act as being contrary to Art. 34, 40 and 43 of the Constitution. While the action was pending the Act expired due to ministerial order, and at the trial it was argued that the claim disclosed no cause of action, owing to the expiration of the Act.

The Supreme Court held that where at the commencement of an action the plaintiff has a cause of action based on the validity of a statute, the expiry of the statute before the hearing of the action does not affect the exercise of the High Court of its constitutional power to review the statute unless the Court is satisfied that a similar statute will not be introduced again.

Case No. 25

Conroy v. Attorney General

The plaintiff was charged with the summary offence of drunken driving contrary to s.49 of the *Road Traffic Act, 1961*. The penalty, on conviction, was imprisonment not exceeding six months, and/or a fine not exceeding £100, and the disqualification from holding a driving licence for a specified period. The plaintiff claimed that s.49 did not create a minor offence but was one which must be tried by jury in accordance with Art. 38 of the Constitution.

The Supreme Court held that the offence of drunken driving was a minor offence and could be tried in a summary manner without a jury. The punishment was not so severe as to exclude it from the category of minor offences. The disqualification was not in the nature of a punishment but the withdrawal of a right granted by the Act.

Case No. 26

Cook v. Carroll

A priest interviewed together a girl parishioner who alleged she had been seduced and the parishioner whom she held responsible. An action for seduction was brought by the girl's mother against the parishioner. The priest, when called to give evidence of what passed at the interview, refused and claimed privilege.

The High Court held that the priest's refusal was not contempt of court because in the light of the Constitution and the special place given to the religion which was adhered to by the majority of the people, communications made in confidence to a priest in a private consultation between him and certain of his parishioners was privileged.

Case No. 27

Cosgrove v. Ireland

The marriage of the plaintiff and a Dutch-born woman deteriorated and the wife requested him to sign forms consenting to the issue of passports to their two young children. He refused and so notified the Department of Foreign Affairs. Nonetheless the passports were issued and the wife took the children to Holland where they remained. The plaintiff claimed that his rights under Art. 40, 41 and 42 of the Constitution and under the *Guardianship of Infants Act, 1964* had been infringed and claimed damages.

The High Court held that the Department, having notice of the plaintiff's objection, should not have issued the passports without an application to the court having been made by the wife. The Department was responsible, with the wife, for her failure to obtain the consent of the court to sole custody. It was not necessary to consider whether the failure to see that the requirements of the 1964 Act, which stated that the father and mother of a child were the joint guardians, were observed, incidentally caused the violation of any of the plaintiff's constitutional rights. The court awarded £1,250 to compensate for expenses incurred and for the mental distress suffered.

Case No. 28

Cowan v. Attorney General

An election petition to have the plaintiff's election to a local authority quashed was brought on the ground that he was disqualified by law because he was at the time an undischarged bankrupt. The High Court assigned a practising barrister to be the election court to try the petition. The plaintiff claimed that the relevant statutory provisions infringed Art. 37 of the Constitution.

The High Court, in declaring the sections unconstitutional, held that the election court was not exercising limited powers and functions because it might make findings which would affect in the most profound and far-reaching way the lives, liberties, fortunes and reputation of those against whom they were exercised. Also, because it might have to exercise criminal jurisdiction, it violated Art. 37 of the Constitution.

Case No. 29

Crowley v. Ireland

All the teachers save one, of three national schools in a parish, withdrew their services because of a dispute. The Department of Education arranged buses to bring children affected by the dispute to and from their homes and schools in neighbouring parishes. The plaintiff, a school-child affected by the dispute, was dissatisfied with these alternative arrangements and sought an order directing the provision of free primary education within the parish in accordance with Art. 42.4 of the Constitution.

The Supreme Court held that Art. 42.4 conferred on the plaintiff a right to receive free primary education but the obligation on the State was to 'provide for' such education and not to supply it. The evidence established that the State had not failed in its duty.

157

Case No. 30

Cullen v. Attorney General

The *Road Traffic Act, 1961* created the summary offence of driving without insurance. On conviction, s.57 empowered the court, in addition to any other punishment, to fine the defendant a sum of damages which were paid to the injured party. The plaintiff was convicted of driving without insurance and the court awarded the injured party £606. He challenged s.57 because the offence it created was not a minor one within the provisions of Art. 38 of the Constitution.

The High Court held s.57 invalid because there was no limit to the amount of the damages which could be imposed. It was therefore not a minor offence which could be tried by a court of summary jurisdiction.

Case No. 31

Deaton v. Attorney General

The plaintiff was charged with offences contrary to s.186 of the *Customs (Consolidation) Act, 1876.* The section empowered the Revenue Commissioners to elect between alternative penalties; either forfeiture of treble the value of the goods, including the duty payable thereon, or £100.

The Supreme Court held that the selection of punishment is an integral part of the administration of justice and as such cannot be committed to the hands of the executive as s.186 purported to do.

Case No. 32

de Búrca v. Attorney General

A list of jurors prepared under the *Juries Act, 1927* consisted of the names of ratepayers in a district. These were persons aged between 21 and 65 years who had land having a rateable valuation in excess of a prescribed minimum. Women were exempt but could, if they otherwise qualified, apply for inclusion in the list. The plaintiff was returned for trial by jury on criminal charges and before the trial she challenged the Act as being unconstitutional.

The Supreme Court held that the exclusion of citizens who were not ratepayers from a jurors list was an invidious discrimination and offended Art. 40.1 of the Constitution; also a jury drawn from a panel so formed is one which offends Art. 38.5 by reason of its lack of representativeness. The conditional exclusion of women, which was based on sex alone, was an invidious discrimination and the virtual elimination of women from jury service resulted in a similar unrepresentativeness.

Case No. 33

Dillane v. Ireland

The plaintiff appeared in the District Court on road traffic offences. When the prosecuting Gárda withdrew the summonses, the plaintiff applied for his costs but was refused them. Rule 67 of the District Court Rules, 1948 states that a District Justice has a general power to award costs and witnesses' expenses against any party to proceedings but he may not make such award, *inter alia,* against a member of the Gárda Síochána acting in discharge of his duties as a police officer. The plaintiff challenged the constitutionality of this Rule.

The Supreme Court held that the discrimination in favour of a member of the Gárda Síochána was justified under Art. 40 on the ground of social function. The Court rejected the claim that the Rule violated the plaintiff's right to property because the eligibility for costs could not be enumerated as one of his property rights.

Case No. 34

Dooley v. Attorney General

The *Prohibition of Forcible Entry and Occupation Act, 1971* provides that a person who forcibly enters land is guilty of an offence unless he is the owner or, if he is not the owner, he does not interfere with the use and enjoyment of the land, or he enters in pursuance of a *bona fide* claim of right. Owner is defined as the lawful occupier, or every person lawfully entitled to the immediate use and enjoyment of unoccupied land, or any person having an estate or interest in the land. The plaintiff on being charged with an offence brought an action claiming that some sections of the Act contravened Art. 40 of the Constitution.

The Supreme Court, in rejecting the claim, held that the sections did not invidiously discriminate between owners and landless persons contrary to Art. 40.1 of the Constitution because the exclusion of the owner from the application of these sections only excludes the person in lawful occupation or the persons entitled to the occupation. All other persons, whether having an estate or interest in the land or not having such interest, were amenable to these sections.

Case No. 35

East Donegal Co-operative v. Attorney General

The *Livestock Marts Act, 1967* made the selling of livestock by auction an offence unless a licence had been granted by the Minister for Agriculture. S.3 enabled the Minister to grant or refuse a licence at his discretion, to attach conditions, and to revoke a licence if the holder was guilty of an offence under the Act. S.4 enabled the Minister to exempt from the provisions of the Act the conduct of any particular business or business of any particular class. The plaintiffs challenged these sections.

The Supreme Court held s.3 constitutional because it must be presumed that all proceedings, procedures, discretions and adjudications which were permitted by the Act were intended by the Oireachtas to be conducted in accordance with the principles of constitutional justice which require that the Minister should consider every case on its merits, that he should consider the submissions of any applicant or licensee, and that an opportunity be given to controvert any case that was made in favour of the course that the Minister intended to adopt. The Supreme Court held s.4 unconstitutional because the power of the Oireachtas under Art. 40.1 of the Constitution to have due regard to the differences of capacity and social function in its legislation could not be delegated to a Minister of State so as to enable him to exempt a particular individual from the operation of the Act.

Case No. 36

Educational Company of Ireland v. Fitzpatrick

Some employees of the company were trade union members and others were not. The trade union members failed to persuade the others to join a union. They then endeavoured to force the company to compel these employees, by the threat of dismissal if necessary, to join a union. When this failed the union members withdrew their labour and picketed the company's premises. The company sought an injunction to prevent the picketing.

The Supreme Court held that while there was a trade dispute in existence, the provisions of the *Trade Disputes Act, 1906* could not be used to coerce persons to join a trade union against their will. The picketing was therefore unlawful.

Case No. 37

Fisher v. Irish Land Commission

The plaintiff was the yearly tenant of an extensive holding vested in the Land Commission. When the Commission took steps to resume the holding, with compensation, the plaintiff challenged the constitutionality of that procedure.

The Supreme Court held that the provisions of the *Land Act, 1923*, which authorised the resumption for specific purposes of holdings vested in the Land Commission, was a purely administrative act, and while all concerned where bound to act judicially, they were not administering justice contrary to Art. 34 of the Constitution.

Case No. 38

Foley v. Irish Land Commission

The plaintiff signed an agreement with the Land Commission for the purchase of certain lands, and a dwelling house was built on the land. The Commission, on learning that the plaintiff had not taken up permanent residence in the dwelling house, warned that unless he did so they would consider retaking the land from him. The plaintiff failed to take up residence, so the Commission demanded possession. The plaintiff then tested the constitutionality of s.2 of the *Land Act, 1923* which permitted the direction of the Land Commission as to residence.

The Supreme Court, in upholding the section, held that the condition as to residence was not an abolition of private property within the meaning of Art. 43.1.2°, but a delimitation of these rights with a view to reconciling their existence with the exigencies of the common good and in accordance with the principles of social justice set out in Art. 43.2 of the Constitution.

Case No. 39

In re Frost, infants

The husband, a Protestant, married the wife, a Roman Catholic. Prior to the marriage he signed an undertaking that their children, of which there were 5, should be reared as Roman Catholics. With the exception of the youngest, the children were baptised as Roman Catholics. As a result of differences the parties separated. By agreement the children under 8 years remained with the mother until that age and meantime they were to be reared as Protestants. The older children remained with the father and he placed them in a Protestant home. Later, because of economic difficulties the mother handed the younger children to the father and he placed them in the same home. The father died and the mother sought custody of all the children.

161

The Supreme Court held that the common law principles had not been altered by Art. 41 and 42 of the Constitution. These provided that where the father is dead and the mother is living, the father's religion is that in which the children are to be reared unless the father's right is displaced by consideration of the children's welfare. The father's right is not abrogated by an ante-nuptial agreement to the contrary with the mother. The question was whether the welfare of the children required that the father's wishes that they be educated as Protestants be disregarded. The answer was no and as the father's wishes would unquestionably be disregarded if the mother gained custody, her application was refused.

Case No. 40

G. v. An Bord Uchtála

The mother of an illegitimate child is the guardian of that child and every guardian is entitled to custody of the child. Proceedings may be taken by the guardian for the restoration of the child's custody. An adoption order cannot be made without the consent of the mother, which consent may be withdrawn at any time before the adoption order is made. Where a consent has been refused or withdrawn an applicant for an adoption order may apply to the High Court. The Court, under s.3 of the *Adoption Act, 1974,* may, if it is satisfied that it is in the best interest of the child so to do, make an order giving custody to the applicant and may authorise An Bord Uchtála (the Adoption Board) to dispense with consent. The plaintiff, an unmarried woman aged 21 years, gave birth to a daughter. While in hospital she was advised to place her child for adoption. She lived in a flat with three other girls and earned a modest salary. She was unable to care for the child, so when it was two months old she placed it with an adoption society and signed a consent. Later, when her parents agreed to help rear the child, the plaintiff withdrew her consent in writing. In the meantime the child had been placed with a married couple. The plaintiff issued proceedings to have her child restored to her and the married couple claimed an order dispensing with the consent of the plaintiff.

The Supreme Court held that the plaintiff had a natural right to the custody of her child, this right being a personal right under Art. 40.3 of the Constitution. It was not absolute because the child had a natural right to have its welfare safeguarded which was also a personal right within Art. 40.3. The test in deciding an application under s.3 of the 1974 Act was whether the mother had refused or withdrawn her consent capriciously or irresponsibly, or whether the welfare of the child overwhelmingly demanded that an order under the section be made. In finding for the plaintiff the Court held that the welfare of the child did not require overwhelmingly that she should remain in the custody of the married

162

couple and that the plaintiff's consent had not been withdrawn capriciously or irresponsibly.

Case No. 41

In re Haughey

Dáil Éireann ordered the Committee of Public Accounts to examine the expenditure of a certain grant-in-aid. The *Committee of Public Accounts of Dáil Éireann (Privileges and Procedure) Act, 1970* was passed. S.3 provided that, if any person being a witness before the Committee should refuse to answer any question to which the Committee might legally require an answer, the Committee might certify that fact to the High Court. The High Court could punish that person as if he had been guilty of contempt of the High Court. The applicant was called by the Committee as a witness. He made a statement and refused to answer any questions because hearsay evidence containing serious allegations had been made against him by another witness. The Committee certified an offence had been committed and the High Court sentenced him to six months' imprisonment.

On appeal the Supreme Court quashed the conviction. The offence created by the Act was not the offence of contempt of court but an ordinary criminal offence. By reason of the unlimited nature of the penalty authorised it was not a minor offence within Art. 38.2 of the Constitution and must be tried by a jury.

Case No. 42

King v. Attorney General

One of the offences created by s.4 of the *Vagrancy Act, 1824* was that of intent to commit a felony when the person in question, being a suspected person or reputed thief, loitered in a public place. The *Prevention of Crimes Act, 1871* provided that in proving the intent it was not necessary to show that the person suspected was guilty of any particular act or acts and that his known character could be proved. The plaintiff was convicted of this offence and challenged these provisions.

The Supreme Court held that the offence conflicted with Art. 38.1 of the Constitution because it allowed evidence of the known character of a person to be used in proving guilt of another offence, which was contrary to our concept of justice. It offended Art. 40.1 because a suspected person could be prevented from doing what was perfectly lawful for other citizens to do, namely to walk slowly, dawdle or stop in a public place.

163

Case No. 43

Landers v. Attorney General

An 8-year-old boy, with an exceptional singing voice, was offered large sums of money to perform publicly. The family, after providing certain safeguards, agreed. Some engagements were performed on licensed premises and the father, convicted of allowing a child under the age of 14 years to perform on licensed premises, challenged the constitutionality of s.2 of the *Prevention of Cruelty to Children Act, 1904.*

It was held by the High Court in dismissing the claim that the purpose of the statute was the protection of children of tender years from exploitation and was not an attack upon the right to choose a career contained in Art. 40.3, or upon Art. 41 because public appearances were outside the scope of family authority; and because the prevention of the exploitation of young children was for the common good, it was not an attack on property rights.

Case No. 44

Loftus v. Attorney General

The *Electoral Act, 1963,* s.13, states that the Registrar of Political Parties shall register any political party which applies to him for registration and which is a genuine political party organised to contest a Dáil or local election. The effect of registration enables the name of the candidate's party to be inserted after the candidate's name on the ballot paper. Otherwise a candidate may have the words 'Non-Party' inserted. The plaintiff's application to have his political party registered was rejected and he challenged this section as to its constitutionality.

The Supreme Court held that the right to have a political party registered was not a personal right within Art. 40.3 of the Constitution. The prevention of the name of a candidate's party from appearing on the ballot paper did not infringe the citizen's right of association guaranteed by Art. 40.6.1°. The discrimination made by the Act, which allowed automatic registration to parties represented in Dáil Éireann when the Act was passed, was not an invidious discrimination contrary to Art. 40.1.

Case No. 45

M. v. An Bord Uchtála

The *Adoption Act, 1952* provided that an adoption order should not be made unless the applicants were of the same religion as the child and, if the child is illegitimate, the same religion as the mother. The plaintiffs were married, the husband being a Roman Catholic and the wife a member of the Church of England. The wife before the marriage had a child of which the husband was not the father. The child was then being reared as a Roman Catholic. The couple applied to adopt the child but their application was refused because the provisions regarding religion were not satisfied.

The High Court held these provisions contrary to Art. 44.2.3° of the Constitution because they imposed disabilities and made a discrimination on the ground of religious profession or belief.

Case No. 46

In re McAllister

The *Bankrupt and Insolvent (Ireland) Act, 1857* provided that it was lawful for a court in bankruptcy proceedings where a person does not fully answer any lawful question to commit him to prison, there to remain without bail, until he subjects himself to the court. During bankruptcy proceedings the High Court was asked to commit the applicant to prison. He objected on constitutional grounds contending that he was entitled to trial by jury under Art. 38.5 of the Constitution and that the Act purported to exclude from the High Court the power to grant bail.

The High Court, in committing the applicant to prison, held that the procedure was not the trial of a criminal charge. The words 'without bail' purported to exclude the jurisdiction of the High Court to grant bail and were inconsistent with Art. 34.3.1° of the Constitution.

Case No. 47

Macauley v. The Minister for Posts and Telegraphs

The *Ministers and Secretaries Act, 1924* provided that the fiat (permission) of the Attorney General had to be obtained before legal proceedings could be validly instituted in the High Court against a Minister of State. The plaintiff intended to commence proceedings against the defendant. The fiat was sought and while never formally rejected was not forthcoming. Having issued proceedings, a defence that the fiat had not been obtained was made.

The High Court held that Art. 40.3.1° of the Constitution implied a personal right in the citizen to have recourse to the High Court to assert and vindicate a legal right. Therefore the procedure of seeking a fiat was unconstitutional.

165

Case No. 48

In re MacCurtain

A Special Criminal Court was set up under Part V of the *Offences Against the State Act, 1939* which part was activated by a Government declaration under s.35 of the Act. The prosecutor was convicted by a Special Criminal Court of murder and sentenced to death. This Court sat in a military barracks and was composed of officers of the Defence Forces, each of whom was not below the rank of commandant. The prosecutor challenged the constitutionality of the Act.

The Supreme Court held that s.35 which authorised the Government to activate Part V was not contrary to Art. 38.3.1° of the Constitution. Notwithstanding that all the members of the Court were military officers, that Court was not a military tribunal within the meaning of Art. 38.4.

Case No. 49

McDonald v. Bord na gCon

The *Greyhound Industry Act, 1957* empowered Bord na gCon, under s.47, to exclude a person from being on any greyhound track or at any public sale of greyhounds. The plaintiff appeared to alter a material document and was summoned to a meeting of the Committee which investigated the charge. An exclusion order was made and the plaintiff challenged the constitutionality of s.47.

The Supreme Court held, in dismissing the claim, that the Committee was not administering justice contrary to Art. 37 of the Constitution.

Case No. 50

McGee v. Attorney General

The *Criminal Law (Amendment) Act, 1935,* s.17, prohibited the sale or importation for sale of artificial contraceptives. The plaintiff attempted to import contraceptives but these were seized by the customs. She was a married woman with 4 children and had been informed by her doctor that another pregnancy would have serious results and would put her life at risk. She challenged s.17 as to its constitutionality.

The Supreme Court held s.17 was an unjustified invasion of the plaintiff's personal right to privacy in her marital affairs contrary to Art. 40.3.1° of the Constitution.

Case No. 51

In re McGrath and Harte

In pursuance of Art. 51 which provided that the Constitution, except certain Articles including Art. 51, could be amended by the Oireachtas within a period of 3 years after the date on which the first President entered into office, the *First Amendment of the Constitution Act, 1939* was passed. It altered Art. 28.3 of the Constitution. A Military Court was eastablished under the *Emergency Powers (Amendment) Act, 1940,* which permitted the trial of persons charged with certain offences. The prosecutors were convicted of murder and challenged the constitutionality of various matters.

The Supreme Court held that the amendment of the Constitution had been within the powers of the Oireachtas. The provisions of Art. 25.2.1° which provided that the President not sign a Bill until the lapse of five days does not apply to a Bill to amend the Constitution. It was not necessary to recite the resolution declaring a state of emergency in a statute provided the statute was expressed to be for the purpose of securing the public safety and the preservation of the State in time of war.

Case No. 52

McMahon v. Attorney General

Art. 16.1.4° of the Constitution provides that the voting at Dáil Éireann elections must be by secret ballot. The procedure according to the *Electoral Act, 1923* was that the voter's number on the register of electors was marked on the counterfoil of the ballot paper immediately before that paper was delivered to the voter. The counterfoil and ballot paper contained an identical number. The plaintiff challenged this procedure.

The Supreme Court held, in finding for the plaintiff, that the words 'secret ballot' meant a ballot which is completely and inviolably secret.

Case No. 53

Maher v. Attorney General

The plaintiff was charged with drunken driving, and in the course of the trial the prosecution produced a certificate which, by virtue of the *Road Traffic Act, 1968,* s.44, was deemed conclusive evidence of the amount of alcohol in the blood at the time the specimen of blood was taken. He was convicted and challenged the constitutionality of s.44.

It was held by the Supreme Court that by giving the certificate this quality of evidential conclusiveness the Oireachtas has invalidly impinged upon the exercise of the judicial power and therefore s.44 was invalid.

Case No. 54

Mayo-Perrott v. Mayo-Perrott

The plaintiff obtained against the defendant in England a decree of divorce *a vinculo matrimonii* and an order for costs. The defendant having come to reside in Ireland, the plaintiff sought judgment for the costs in the High Court.

The Supreme Court held that the public policy of this country as reflected in the Constitution did not favour divorce *a vinculo* and because the order for costs was not severable from the divorce the action was dismissed. Our courts would not give assistance to the process of divorce by entertaining an action for the costs of such proceedings.

Case No. 55

Melling v. Ó Mathghamhna

The plaintiff was charged with the summary offence of smuggling. The Revenue Commissioners, under s.186 of the *Customs Consolidation Act, 1876* elected to press for a penalty of £100. The plaintiff claimed that this offence was not a minor one and could only be tried by a jury.

The Supreme Court held that this smuggling offence was a minor one which could be tried summarily under Art. 38.2 of the Constitution.

Case No. 56

Meskell v. C.I.E.

The company agreed, following negotiations with four unions, to terminate the employment contracts of some of their employees and to offer each employee immediate re-employment on the same terms if each agreed. As a special and additional term the employee must be at all times a member of one of the four trade unions. The plaintiff's contract was terminated by the company and he was not re-employed as he refused to accept the special condition. At his dismissal the plaintiff had been employed by the company for fifteen years and had been a member of one of the four unions. The plaintiff sued the company for damages for breaching his constitutional rights.

168

The Supreme Court, in finding for the plaintiff, held that this attempt to coerce the plaintiff into abandoning his constitutional right of dissociation was a violation of the Constitution.

Case No. 57

Moynihan v. Greensmyth

The *Civil Liability Act, 1961,* s.9 provides that proceedings cannot be commenced against the estate of a deceased person unless begun within a 2-year period of his death. In August 1966 a motor car driven by the deceased, in which the plaintiff was a passenger, collided with a bridge and as a result the deceased was killed. In August 1969 the plaintiff sued the deceased's estate for negligence and when the defence pleaded that the action was barred by s.9, the plaintiff challenged its constitutionality.

The Supreme Court held there was no failure to protect from unjust attack the property rights of the plaintiff, guaranteed by Art. $40.3.2^{\circ}$ of the Constitution, because of the State's other duty to citizens interested in the early completion of the administration of the estates of deceased persons.

Case No. 58

Mulloy v. Minister for Education

The Minister for Education established a scheme for the payment of salary increments to secondary school teachers. Teaching service abroad by lay teachers was treated as teaching service under the scheme. The plaintiff was a priest and a secondary school teacher with teaching experience abroad. The Minister, in considering whether the plaintiff was qualified to receive incremental salary, ignored his teaching abroad.

The Supreme Court held that the rule restricting the scheme to lay secondary school teachers was repugnant to Art. $44.2.3^{\circ}$ of the Constitution wherein the State guaranteed not to make any discrimination on the ground of religious status.

Case No. 59

Murphy v. Dublin Corporation

The plaintiff owned land on which the Corporation made a compulsory purchase order. The plaintiff objected and a public inquiry was held. A report of this was made to the Minister for Local Government. The plaintiff issued proceedings to invalidate the purchase order and sought production of the report. The Minister refused on the ground of public policy and being contrary to the public interest.

The Supreme Court held that if the Minister's claim was based on executive privilege a conflict existed between the interests of the State in the exercise of the executive power of the State and the interest of the State in the administration of justice and that conflict had to be resolved by a decision of the High Court which was charged with the administration of justice under the Constitution.

Case No. 60

Murphy v. Stewart

The plaintiff wished to change trade unions. The second union, the Irish Transport & General Workers Union, was agreeable to accept his membership provided the first union, the National Union of Vehicle Builders had no objection, but it had. He claimed that the refusal of the N.U.V.B. to give consent to his transfer to the I.T.G.W.U. was an infringement of the right guaranteed by Art. 40.6.1° of the Constitution.

The Supreme Court held that the refusal of one union to consent to the plaintiff's transfer to another union was not an infringement of his right to form associations and unions.

Case No. 61

Murphy v. Attorney General

The plaintiffs, a married couple with one child, were teachers. They claimed that ss.192 to 198 of the *Income Tax Act, 1967,* which aggregated the wife's income with that of her husband's for the purpose of assessment to income tax, infringed Art. 40 and 41 of the Constitution.

The Supreme Court held the sections unconstitutional because the nature and potentially progressive extent of the burden created by them was a breach of the pledge by the State to guard with special care the institution of marriage. Art. 40.1 was not violated because the inequality for income tax between couples living together and married couples living apart was justified on the ground of social function.

170

Case No. 62

Murtagh Properties Ltd. v. Cleary

The plaintiffs were publicans and employed some part-time waitresses. The union representing bar waiters objected to the employment of women and its members picketed the plaintiffs' premises. The plaintiffs sought an injunction to prevent the picketing.

The High Court, in granting the injunction, held that although the picketing was in furtherance of a trade dispute it was unlawful because its purpose was to compel the plaintiffs to dismiss the bar waitresses in breach of the latters' personal right to earn a livelihood, which was enshrined in Art. 40.3 of the Constitution.

Case No. 63

National Union of Railwaymen v. Sullivan

Part III of the *Trade Union Act, 1941* established a trade union tribunal with power, on the application of any trade union claiming to organise a majority of the workmen of a particular class, to grant a determination that such union alone should have the right to organise workmen of that class. Where such determination is unrevoked no other union could accept as a new member any workmen of that class. The Irish Transport & General Workers Union applied to the tribunal but before the hearing the plaintiffs, a rival union claimed that Part III was unconstitutional.

The Supreme Court held that Part III of the Act, by purporting to deprive citizens of the choice of persons with whom they might associate, was at variance with the emphatic assertion in Art. 40.6.1° of the Constitution of the citizen's right to form associations and unions.

Case No. 64

Norris v. Attorney General

The *Offences Against the Person Act, 1861* and the *Criminal Law (Amendment) Act, 1885* provide for the criminalisation and punishment of certain sexual acts regarded as unnatural. The plaintiff, a homosexual, challenged their constitutionality.

The Supreme Court by a majority upheld these provisions. There was no invidious discrimination under Art. 40.1 because the legislature could prohibit certain sexual conduct between males while not prohibiting the same sexual conduct between females. Freedom of association under

171

Art. 40.6 was not infringed. Because of the Christian nature of the State, and on the ground that the deliberate practice of homosexuality was morally wrong and damaging to the health of the individual and the public and potentially harmful to the institution of marriage, there was, in such circumstances, no constitutional right to sexual privacy.

Case No. 65

Northampton County Council v. A.B.F.

An English local authority sought the return to its custody of a child who had been removed by its father from England and given to the defendant. Both parents were British citizens, had married and were domiciled in England where the child was born. The father took the child to Ireland because it was proposed to have her legally adopted, which was permissible in England but was against the father's wishes.

The High Court refused the order because to grant it would been a breach of Art. 41 of the Constitution which recognised the family as the natural, primary and fundamental group of society. It was inconceivable that, because of his British nationality, the father of the child could not rely on the recognition of the family for the purpose of enforcing his rights as the lawful father.

Case No. 66

O'Brien v. Bord na Mona

The *Turf Development Act, 1946* empowered Bord na Mona to acquire compulsorily certain lands. When the Board sought to acquire some land of the plaintiff, he challenged the constitutionality of the statute on the ground that the Board was acting judicially.

The Supreme Court held that the Board in making a decision to acquire land was not acting judicially but administratively because the purpose of the statute was to permit the acquisition of bogland for the common good.

Case No. 67

O'Brien v. Keogh

The *Statute of Limitations, 1957* provides that an action for negligence resulting in personal injury must be commenced within 3 years. S.49 permitted an infant to bring an action within 3 years of reaching his majority.

This exception did not apply if the infant was in the custody of a parent. The infant plaintiff suffered personal injuries in 1963 while in the custody of his parents. When in 1968 he brought an action the defendant claimed it was statute-barred and the plaintiff challenged the constitutionality of s.49.

The Supreme Court held that s.49 failed to protect and vindicate the personal rights of the plaintiff contrary to Art. 40.3.2° of the Constitution.

Case No. 68

O'Brien v. Manufacturing Engineering Co. Ltd.

The *Workmen's Compensation Act, 1934,* as amended, permitted a workman injured by his employer's negligence to claim compensation or to take court proceedings. If he claims compensation and wishes to sue he must generally do so within one year. The plaintiff was injured in 1963 and accepted compensation. On commencing court proceedings in 1966 the defence claimed the action was statute-barred and the plaintiff challenged the constitutionality of the statute.

The Supreme Court held that the statute did not discriminate against the plaintiff because it gave the advantage of drawing compensation while it gave time to take an action. The one-year period was not unreasonably short and did not offend Art. 40.1 of the Constitution.

Case No. 68a

O'Brien v. Stoutt

The deceased entered into a permanent relationship with a woman but could not be married because the woman already was married. There was a child of the relationship, which the deceased supported, maintained and educated. The deceased was survived by that daughter, with whom he lived, and by two sisters and a brother. He died intestate and the *Succession Act, 1965* provides that if an intestate dies, leaving neither spouse nor issue nor parents, the estate is to be distributed between his brothers and sisters equally.

It was held by the High Court that the expression 'issue' did not include illegitimate issue nor did Art. 40 of the Constitution confer any express right of inheritance on illegitimate issue. The provisions of the Act were not unconstitutional and a claim by the daughter failed.

173

Case No. 69

O'Byrne v. The Minister for Finance

A judge while in office paid income tax and surtax. The plaintiff, as executrix of his estate, claimed that these deductions were contrary to Art. 35.5 of the Constitution.

The Supreme Court held that the purpose of Art. 35.5 was to safeguard the independence of the judiciary from the control of the executive and not to exempt the remuneration of judges from taxation common to all citizens. To require a judge to pay taxes on his income on the same basis as other citizens could not be said to be an attack upon his independence.

Case No. 70

O'Donovan v. Attorney General

The *Electoral (Amendment) Act, 1959* purported to revise the constituencies and the number of members to be returned to Dáil Éireann from each such constituency. The plaintiff claimed the Act was unconstitutional.

The High Court held that the Act offended Art. 16.2.3° because it departed substantially from the ratio of members of Dáil Éireann to the population, thus causing grave inequalities of representation for which no justification or genuine administrative difficulty existed. It offended Art. 16.2.4° because when revising the constituencies the legislature did not have due regard to the changes in the distribution of the population.

Case No. 71

In re O'Farrell

The *Solicitors Act, 1954* empowered a disciplinary committee of the Incorporated Law Society, on hearing a complaint against a solicitor, to strike his name off the roll of solicitors. On being struck off, the plaintiff challenged the constitutionality of this power.

The Supreme Court held that the power to strike a solicitor off the roll of solicitors is an administration of justice. The infliction of such a severe penalty is a matter which calls for the exercise of the judicial power of the State. To entrust this power to persons other than judges is an interference with the proper administration of justice which is reserved to courts established under the Constitution.

Case No. 72

In re Ó Láighléis

The applicant was arrested and interned without trial under s.4 of the *Offences Against the State (Amendment) Act, 1940.* He claimed his detention was unlawful because it offended the European Convention on Human Rights.

The Supreme Court held that the Convention was not part of the domestic law of the State because the Oireachtas, in accordance with Art. 29.6 of the Constitution, had not determined that the Convention be part of the domestic law. The primacy of domestic legislation was not displaced by the State becoming a party to the Convention nor was the executive estopped in the courts from relying on the domestic law.

Case No. 73

The People (Attorney General) v. Conmey

The appellant was convicted in the Central Criminal Court, which is the High Court dealing with criminal matters, and appealed to the Court of Criminal Appeal, which dismissed his appeal. He then appealed to the Supreme Court and raised the question as to whether an appeal lay from the Central Criminal Court directly to the Supreme Court.

The Supreme Court held that by virtue of Art. 34.4.3° of the Constitution the Supreme Court had appellate jurisdiction from all decisions of the High Court unless prohibited by statute law. No law prevented an appeal from the Central Criminal Court but in this instance no appeal lay, because the appellant had already appealed to the Court of Criminal Appeal.

Case No. 74

The People (Attorney General) v. O'Brien

Members of the Gárda Síochána, on foot of a search warrant which contained the incorrect address, raided the home of the appellant. On conviction he appealed on the ground that the production at his trial of property found at his home should not have been allowed because it was obtained without a valid search warrant in violation of Art. 40.5 of the Constitution.

The Supreme Court dismissed the appeal. The mistake in the warrant was an oversight. Had the evidence been obtained as the result of a deliberate and conscious violation of the constitutional rights of the appellant it would have had to be excluded in the absence of extraordinary excusing circumstances.

Case No. 75

The People (Attorney General) v. O'Callaghan

The applicant was returned for trial on various charges. He was refused bail because it was claimed he would interfere with witnesses.

The Supreme Court in granting bail held that bail cannot be refused merely because there is the likelihood of the commission of further offences while on bail. To do so would be a form of preventive justice unknown to our legal system.

Case No. 76

The People (Director of Public Prosecutions) v. Farrell

S.30 of the *Offences Against the State Act, 1939* permits the arrest and detention of a person for twenty-four hours. An order to extend this period for a further twenty-four hours must be made by an officer of the Gárda Síochána not below the rank of chief superintendent, though this power may be exercised by a superintendent who is so authorised in writing by the Commissioner. The appellant's conviction of causing an explosion was based on incriminating statements made by him during the extended period of detention.

The Court of Criminal Appeal, in quashing the conviction, held that since there was no evidence of the superintendent's authority to extend the appellant's detention for a further twenty-four hours, the statements were made while he was unlawfully detained and in deliberate and conscious breach of his constitutional rights.

Case No. 77

The People (Director of Public Prosecutions) v. Lynch

The appellant volunteered to go to a Gárda station to make a statement. After doing so, he remained overnight, was subjected to successive bouts of questioning by different groups of Gárdaí and was not given an opportunity to sleep or rest. The appellant made incriminating statements which were admitted into evidence at his trial.

The Supreme Court quashed the conviction. Because the appellant

176

had not been at liberty to leave the station, his detention was unlawful and unconstitutional under Art. 40 by the time the statements were made.

Case No. 78

The People (Director of Public Prosecutions) v. Madden

The appellant was arrested under s.30 of the *Offences Against the State Act, 1939* which permits detention for twenty-four hours. Shortly before this period was due to expire he began making an incriminating statement which was not completed until three hours after the twenty-four hour period had expired. This statement was admitted in evidence and on conviction the appellant appealed.

The Court of Criminal Appeal, in quashing the conviction, held that because this statement was completed after the expiration of the period of lawful detention the appellant was then in unlawful custody which was a deliberate and conscious breach of his constitutional rights.

Case No. 79

The People (Director of Public Prosecutions) v. O'Loughlin

The appellant, after the Gárdaí found some stolen machinery on his land, went voluntarily to the Gárda station so that the Gárdaí might confirm his explanation. Some hours after the explanation was found to be false, the appellant made an incriminating statement. On conviction, he appealed.

The Court of Criminal Appeal, in quashing the conviction, held that from the time the Gárdaí realised that the explanation was false, the appellant's detention was unlawful because he had neither been charged nor released and so his detention amounted to a deliberate and conscious breach of his constitutional rights.

Case No. 80

The People (Director of Public Prosecutions) v. O'Shea

The defendant was tried in the Central Criminal Court by a judge and jury. He was acquitted by direction of the judge. The DPP appealed to the Supreme Court thus raising the question whether an appeal lies from a verdict of not guilty recorded by a jury at the direction of the judge.

The Supreme Court held an appeal lay by virtue of Art. 34.4.3° of the Constitution which gives to the Supreme Court jurisdiction to hear all appeals from the High Court unless prohibited by statute law.

Case No. 81

The People (Director of Public Prosecutions) v. Shaw

The appellant was arrested at 11.30 on a Sunday evening. Shortly after his arrest he was suspected of involvement in the disappearance of two women. He was not brought before a court until the following Thursday evening. While in custody he made incriminating statements which were admitted in evidence, and on conviction for murder he appealed.

The Supreme Court, in dismissing the appeal, held that while there had been a deliberate and conscious violation of the appellant's right to liberty by his not being charged or released, there existed extraordinary excusing circumstances in that attempts were being made to vindicate the right to life of another.

Case No. 82

Pigs Marketing Board v. Donnelly (Dublin) Ltd.

The plaintiffs were empowered to fix the price of pig-meat. The defendants were prohibited from purchasing pigs at prices other than those fixed. If they did they were liable to the plaintiffs for the difference. On being sued for a large sum of money the defendants challenged the constitutionality of this power on the ground that it infringed property rights.

The High Court held that legislation interfering with trade competition or with contractual or proprietary rights was not *per se* unconstitutional.

Case No. 82a

Private Motorists Provident Society Ltd. v. Attorney General

The plaintiffs, incorporated in 1958, carried on a banking business which consisted in taking deposits from, and making loans to, members. Deposits grew to £135 million. The *Industrial and Provident Societies (Amendment) Act, 1978,* prohibited industrial and provident societies from accepting or holding deposits after the end of a period of five years commencing at the passing of the Act. The plaintiffs challenged the constitutionality of the Act.

The Supreme Court, in rejecting the claim, held that the Act, far from expropriating the business of a plaintiff, was a regulation and control of the range of business which they could carry out and was not contrary to Art. 40.3 because it was for the common good.

178

Case No. 83

Quinn's Supermarket Ltd. v. Attorney General

The plaintiffs were prosecuted for keeping a meat shop open on the evening of a week-day, which was contrary to a statutory order. Meat shops which sold only kosher meat were exempt from the order. The plaintiffs challenged the constitutionality of the order.

The Supreme Court held that the order, by exempting kosher meat shops from its application, contained a discrimination on the ground of religious profession, belief or status and was contrary to Art. 44.2.3° of the Constitution.

Case No. 84

Ryan v. Attorney General

The *Health (Fluoridation of Water Supplies) Act, 1960* imposed an obligation on a health authority to arrange for the fluoridation of water supplied to the public. The plaintiff, a mother of five children, whose home was connected to a public piped water supply, claimed that some provision of the Act were unconstitutional.

The Supreme Court held that the right to bodily integrity, while not expressed in the Constitution, was an implied right under Art. 40.3.2°, not infringed by the addition of fluoride to drinking water. Nor did the Act violate the guarantees given to the family in Art. 41.1.2°.

Case No. 85

Somjee v. The Minister for Justice

The plaintiff, an alien, married a woman who was an Irish citizen. S.8 of the *Irish Nationality and Citizenship Act, 1956* provides an almost automatic conferment of citizenship on alien women who marry Irish citizens. There was no similar provisions available to alien men. The plaintiff claimed that this differentiation between alien men and women constituted an inequality before the law contrary to Art. 40.1 of the Constitution.

The High Court held that s.8 did not create an invidious discrimination but a diversity of arrangements which was not contrary to Art. 40.1.

Case No. 85

The State (Burke) v. Lennon

S.55 of the *Offences Against the State Act, 1939* empowered a Minister of State to order the arrest and internment without trial of a person if he was satisfied that person was engaged in activities calculated to prejudice the preservation of the peace, order or security of the State. The applicant contended that his arrest and internment were unconstitutional.

The High Court held that internment without trial did not respect the citizen's right to personal liberty guaranteed by Art. 40.4, and that in signing a warrant under the section the Minister was administering justice, which was a judicial function confined to courts established under the Constitution.

Case No. 87

The State (C.) v. Frawley

The prosecutor was sentenced to imprisonment. He had a sociopathic personality disturbance, was strong physically, was aggressive and hostile to any form of authority, made repeated attempts at escape and had a record for swallowing metal objects that had to be removed by surgery. He was kept in solitary confinement and deprived of most of the equipment of an ordinary prisoner. The prosecutor sought his release.

The High Court, in dismissing his application, held that the rigorous conditions were imposed to diminish the possibility of the prosecutor injuring himself and were not a breach of the implied right to bodily integrity.

Case No. 88

The State (C.) v. The Minister for Justice

The prosecutor was charged and remanded in custody until a stated date. Before that date he was removed to a mental hospital pursuant to s.13 of the *Lunatic Asylums (Ireland) Act, 1875* on the direction of the Minister for Justice. The court was thus prevented from exercising its jurisdiction in relation to the charge.

The Supreme Court held that s.13 of the Act constituted a legislative interference with an exercise of the judicial power to administer justice and was unconstitutional.

Case No. 89

The State (Commins) v. McRann

The prosecutor failed to obey a civil order of the Circuit Court and was committed to prison for contempt of court. He claimed that this contempt was a criminal charge, was non-minor and only triable by a jury by virtue of Art. 38.5 of the Constitution.

The High Court held that even if it were assumed that the contempt was a criminal offence to which Art. 38.5 applied, the terms of Art. 34 constituted a qualification upon Art. 38 and authorised the Courts to adjudicate in a summary manner the issue of contempt and to impose sanctions in the event of disobedience to their orders.

Case No. 90

The State (Director of Public Prosecutions) v. Walsh

Two persons were convicted of capital murder by a non-jury Special Criminal Court and sentenced to death. The defendant issued a statement referring to the Special Criminal Court as a sentencing tribunal which was published by a newspaper. When cited for contempt in the High Court the defendant claimed a jury trial as the offence was a non-minor one.

The Supreme Court held that in proceedings for criminal contempt committed other than in the face of the court the defendant has a *prima facie* right under Art. 38.5 of the Constitution to trial by jury provided there are live and real issues of fact to be decided. Where the facts are admitted the matter can be disposed of summarily.

Case No. 91

The State (Healy) v. Donoghue

The *Criminal Justice (Legal Aid) Act, 1962* provided that a court may, on an application being made to it, grant legal aid where the means of the person charged are insufficient to enable him to obtain legal aid and the offence is grave. The prosecutor was charged, unable to pay for legal aid, and was not informed by the court of his right to apply for legal aid. He was convicted.

The Supreme Court quashed the conviction. Art. 38 of the Constitution, in requiring a criminal trial to be conducted in due course of law, imports the requirement of fair procedures. Where an accused faces a serious charge and by reason of lack of education requires the assistance of a

181

qualified lawyer in the preparation and conduct of a defence, the administration of justice requires that the accused should be afforded the opportunity of obtaining such assistance at the expense of the State even though the accused has not applied for it.

Case No. 92

The State (K.M.) v. The Minister for Foreign Affairs

The prosecutor, an unmarried citizen, gave birth to a child which was registered in the name of its father, an alien. These parties did not intend to marry each other. Due to the inability of the mother to care for the child and because it had inherited the father's racial characteristics, it was decided in the best interest of the child to allow it to be reared by the father's parents in his native country. A passport application by the mother was refused on the ground that s.40 of the *Adoption Act, 1952* prohibited the removal from the State of an illegitimate child under 1 year unless it was for the purpose of residing with the mother outside the State.

The High Court held that, subject to public order and the common good, every citizen has the implied right under Art. 40.3.2° of the Constitution to travel outside the State. The prohibition in s.40 was unconstitutional, though where the exercise of that right by or on behalf of an infant affects its welfare adversely the Courts may intervene to protect the welfare of the child.

Case No. 93

The State (Lynch) v. Cooney

Radio Telefís Éireann in its coverage of a general election allowed time on television and radio for political broadcasts by political parties. To qualify for time it was necessary to have at least seven candidates. Provisional Sinn Féin were allotted two minutes. The defendant, the Minister for Posts and Telegraphs, made an order under s.31 of the *Broadcasting Act, 1960,* as amended, restraining RTE from broadcasting any party political broadcast on behalf of Provisional Sinn Féin. The prosecutor, one of the candidates, challenged the constitutionality of s.31.

The Supreme Court upheld s.31. The guarantee contained in Art. 40.6.1° of the Constitution was qualified in the interests of public order and morality. The use of the organs of public opinion for the purpose of securing or advocating support for organisations which seek by violence to overthrow the State, which Provisional Sinn Féin did, is a use prohibited by the Constitution and places on the State the duty to ensure that these organs are not so used.

182

Case No. 94

The State (McFadden) v. The Governor of Mountjoy

The prosecutor was arrested on foot of an English warrant and brought before the District Court where an order for his extradition was made. At no time was he given a copy of the warrant, or asked if he wished to be legally represented, or if he wanted an adjournment to obtain legal advice or representation. He claimed that these procedures in the District Court were unfair.

The High Court held that in extradition proceedings, because the liberty of the person was in jeopardy, he ought to be given an opportunity to prepare his case. The procedures fell short of the constitutionally accepted standard of fairness.

Case No. 95

The State (Murray) v. McRann

While being lawfully detained in prison the prosecutrix was charged with committing a breach of prison discipline by assaulting a prison officer. After a proper investigation the prosecutrix was punished in a manner authorised by the prison rules. She claimed that this power was unconstitutional.

The High Court held that the exercise by the governor of his functions, upon the breach of prison discipline charged against the prosecutrix, was not transformed into an exercise of the functions and powers relevant to a criminal matter, within Art. 37 of the Constitution, by the fact that such breach happened to be also a criminal offence.

Case No. 96

The State (Nicolaou) v. An Bord Uchtála

The prosecutor was the natural father of a child. He wished to marry the mother but she was unwilling. The mother gave the child for adoption and the father challenged the *Adoption Act, 1952.*

The Supreme Court held that the Act which permitted the making of an adoption order for an illegitimate child without the consent of the natural father was not contrary to the Constitution.

Case No. 97

The State (Quinn) v. Ryan

The prosecutor was arrested on foot of an English warrant but released because of a defect in it. A second warrant was prepared. The prosecutor was re-arrested and immediately removed from the jurisdiction. The *Petty Sessions (Ireland) Act, 1851* permitted the immediate removal of a person from the jurisdiction of the Irish courts who had been arrested under a warrant issued in England.

The Supreme Court held that s.29 was unconstitutional because it prevented an arrested person from testing the validity of his arrest contrary to Art. 40 of the Constitution.

Case No. 98

The State (Richardson) v. The Governor of Mountjoy

The prosecutrix was imprisoned. Prisoners in the morning emptied their chamber pots into a toilet and washed them in a cold water sink. Some prisoners emptied these pots into the sink, in which human waste had been found. The prosecutrix claimed that these facilities failed to regard her right to health and human dignity.

The High Court held that the State failed in its duty under the Constitution to protect the prosecutrix's health and to provide her with appropriate facilities to maintain proper standards of hygiene and cleanliness.

Case No. 99

The State (Shanahan) v. Attorney General

Information having been refused in the District Court, the Attorney General, under s.62 of the *Courts of Justice Act, 1936,* directed that the prosecutrix be sent forward for trial to the Circuit Court.

The Supreme Court held that the Attorney General in exercising this power was not administering justice contrary to Art. 34 of the Constitution.

Case No. 100

The State (Sheerin) v. Kennedy

The prosecutor was convicted summarily and sentenced by virtue of s.2 or the *Prevention of Crimes Act, 1908* to two years in a borstal institution.

The Supreme Court held that the offence was not a minor one because an offence which attracts the deprivation of liberty for a period up to three years could not be regarded as minor under Art. 38.2 of the Constitution.

Case No. 101

In re Tilson, infants

The parents were married in a Roman Catholic Church, the husband being a Protestant and the wife a Catholic. The husband signed an ante-nuptial agreement that all issue of the marriage would be reared as Catholic. There were four children and all were baptised Catholics. Differences arose between the parties and the husband placed the children in a Protestant institution. The wife sought their custody.

The Supreme Court held, in granting the mother custody, that under the Constitution both parents have a joint power and duty in respect of the religion of their children. If they together make a decision and put it into practice, it is not within the power of either parent to revoke such decision against the will of the other.

APPENDIX

As explained on p. 105 the purpose of an arrest is to bring the arrested person before a court on a criminal charge. The one statutory exception is s. 30 of the Offences Against the State, 1939 (see p. 106). The Criminal Justice Bill, s. 3 proposes detention without charge where a person is arrested without a warrant on suspicion, with reasonable cause, of having committed an offence which is punishable by five years imprisonment. Detention is only to be permitted if the member of the Gárda Síochána in charge of the station to which the arrested person is taken has reasonable grounds for believing that it is necessary for the proper investigation of the offence. Detention will be for six hours though this may be extended for a further six hours on the authority of a chief superintendent or, if he is absent, the superintendent acting for him. The hours between midnight and 8 am, during which questioning in general may not take place, are excluded when calculating the period of detention.

As explained on p. 101 a person, whether arrested or not, is under no obligation, in general, to answer any question. The Bill does not propose to alter this rule but s. 16 will allow a jury or court to draw an inference which appears proper if a person at his trial offers an explanation which he could reasonably have been expected to mention to the Gárdaí when being questioned or charged. An inference can also be drawn where a person fails or refuses to account for any object, substance or mark, or for his presence in a particular place at or about the time the offence for which he was arrested was committed which the Gárdaí reasonably believe may be attributable to his participation in the offence.

S. 5 of the Bill proposes that where a person is detained his name and address may be demanded, he may be searched, photographed, finger and palm printed, and may be tested to ascertain whether he has been in contact with any firearm or explosive substance, and for that purpose swabs from the skin and samples of the hair may be taken. But the photographing and finger-printing can only be done on the authority of a Gárda officer not below the rank of superintendent.

S. 24 of the Bill proposes that the verdict of a jury in a criminal trial shall be that of a majority of ten jurors.

Because this Bill, if enacted, will curtail constitutional rights the courts will interpret it in the way explained on pp. 106 and 109.

NOTES

1. K. C. Wheare, *Modern Constitution*, London 1966.
2. The Preamble and Art. 45 entitled 'Directive Principles of Social Policy': '. . . the Constitution . . . expresses not only legal norms but basic doctrines of political and social theory,' per O'Higgins C. J. in *Art. 26 and the Criminal Law (Jurisdiction) Bill, 1975* (Case No. 3).
3. Unlike the Constitution of Saorstát Éireann, 1922 which was vetted by the British Government.
4. At a plebiscite held on 1 July 1937, 685,105 voted in favour and 526,945 against. The Constitution came into effect on 29 December 1937.
5. 'The Draft Constitution shall be submitted to a plebiscite of the people' — Plebiscite (Draft Constitution) Act, 1937, s. 2(1). The Act is silent as to whether a simple, or other weighted majority, was necessary for its enactment.
6. 'Redolent as they are of the great papal Encyclicals': per Gavan Duffy P. in *In re Tilson* (Case No. 101) though this marked leaning towards one Church had waned by the time of *Ryan v. Attorney General* (Case No. 84) where Kenny J. referred to 'the Christian and democratic nature of the State'.
7. 'In the absence of convincing evidence that the Constitution of 1937 does not reflect the moral views, and the political and social culture of the majority of the Irish people, I believe it would be unnecessary, premature and unwise to repeal the Constitution or to alter it in any fundamental way' — Mary Redmond in 'Fundamental Rights in Irish Constitutional Law' published in *Morality and the Law*, Dublin 1982.
8. Declan Costello, 'The Natural Law and the Constitution' in *Studies*, Vol. XLV, 403-14, and Vincent Grogan, 'The Constitution and the Natural Law', in *Christus Rex*, Vol. 8, 201-8.
9. '. . . it was also the fundamental charter of the new State meant to be read and understood by the educated layman, and, where the language is that of an ordinary educated layman, it would be wrong to attempt to divorce it from its plain and ordinary meaning . . .' said Kingsmill Moore J. in *In re Employers' Mutual Insurance* [1955] I.R. 176 speaking of the 1922 Constitution.
10. The Supreme Court decided in *The State (Quinn) v. Ryan* (Case No. 97) that in constitutional cases it was not bound by its own previous decisions.
11. See *O'Donovan v. Attorney General* (Case No. 70) and *Crowley v. Ireland* (Case No. 29).
12. Byce, *Studies in History and Jurisprudence*, Vol. I, Essay 3.
13. The Third Amendment to the Constitution Bill, proposing change in

the system of proportional representation, was defeated in the Seanad but was deemed by a resolution of Dáil Éireann to have been passed by both Houses of the Oireachtas.

14. Art. 43 of the Constitution of Saorstát Eireann provided for an Initiative which permitted a minimum number of votes to initiate a constitutional amendment. This was abolished in 1928.
15. Signed on 26 December 1933.
16. *80 Hague Recueil*, 1952, I, 80-96.
17. *Principles of Public International Law*, Oxford 1979.
18. *Introduction to International Law*, London 1979, chapter 5.
19. *A Manual of International Law*, 1976.
20. 1,041,890 voted in favour; 211,891 against.
21. See *Bank of Ireland v. Caffin* (Case. No. 10).
22. O'Higgins C. J., himself, said it was not [1977] I.R., 148.
23. *Macleod v. Attorney General for New South Wales [1891]*, A.C. 455.
24. (1927), P.C.I.J. Ser. A, No. 10.
25. For example, Brierly, *58 Hague Recueil*, 1936, IV, 146-8; 183-4.
26. The Fisheries Case, I.C.J. Reports 1951, 116, and the Nottebolm Case, I.C.J. Reports, 1955, 4.
27. The date on which the Constitution of Saorstát Éireann came into effect.
28. Citizenship was thus conferred on Sir Alfred Chester Beatty and Dr T. Herrema.
29. *L'Esprit des Lois*, 1748, Book XI, chapter 6.
30. Charles Louis de Secondat, Baron de la Brède et de Montesquieu (1689-1755).
31. This definition, found also in Art. 35 of the Constitution of Saorstát Éireann, is originally to be found in the Parliament Act, 1911.
32. This procedure has never been resorted to. The Certificate of the Ceann Comhairle is omitted from Money Bills when enacted and printed.
33. All the referrals to date have been decided within the sixty days; details of the time taken are given in notes 36-41 below. Most were given within a short period; the exception, the Criminal Law (Jurisdiction) Bill, may be because of disagreements among the members of the Court.
34. The Oireachtas Committee on the Constitution, 1967 suggested in Par. 99 that this prohibition should expire seven years after the decision.
35. *The State (Quinn) v. Ryan* (Case No. 97).
36. Referred 8 January 1940; decision 9 February 1940.
37. Referred date unknown; decision 15 April 1943.
38. Referred date unknown; decision 14 July 1961.
39. Referred 10 March 1976; decision 6 May 1976.
40. Referred 24 September 1976; decision 15 October 1976.
41. Referred 24 December 1981; decision 19 February 1982.
42. There have been six Presidents of Ireland: *Douglas Hyde*, 1938-45 — no election; *Seán T. O'Kelly*, 1945-59 — elected in 1945, agreed in

1952; *Éamon de Valera*, 1959-73 — elected both occasions; Erskine Childers, 1973-4 — elected. Died in office; Cearbhall Ó Dálaigh, 1974-6 — agreed candidate, resigned; Patrick Hillery, 1976-present — agreed candidate.

43. Andrew Johnson (1865-69) was impeached by the House of Representatives but not by the Senate. Richard Nixon (1969-74) resigned after the House Committee on the Judiciary voted three articles of impeachment.

44. In June, 1982 an attempt to injunct the President from dissolving Dáil Éireann, while successful in the High Court, failed in the Supreme Court.

45. It has met on only nine occasions since 1937.

46. The Electoral Act and the number of deputies is: 1947 — 147; 1961 — 144; 1969 — 144; 1974 — 148.

47. 423,496 in favour, 657,898 against.

48. The number of constituencies provided by the Electoral Acts were as follows: 1947 — 40; 1961 — 38; 1969 — 42; 1974 — 42.

49. The members were a judge of the Supreme Court as Chairman; the Secretary of the Department of the Environment; and the Clerk of Dáil Éireann.

50. By comparison the salary of a District Justice was £1,000: *Courts of Justice Act, 1924*.

51. This is called the 'Droop' quota after H. R. Droop who first evolved it in 1872.

52. 1959: 453,322 in favour; 486,989 against. 1968: 424,185 in favour; 657,898 against.

53. 1943 and 1944.

54. For example, the Vienna Convention on Diplomatic Relations is incorporated into the Diplomatic Relations and Immunities Act, 1967.

55. Report dated April 1974. Irish members were Brian Walsh, Seamus Henchy (both judges of the Supreme Court), T. A. Doyle and D. Quigley. The British members were Robert Lowry, Lord Scarman, Kenneth Jones and J. B. Hutton.

56. The granting of legal aid is such a function.

57. The constitutional point was not argued in the High Court.

58. Salmond, *Jurisprudence*, London 1966, chapter 27.

59. See Chapter 1 and note 8 above.

60. Op. cit., chapter 27.

61. See also *Northampton County Council v. A.B.F.* (Case No. 65).

62. April 1978. Members were Barra Ó Briain, retired President of the Circuit Court, Ruaidhrí Roberts, a trade union official, and Patrick Malone, former Commissioner of the Gárda Síochána.

63. Printed in the Ó Briain *Report*.

64. *McCarrick v. Leavy* 99 I.L.T.R. 163 and *The People* (A.G.) v. *Cummins* 108 I.L.T.R. 5.

GLOSSARY

*Each of the terms defined below is signalled by an asterisk the first time it appears in the text.

appellate jurisdiction: the jurisdiction exercised by a court when hearing appeals from a lower court.

appellant: the party complaining to a superior court of an injustice done by an inferior one. The other party is styled the respondent.

applicant: the party applying for any State-side Order such as *certiorari*, prohibition, *mandamus* (q.v.) or an order under Art. 40. If a conditional order is granted the party is then styled the prosecutor (q.v.). The term applicant is also applied to those who apply for bail to the High Court and to those who apply to the Court of Criminal Appeal for leave to appeal. If leave is granted they are then styled appellants.

artificial person: term applied to a corporation to distinguish it from a natural person.

certiorari: a High Court order commanding proceedings to be removed from an inferior court into the High Court for review.

collateral proceeding: in constitutional matters where a challenge is not made directly to a statute but to some order or decision given under a statute.

consultative jurisdiction: the jurisdiction exercised by a superior court when advising an inferior court on a point of law.

defendant: a person sued in a civil action or charged with a minor criminal offence. A person charged with a serious crime is styled the accused.

felony: a serious crime such as murder, rape and robbery.

Gárda Síochána: the civilian police-force.

habeas corpus: the deliverance from illegal confinement. This was its common law term. Now the procedure is more properly entitled an application under Art. 40 of the Constitution.

Iris Oifigiúil: the official Government gazette in which all constitutional and legally important announcements are made.

locus standi: signifies a right of appearance in a court of justice.

mandamus: a command issuing from the High Court and directed to any person, corporation or inferior court requiring them to do some particular act which pertains to their office and duty.

Oireachtas: Parliament, a deliberative assembly.

original jurisdiction: the jurisdiction exercised by a court when hearing and determining an issue at first instance.

plaintiff: the party seeking relief in civil proceedings.

privilege: by which certain communications are protected from disclosure in legal proceedings.

prohibition: an order of the High Court forbidding an inferior court from proceeding in a case there pending.

prosecutor: means properly any person who prosecutes any proceeding in a court of justice but usage has confined it to denote the complainant in *certorari*, prohibition and *mandamus* proceedings and in applications under Art. 40 of the Constitution. The defending party is styled the respondent.

seisin: is the feudal possession of freehold land but is applied generally to denote custody or control of legal proceedings.

statutory instrument: a form of delegated legislation. Statute empowers a designated party to make statutory instruments, which are a form of law, in order to further operate the statute.

sui juris: a phrase used to denote a person who is under no disability affecting his legal power to make conveyances of his property, to bind himself by contracts and to sue and be sued: as opposed to persons wholly or partially under disability, such as infants, mentally disordered persons and prisoners.

Taoiseach: Prime Minister (first in order of rank, leader, chief).

Tánaiste: Deputy Prime Minister (second in order of rank, heir presumptive).

INDEX

administrative action, review of, 85
adoption, 136
aliens, 18, 91
amendment to Constitution, 6, 10, 48, 56, 58, 88, 91
appeal, right of, 78
Application under Art. 40, 76, 114ff., 81
arrest, power of, 102ff., 186
assembly, freedom of, 121ff.
association, freedom of, 117ff.
Attorney General, 43, 45
audi alteram partem, 99
Australia, Constitution of, 3, 15

bail, 111
ballot paper, 59
Belgium, 36
blasphemy, 128
bodily integrity, right to, 116
Britain, Constitution of, 6, 19, 23, 25, 32, 36, 40
broadcasts, 54

censorship, 125, 128, 129
census, 47
Central Criminal Court, 73
certiorari, 76, 81
Chairman of Dáil Éireann, 25, 28, 39, 45, 46, 50, 56, 57
Chairman of Seanad Éireann, 39, 45, 46, 50, 59
Chief Justice, 38, 45, 46, 70, 71
children, rights of, 138
Circuit Court, 59, 81
citizenship, 11, 16ff., 36, 39, 46, 51, 58, 91, 92
Clerk of Dáil Éireann, 50, 52, 53, 56, 57, 59, 61
Clerk of Seanad Éireann, 59, 61
Committee of Privileges, 28
Comptroller and Auditor General, 41, 43, 47, 65
conspiracy, 76, 119
constituencies, 38, 48ff., 54
constitutional rights, 86ff.
Constitution of Ireland, 3ff.
constitutions, 1ff.
Council of State, 43, 44, 45ff., 70

county councils, 37, 49, 61
Court of Criminal Appeal, 73
courts, 19, 20, 21, 67ff.
courts martial, 83
crimes, classification of, 80
criminal trial, 79ff
custody of children, 133

Dáil Éireann, 6, 19, 23, 24, 25, 26, 27, 28, 31, 32, 43, 44, 46ff., 57, 61, 63, 64, 65
Dáil, First (1919), 16
declaratory action, 76
Defence Forces, 25, 43, 47, 51, 83, 101, 116, 120
demands, 101, 102
democracy, 13ff, 48
departments of State, 64
deposits in elections, 38, 52, 57
Director of Public Prosecutions, 83
dissociate, right to, 117
District Court, 81
divorce, 130
domicile, 11, 12
due course of law, 80
duty, constitutional, 89
dwelling, inviolability of, 143

East Germany, 14
educational institution, property of, 143
education, right to, 134
Éire, 15
elections, 38, 51, 58, 59
Electoral Commission, 47
electoral court, 57
emergency, *see* national emergency
equality before the law, 95ff
European Convention on Human Rights, 66
European Economic Community, 10
evidence unconstitutionally obtained, 109ff.
executive, *see* government
expression, freedom of, 124ff.
external sovereignty, 10
extradition, 67, 112
extra-marital family, 137
extra-territorial jurisdiction, 12

192

fair procedures, 80, 98
family, the, 133ff.
family, extra-marital, 137
family rights, 130ff.
fingerprints, 107, 186
France, Constitution of, 24, 36

Gárda Síochána, 35, 51, 54, 101ff.,
   120
Germany, Federal Republic of, 36
general election, *see* election
government or executive power, 18, 19
Government, 25, 26, 40, 42, 43, 44, 62ff.,
   69, 70, 83
guardianship, 133
habeas corpus, see Application under
   Art. 40
High Court, 52, 74ff., 114ff.
Houses of Oireachtas, 6, 23, 37, 40ff.,
   43, 44, 45, 70, 82

impeachment, 40
implied constitutional rights, 90
imprisonment, 112, 114
independence of judiciary, 70
indecency, 128
India, Constitution of, 3
injunction, 76
internal sovereignty, 11
international agreements, 26, 66
internment without trial, 113
Irish Free State, *see* Saorstát Éireann
invidious discrimination, 95ff.

judges, 39, 41, 43, 47, 69
judicial powers and functions, 18, 68, 84
judicial power of Oireachtas, 32
judiciary, 67ff
Judges' Rules, 108
jurisdiction, of State, 11ff., personal, 11;
   territorial, 11
jury trial, 82
justice, administration of, 67ff, 84

languages, 7
law, positive, 4, 86
laws, system of, 78
legislation, enactment of, 26ff.
legal advice, right to, 108
legal aid, 99
legislative function, 18, 20
liberty, personal, 101ff.
life, right to, 116
limited judicial power, 84
litigate, right to, 142
locus standi, 91ff.

mandamus, 81
marriage, 130
military trial, 83
Minister for Defence, 43
Minister for the Environment, 38, 54, 59
Minister for Finance, 63, 65
minor offence, 80
Money Bills, 27, 44, 45
Montesquieu, 18

national emergency, 32ff.
nationality, *see* citizenship
nationhood, 7ff.
natural justice, *see* fair procedures
natural law, 4, 86, 88
nemo judex in sua causa, 99
Northern Ireland, 9

offences relating to Oireachtas, 35
offences relating to President, 44
offences, trial of, 79ff
Oireachtas, 19, 23ff, 47, 61, 62, 63, 65
   70, 89, 94

parents, right of, 133
People, the, 3, 4, 6, 7ff., 9, 18, 19, 22,
   36, 46, 47, 56
photographing suspects, 107, 186
picketing, 124
political parties, 49, 50
poll, *see* election
population, 47
powers, separation of, 18ff.
President of High Court, 37, 45, 46
President of Ireland, 15, 17, 23, 24, 25,
   29, 30, 31, 32, 36ff, 51, 63, 65, 69,
   70, 71, 82
Presidential Commission, 46
Proclamation of 1916, 16
prohibition, 81
property rights, 138ff.
proportional representation, 38, 55, 59
public morality, 121, 124, 127
public order, 119, 122, 127
referendum, 6, 10, 44, 46, 48, 56

register, of electors, 51, 82; of political
   parties, 49
religion, and family, 135; freedom of,
   129
religious denomination, property of, 143
representation, uniformity of, 48
rights, in general, 88ff.; personal 86ff.;
   see also under each right
riot, 122

194